THE SEA OF FAITH

Jack W. Moore

Order another copy of

Maurice Wiles, *Faith and the Mystery of God*. London, SCM Press Ltd, 1982,

address: SCM Press Ltd
58 Bloomsbury St
London WC 1

THE SEA OF FAITH

DON CUPITT

BRITISH BROADCASTING CORPORATION

For Peter Armstrong

Published by the British Broadcasting Corporation
35, Marylebone High Street, London W1M 4AA

ISBN 563 20398 6

First published 1984

This paperback edition first published 1985

© Don Cupitt 1984

Printed in England by
Jolly & Barber Ltd, Rugby, Warwickshire.

CONTENTS

INTRODUCTION

For those caught up in it, a time of religious upheaval is peculiarly hard to understand. People's deepest convictions, their philosophy of life and their form of religious consciousness are all in turmoil. All seems darkness, confusion and a Babel of conflicting voices. Only with hindsight, after the dust has settled, will it be possible to see clearly what are the gains, the losses – and also, the unexpected continuities.

Yet we live in such a time and this book is an attempt to show, step by step, what has happened and what new forms are emerging. An impossible task; but there are reasons for attempting it. For our modern industrial civilisation which now rules the whole world was forged in just one particular place and period, and influenced by just one religious tradition. We are speaking, of course, of Europe between the seventeenth and early twentieth centuries, and of Western Christianity. The domain is limited, and the story can be told. The slow process of secularisation, the impact of science and then of biblical and historical criticism, the shift to an ever more man-centred outlook, the encounter with other faiths, and then finally the awesome and still incomplete transition to modernity – all this makes up a story which for Christians has extended over some three or four centuries. There are people in other traditions, and most notably in Islam, who say that the story is a purely Christian one that reflects only Christianity's weakness in controlling developments in its own culture and its failure to resist the corrosive effects of scepticism. They flatter themselves that they will be able to escape the fate that has overtaken Christianity, some Muslims even adding that they will be able to create an Islamic science free from the undercurrent of scepticism that has marked Western science. They are, I fear, mistaken. The story we have to tell may be local, but its moral is universal. Christianity has had the great advantage of a long period in which to understand and in some measure to adjust itself to what has happened, whereas in other cultures the process of modernisation is all the more abrupt, confusing and traumatic for being telescoped to within the span of a single lifetime. It is not surprising that so many people should be seeking out ways of insulating themselves from the truth, using the shreds and tatters of the old order to protect themselves from the blast of the new.

Periods of rapid religious change have always been highly stressful. In the third century of our era the Romans had so large an empire, embracing so many different peoples and faiths, that in the great cities where the trade routes met there were dozens of religions and philosophies competing for the public's favour. In times already insecure and pessimistic the very diversity of religions, of which people were so highly conscious, served only to make religious striving the more frenzied. The divine seemed to have withdrawn itself from the world, people were vulnerable to ideas of demonic possession, and religion could readily become extravagantly ascetical or mystical.

Our situation is not so very different. What the Roman Empire then did for the lands around the Mediterranean, mass travel and modern communications have now done on a global scale, creating a ferment of ideas and a great deal of religious experimentation, borrowing and innovation.

At the same time, people everywhere are today experiencing the disruptive effect of modern knowledge upon traditional religious worldviews and values. Science is now vast in scope and very powerful. Recession or not, the engine of new research and technical innovation keeps turning unstoppably. Being consciously value-neutral and independent of local political or religious beliefs, it penetrates all cultures with equal ease. It inevitably has a strong secularising influence, for it opens up such wide possibilities of non-religious knowledge and effective action. Yet how can you keep it out? However stable and beautiful your traditional culture and values may be, the fact remains that science-based Western medicine (to quote one very impressive example) visibly works. Suppose you are a tribesman and you see a medical team arrive in your area and cure the blind in hundreds, at a few dollars a time. You are bound to be impressed – and your gods are bound to shiver in their shrines. Your traditional beliefs and values no longer seem quite so all-inclusive and immutable and perfect as they used to be. Suffering which you have traditionally regarded as sent by the gods in punishment for ritual offences now turns out to be caused by things like parasites and bacteria and to be curable quickly and cheaply, without any reference to religion. What do you make of that?

But the impact of half-understood new technologies, impressive though they may be, is as nothing compared with the impact of the new ways of thinking that underlie those technologies and have made them possible. When people first experience a scientific education they learn about a new method of arriving at truth whose procedure is the very opposite of that traditionally taught in religious communities. Instead of gaining wisdom by swallowing whole and digesting slowly, they are taught to be extremely finicky, to pick and choose, to dissect and to prove item by item. Complex wholes are not accepted as sacrosanct totalities, but are broken down into their constituent parts and rigorously tested. The method is systematically sceptical. What survives the test-procedure is kept for the present, and what fails is ruthlessly discarded, however widely it has been believed and however great the authority who has taught it. It is continually hammered into one's head that all theories are merely man-made and provisional. Sooner or later the time will come when they will be found wanting, and be either scrapped or reformulated. The great power and beauty of scientific knowledge lies in the fact that it is built on a firm foundation of doubt, and the strength and vitality of a scientific community depends upon its being (ideally, at least) a society in which the old men rejoice to see the young men prove them wrong. How far actual scientists live up to this ideal may be disputed: what is indisputable is the novelty and extraordinariness of the ideal itself.

Natural science may be the most visible product of this new ethic of knowledge, but it is by no means the only one. The critical spirit that underlies science can equally be applied to history and other arts subjects, and to religious belief as well.

This happened in the age of the Enlightenment, which approximately coincides with the eighteenth century. The methods by which Galileo had demolished Aristotle's natural philosophy were generalised by Descartes, the first modern critical thinker. His supreme confidence in the power of unaided human reason, employing the method of doubt and applied mathematics, to create a complete fundamental science of nature may not have been justified by his own achievements, but it was later to be strikingly vindicated by the triumph of Newton. In the following generations the scholars of the Enlightenment, applying similar principles to all other branches of knowledge, carried out a comprehensive critique of tradition. Since critical thinking on principle cannot accept dogmas at all, but must invariably question and undermine them, the effect on the supernatural dogmatic beliefs of Christianity was very severe, and theologians have been attempting ever since to pick up the pieces with – on their own admission – only limited results. Their lack of success may be partly explained by the sheer unpopularity of their labours. From the front they are under continuous attack by people who do not share their loyalties, for not conceding enough; while from the rear they are accused of treason by fellow-believers who do not understand their problems. On all sides they are charged with causing the very disease they are trying to cure.

Yet in time truth will out, and here is a rather brutal illustration of the trouble we are in by now. From its Protestant background American popular culture has inherited a craving for supernatural redeemer-figures, beings who descend to earth and live incognito until the moment when they are called upon to reveal their true identity and use their superhuman powers in the cause of truth, justice and the American way. Until as recently as forty years ago comic books about such characters were produced and read in all seriousness. If people were troubled by a sense of absurdity, they could doubtless excuse themselves by saying that after all such tales were only fictions, that it was a harmless indulgence in fantasy to read them, that nobody was seriously expected to base his whole life on such ideas, and that in any case the heroes were not strictly speaking supernatural beings or demigods but mere extra-terrestrials, immigrants from other planets. But today these excuses are no longer sufficient, and when the stories are revived – as they still are – they have to be presented in a consciously self-mocking form. By now we cannot help recognising infantile fantasies of omnipotence for what they are. So the myth of a supernatural redeemer, even when transposed and given a modern science-fiction dress, can no longer be presented with full serious-ness; and if this has happened to the myth, then what has happened to the Christian creeds that incorporate it in its original and most uncompro-mising form? Can it be that the faith on which a great civilisation was built has deteriorated within a few generations into a popular superstition, treated with indulgent tolerance? Of course, theologians have been saying for 150 years and more that Jesus should not be regarded as an extra-terrestrial visitant, that phrases like 'he came down from heaven' and 'he ascended into heaven' should not be read literally, and that he really was a human being, of human ancestry. But the Creeds and the Christmas carols that people flock to sing seem to say otherwise, and the language of worship has changed little. The theologians' efforts to de-mythologise Christianity in order to prevent it from decaying into super-stition have so far had little lasting success because most people have instinctively felt that the heart of the matter lies in the myth, understood literally, and have persisted in thinking so even while the authority of the myth has been visibly deteriorating all around them.

Religious change happens willy-nilly, even to those who deny and resist it; for even if the beliefs, the language and the practices are most jealously conserved intact, their effective significance is altered by changes in the surrounding culture. A science-fiction story about a person who under his incognito is really an extra-terrestrial with superhuman powers who has come down from the heavens alters the way the story of the incarnation is perceived, and obliges Christians to decide whether they do or do not mean something like *that*. Again, in the period when Christian doctrine was framed there was little expectation of secular progress, but in recent times there have appeared great movements inspired by the hope of constructing a better society here on earth; and Christians who have for nineteen centuries prayed 'Thy Kingdom come on earth' are forced to ask themselves whether their own hopes for the human future are or are not something like *that*. Another example: since the Second World War we have lived with the knowledge that it lies within our own power to extinguish all life on earth very quickly, and this new realisation is bound to alter the way we understand and respond to traditional apocalyptic language about the imminence of the end of the world.

Religious change is forced because, whether we like it or not, religious meanings are changed by changes in the surrounding culture; and the tendency of such forced, involuntary change has generally been to degrade faith into superstition. As the body of available scientific knowledge and technology grows ever larger and more powerful, science progressively takes over from religion, in one area of life after another, the task of explaining what is happening and prescribing what is to be done. Even in fields whose precise scientific status is disputed, such as economics, social science and psychology, it is still the case that secular, utilitarian and 'engineering' or instrumental ways of thinking have taken over. The older supernaturalist types of explanation have progressively diminished in effectiveness, and looking back we can now see that since about the time of Darwin they have played no part in any major branch of knowledge. Inevitably, religious belief and practice have been left looking like a hobby, a minority world-view and an optional but basically unimportant leisure-time pursuit on the part of those who have a psychological need for 'roots' in an ethnic past or a cultural tradition. Doctrine, supernatural belief, may be tenaciously maintained, but it becomes psychologised, privatised, a matter of one's secret identity and no longer effectively connected with the way one behaves in one's real social and economic life. Like a coat of arms, such belief may anchor us reassuringly in the past; but it is of little use in the present.

Nobody who takes his faith seriously can be happy about this process, but in our tolerantly secular Western democracies how do we resist the relegation of religion to the margins of life? The answer is surely, by demythologising religious belief and attempting systematically to connect traditional patterns of religious thought and action with analogous patterns of challenge that can be discerned in the modern cultural situation. This not only can be done, but is being done. Thus, in the traditional language of faith there was an injunction to 'Repent, for the Kingdom of God is at hand.' The idea was that because of human sinfulness a great catastrophe overhung humanity. God would come in judgment, and people must purify themselves and change their lives if they were to have any chance of surviving. Now although this ancient archetype is no longer a live option in its original supernaturalist form – for we have good scientific grounds for expecting that the Universe will continue in existence for billions of years yet – there is nevertheless a situation and a challenge in modern culture that is analogous to it and may reawaken it. For unless human behaviour changes considerably, human life on earth may extinguish itself in a nuclear war. So at this point the traditional religious message about impending Judgment and the need for repentance in the face of it is able to find an effective and socially relevant modern expression. There is no need for supercilious persons to sniff at such language: where there is faith seeking an outlet in action, it can and it must pour itself out along the most appropriate available channels. So the Churches can and will commit themselves to the cause of peace and disarmament, using their moral authority and their accumulated insight into the human heart to diagnose the sources of nationalism, militarism and the like, and prescribing effective remedial action.

This they are doing. Modern Christianity is already radically different from the Christianity of earlier periods in that it already sees its prime function in terms of social ethics, the defence of individual human rights, and the protection of the human person in his (and her) full moral and religious dignity against the pervasive dehumanising tendencies in the modern State and modern technology. Already Christianity feels itself to be, and is perceived to be, most effective in precisely these areas. And this implies that, in fact if not in theory, the demythologising of Christianity in order to connect it effectively with the modern situation and its challenges has already taken place, simply through faith's proper striving to find an effective public outlet. The old supernaturalism has been tacitly abandoned at the ethical level, as where the energies and the rhetoric that were once deployed in the battle against demons are now directed against dehumanising forces in modern society, or where the old doctrine of a supernatural redemption is translated into a practical struggle to create a society which realises the full moral and religious potential of each one of its members. So evidently I was too one-sided in suggesting earlier that the efforts of theologians to demythologise Christianity have had little success. In the ethical realm, a large measure of demythologisation has already occurred. Christianity in its effective practice has already been extensively translated into a movement of radical religious humanism which strives to realise a particular vision of what human life should be, and resists the threats to that vision posed by racism, totalitarianism and every other kind of oppression. The present Pope, in the days when he was Karol Wojtyla, published a book, *The Acting Person*, along just these lines.

However, what he did not propose, and is not at all likely to propose, was a parallel modernisation of Christian doctrine; and there's the rub. The modernisation of Christian ethics may be controversial and may irritate right-wing journalists, but from the believer's point of view it is not too painful. It is easy to recognise that a traditional Christian ethic of unobtrusive private philanthropy is inadequate to the scale of modern world poverty, and to see that the Church has perforce to become a noisy pressure-group urging action at government level, because only governments nowadays have the necessary power and resources to bring about effective social change. At that level and on that kind of issue the so-called shift to the Left is uncomplicated, and is being made. Personal ethics may be a little more difficult for historical and psychological reasons (and not least in the Roman Catholic Church), but nevertheless in this sphere also rapid modernisation is undoubtedly taking place. Since the time of Darwin, Nietzsche and Freud we have become much more conscious of the biological roots of human nature and much more psychologically aware. It is not difficult to recognise that a great deal of the old pre-modern spirituality, whether of Baroque Catholicism or Evangelical and Reformed Protestantism, was too often crude and oppressive, inhibiting rather than liberating, and with disagreeable sado-masochistic undertones. Imprisoning myths that used to constrain Christian attitudes to the Jews, to women, to children, to sexual behaviour and so on have one after another been criticised and dispelled, with results that have been wholly beneficial.

I do not say that these changes in social ethics, personal ethics and religious psychology have either been uncontroversial or that they are yet completed. They have been sharply contested, and the battles are not ended. But if we compare Christian attitudes today with what they were a century ago it is obvious that vast changes were inevitable, have already taken place, and are still continuing. Through them the Churches have become culturally partly disestablished as they have become more clearly aware of their own distinctive values, and of their proper critical mission *vis-à-vis* civil society. All this has been pure gain.

But what of doctrine? That is a different matter entirely, for the old supernatural doctrine is deeply embedded in creed and liturgy and institutional structures, and in people's deepest affections as well. The whole of what sociologists call the 'institutional drift' of the Churches both protects and perpetuates it. It acts as a sheet anchor and a guarantee of continuing identity. Its preservation intact is used to allay the fears of those who suspect that the process of ethical modernisation may be transforming Christianity into a version of secular humanism. In Rome as elsewhere it has been found politically convenient to combine rather advanced social ethics with a very conservative posture in matters of doctrine. Intellectually, doctrine may be in appalling difficulties, and not even the Pope himself can wave a wand and make his doctrinal pronouncements as interesting and important as his pronouncements in social ethics; but that is not the prime consideration. Whatever its intellectual problems, doctrine must be defended as a matter of obedience and communal loyalty. The leadership in the Churches has some freedom publicly to innovate and modernise in matters of ethics, but it has no such freedom in matters of doctrine, even though it is well aware that it is precisely the supernatural doctrines of the faith which cause the greatest difficulty and distress to the ordinary person in the pew – or, more likely, no longer in the pew, because he has voted with his feet.

The real and continuing crisis, then, is in the area of doctrine, and it is with this that *The Sea of Faith* is mainly concerned. Until the seventeenth century, in almost all societies the world over, the explanation of the course of events in this world, and the guidance of human life in it, were ultimately referred to a higher and more perfect world. Power and authority came down from above, an 'above' that was variously described in terms of God, of a whole world of supernatural beings, or of an ideal metaphysical order. The distinction between the natural world about us and the higher realm above was ultimately derived from Plato and became fundamental to the way Christian belief was formulated for fifteen centuries; and it is just this distinction which has come under the most sustained attack in the modern period. Even as early as the 1580s the Dominican friar Giordano Bruno studied Copernicus, and realised that to put the Sun at the centre of the world and have the Earth flying through the heavens around it meant that the old distinction between the earthly world below and the heavenly world above was no longer tenable. The Earth was itself a heavenly body, and part of the heavens. Furthermore, since the stars all appear to remain in the same relative positions when viewed from opposite ends of the Earth's great orbit, the universe must (as Copernicus had pointed out) be far vaster than anyone had hitherto imagined. Indeed, Bruno supposed it must be infinite, with innumerable inhabited planets circling uncountable suns. So for him the universe began to have some of the attributes hitherto ascribed only to God: infinity, eternity and creative fecundity. As he had begun by merging the Earth into the heavens, so Bruno ended by merging God and the universe together. The universe itself was the one and only incarnate divine being, God's unique self-expression, and all ideas of particular local revelations and divine interventions became redundant.

Two generations later the heterodox Jewish philosopher of Amsterdam, Baruch Spinoza, stated similar ideas in a far more rigorous and well thought-out form. Spinoza lived after Descartes, at a time when the scientific revolution was well under way, and he saw that the idea of the universal reign of physical law implied a unitary and self-sufficient cosmos which he called 'God or Nature'. An early biblical critic, he explained all ideas of divine intervention as products of pre-scientific ways of thinking, and was led to an outlook that was both profoundly mystical and also thoroughly rationalist and naturalistic.

Such figures as Bruno and Spinoza were far ahead of their times, and the mainstream of thought moved more slowly; but in many ways it moved in the same direction. Scientific and critical ways of thinking do in the long run move towards naturalism, the doctrine that the only way we can satisfactorily explain any phenomenon in nature is to connect it up in a regular way with other phenomena and thereby show it to be just one instance of a recurrent pattern. At any rate, the whole way of thinking that looked to supernatural causes of events and supernatural backing for social institutions became gradually weaker. Natural explanations for the occurrence of comets, earthquakes, disease and crop-failure became available, and seemed demonstrably more powerful and effective. And as the habit of seeing everyday events as signs of God's wrath or favour became weaker, so Christians' own ideas of God became less fearsomely immediate and personal, less interventionist, vaguer and woollier. We can see how far this process has now gone if we examine the doctrines of God that are taught by the leading theologians of today. God has become no more than the expression of a diffuse cosmic optimism, a 'fundamental trust' that, deep down and despite appearances, the universe is friendly to us, a pious hope that since human beings are the most complex objects in the known universe and love is the supreme human value then the universe itself or the 'ground of all being' must itself be in a mysterious way somehow also loving. So ambiguous, so destitute of real explanatory value, and so utterly lacking in living religious power is such language that it is evident that there is today a looming crisis of belief in God even within the Churches.

Among the public at large there is a tendency to see in this process a gradual 'decline of religion' and loss of faith. But I shall try to show that there is a profound misconception here. The trouble is that people's perception of religious meanings is too rigid. As we saw earlier when talking about involuntary and forced religious change, the attempt to hold religious meanings fixed must fail, because the process of historical change slowly evacuates them and turns them into superstitions. By this process the faith of men like Luther and Bunyan – a faith that in them was new-minted, first-hand and of superlative quality – when made into a dogma declined into the bigotry of redneck fundamentalism. In the Christian tradition at least, religious meanings cannot be transmitted unchanged. Conservative Christianity is a contradiction in terms.

Hence I reject utterly the common conceptions of the gift of faith and the loss of faith, with the associated idea that there is a permanent, distinct and clear line between believers and unbelievers. Where people attempt to hold religious meanings unchanged, their notion of faith ineluctably becomes increasingly irrational and authoritarian. Soon we hear them speak of faith as being like romantic love, something that may be gained or lost quite inexplicably and involuntarily, a state of the soul that may be granted to us or may be withdrawn from us, we know not how or why. In Grahame Greene's writings of the 1930s to 1950s a supernaturalism that is under increasing strain produces just this conception of faith in a way that reaches a repellent climax in the play, *The Potting Shed* – and then something snapped. The sheer absurdities to which the idea of faith as divinely-produced assent to truths beyond reason had led became at last too great. Greene could no longer build such ideas into convincing works of art. He had to find new ways of thinking, and he did.

So we are not talking about two fixed and permanent camps with a clear line between them. On the contrary, the history of thought shows that all such lines and distinctions are shifting things, and the great thinkers continually redraw them. So far as religion is concerned, this means that the only way to a first-hand personal faith is always through what many people call 'the loss of faith'. You have to go through inner turmoil; you have to descend into the primal chaos, into that nameless region in the depths of the human soul where all meanings are unmade and remade. There at the source of the creative energy that makes us and our world, you pass through a kind of death and rebirth. The more you lose, the more you will gain.

It is through this process of death and rebirth that Christianity must continually pass to renew itself. A living faith never was found and never will be found in any other way. We have to dispense entirely with all ideas of holding on to the truth of old meanings. Supposed truths received at second hand and held on to in that way evaporate, turn into clouds and melt through our fingers like Jupiter in the arms of Io. People say that we live in a time when old certainties are dissolving away; but this is no matter for lament, for it is the nature of all certainties so to dissolve. To a deep existential thinker it is always the case that he must descend into the underworld, the primeval chaos, and there await the remaking of meanings and the emergence of a new reality. And so, returning to the question of what has happened and is happening to belief in God, it should be clear now that one particular *meaning* of God is evidently passing away, evaporating in the hands not of its enemies but of its own best proponents. People have been struggling for too long to hold on to a meaning of God which is passing away, no doubt because they think that this meaning is *the* meaning, the only possible meaning. But if meanings change and must be reminted then we should be looking for signs of a profound mutation of Christianity, a reforging of all its meanings.

It has all happened before. The Gospel message began in the Palestinian Aramaic world of Jesus and the first generation of his followers, a thought-world that was even then almost as strange and remote to contemporary Greeks and Romans as it now is to us. The New Testament itself is the record of the deep transformation of the earliest faith so that it could become a message intelligible to the Graeco-Roman world. There were similar shifts of meaning in the time of Constantine and at the Reformation. In a long historical perspective it would seem likely that the arrival of modern culture will demand the greatest meaning-shift yet, and the most difficult; but precedent suggests that we should not despair of its possibility. Human beings can never wholly lose touch with the forces of re-creation. When an order of meanings and values, a 'reality' that people have lived by, begins to fall into disrepair there are always a few prophetic spirits who sense what is happening and know as if instinctively what they themselves are called upon to undergo. Through the inner turmoil that they enter, a new order begins to take shape.

That is why, in discussions that went on intermittently for some years, *The Sea of Faith* increasingly took the form of a series of studies of outstanding individual figures. We might have cast the project in a much more broadly historical form, by attempting in a series of programmes to reconstruct the faith and the world-view of ordinary believers as it has slowly evolved over the centuries and is still evolving today. An interesting project, if it could be carried out; but I suspect that the story is too complex, and as yet too imperfectly understood by historians, for it to be feasible. By contrast, the exceptionally creative and prophetic characters we eventually chose for study are much more easily accessible. They admit us to their own inmost thoughts, and allow us sometimes to glimpse the emergence of a new order. But it is still the case that if you read this book with fixed and preformed religious meanings in your mind and with clear ideas about the frontier between belief and unbelief, then you will see only the tide receding. It is those who are prepared to abandon their preconceptions and to become as ignorant and innocent as Socrates himself who will be able to see the tide returning. The sea of faith, in Matthew Arnold's great metaphor, flows as well as ebbs; but the tide that returns is not quite the same as the tide that went out. It will rise equally high; and there is continuity. The very metaphors that we have used, of dissolution and recreation, of death and rebirth, of loss and gain, are themselves pointers to continuity at the deepest archetypal level. But to expect the new to be the same as the old is to miss the point.

Although, as we shall see, the new point of view has been taking shape for a very long time it remains obstinately difficult to grasp, or perhaps we remain obstinately reluctant to grasp it. A first sketch may be a useful clue through the labyrinth ahead.

Most people begin by thinking of their own religious beliefs as being 'literally' or descriptively true; as describing – however inadequately – real beings, forces and states of affairs. Thus there is supposed to be an objective God, another and higher world, a life after death and so forth. We call this naive kind of belief theological realism. Natural though it seems, there must be something wrong with it, for nowadays we have highly refined tests and standards for what is to count as knowledge, and by those criteria no religious belief whatever today belongs to the public body of tested knowledge.

It may be objected that there are a few factual elements in religious belief. For example, secular historians may judge it probably true that Jesus of Nazareth was executed by order of Pontius Pilate. But that only shows that the mere historical statement by itself is not religious. It only gets to be religious when people make it their own in a very special way and thereby come to affirm that Jesus died 'for us'. A belief is made religious, not so much by its content, as rather by the way it is held.

This suggests that religious beliefs should be understood not in the realist way, but rather as being more like moral convictions. They are not universal truths but community-truths, and they guide lives rather than describe facts. They belong together in systems, and each system in turn belongs to just one community. They express what it means to belong to that community, to share its way of life and to owe allegiance to its values. No religious beliefs are free-floating; they are all tied to communities, in such a way that every member of a community may be expected to accept a whole set of them, and those who do not belong to the community are not expected to accept any of them. So it comes about that we expect every Christian to affirm Christ's resurrection, but no Muslim to do so; and what is more, it would be against the very nature of religious beliefs to suppose that the content of faith in Christ's resurrection could ever be established as part of the public body of tested knowledge. You need faith to believe a thing of that kind; that is, you need to be committed to a certain community and its way of life.

All this is obvious today, and everyone takes it for granted. The revolution comes when we carry it through and apply it consistently to ourselves. We then see that realism has been abandoned. Our beliefs are rules of life dressed up in pictures, giving symbolic expression to our commitment to a particular community, its values, its sense of the shape and direction a human life should have – in a word, its spirituality.

There are in the human world many complete and coherent spiritualities or ways of life. Their values may overlap, but as wholes they are distinct; and there is no Archimedean point independent of them all from which they can be evaluated. For as soon as you begin to evaluate them, you have joined one of them.

Thus our most fundamental beliefs have simply to be chosen. Their 'truth' is not descriptive or factual truth, but the truth about the way they work out in our lives. They are to be acted upon.

If nothing can be prior to the acts of choice by which values and life-policies are adopted, then we see that religion is completely human, bound up with the cultures and the histories that it creates. Ordinary folk may think mythologically that their religious beliefs express timeless and objective truths, but specialists know that every last detail of every religion is human, evolved in human societies and having a purely human history that can in principle be reconstructed.

In the past those who came to see that religion is just human became themselves non-religious. Today this is no longer the case. The first *conscious* believers are appearing, people who know that religion is just human but have come to see that it is no less vital to us for that. Religion has to be human; it could not be otherwise, for it would not work as religion unless it were simply human.

Coupled with all this is a large-scale philosophical shift, the so-called 'end of metaphysics'. We have come to see that there can be for us nothing but the worlds that are constituted for us by our own languages and activities. All meaning and truth and value are man-made and could not be otherwise. The flux of experience is continuous and has no structure of its own. It is we who impose shape upon it to make of it a world to live in.

We will meet various forms of this doctrine – radical humanism or anthropocentrism – as it was taught by Marx, Nietzsche, Wittgenstein and others. Nietzsche in particular regarded its full implications as being catastrophic and revolutionary. So they are perhaps, and yet in another sense the idea is an old one, implicit not only in Greek humanism but also in Christianity's image of the ascended and glorified Christ, and in its doctrine of the will. The convert at baptism simply chose his new life, his new allegiances and values, his new world. Alongside the tradition of intellectualism which sees religious belief as assent to truths there is also a strain of voluntarism which stresses the primacy and the creativity of the will. We must choose what to be, what to value, and what world to constitute about ourselves, and that fearsome responsibility is absolutely primal. The chief task of religion is to reveal that originative moment of decision in which all things are created out of nothing – and *we* have to do it all.

This anthropocentric and voluntarist interpretation of religion will clearly involve drastic revision of the popular understanding of religious belief; but there will not be anything forced or unnatural about it. Those who think a fully demythologised version of Christianity far-fetched are misrepresenting the matter. On the contrary, we restore simple and plain meanings. Your 'future life', for example, will just be . . . your future life; and God . . . your god. It's as easy as that.

The editors of *Theology* have kindly allowed me to re-use some material they first published in 1983. My thanks go also to Peter Armstrong, to whom this book is dedicated, and to all those who worked with us on *The Sea of Faith*.

D.C.

Chapter 1

DOVER BEACH

The sea is calm to-night.
The tide is full, the moon lies fair
Upon the straits; – on the French coast the light
Gleams and is gone; the cliffs of England stand,
Glimmering and vast, out in the tranquil bay.
Come to the window, sweet is the night-air!
Only, from the long line of spray
Where the sea meets the moon-blanch'd land,
Listen! you hear the grating roar
Of pebbles which the waves draw back, and fling,
At their return, up the high strand,
Begin, and cease, and then again begin,
With tremulous cadence slow, and bring
The eternal note of sadness in.

Sophocles long ago
Heard it on the Aegaean, and it brought
Into his mind the turbid ebb and flow
Of human misery; we
Find also in the sound a thought,
Hearing it by this distant northern sea.

The Sea of Faith
Was once, too, at the full, and round earth's shore
Lay like the folds of a bright girdle furl'd.
But now I only hear
Its melancholy, long, withdrawing roar,
Retreating, to the breath
Of the night-wind, down the vast edges drear
And naked shingles of the world.

Matthew Arnold published 'Dover Beach' in 1867, in his last collection of poems. It expressed the sense, common in his time, that the ancient supernatural world of gods and spirits which had surrounded mankind since the first dawn of consciousness was at last inexorably slipping away. The English social and religious order had until quite recently seemed strong enough to be able to resist the encroachment of unbelief by isolating and containing it, but it was becoming apparent that the long rearguard action was being lost. From now on thinking Christians would either be revisionists of some kind, or else be consciously in a dissenting minority.

Arnold himself was a revisionist, for after turning away from poetry he published in the 1870s four books of what would now be called radical theology. But he was not primarily a thinker. In the English manner he was a mixture of poet and shopkeeper, combining an intuitive, imaginative mind with a sharp sense of social reality. What moved him was not philosophical argument, but his sense of the social and cultural changes that had come about with the French Revolution. In Britain intuitive thinking, acute social perceptions and a uniquely long experience of industrialism have ensured that even today events in the heart of the great cities are still seen as peculiarly challenging and significant.

Secularism

On Trinity Sunday 1959 I was ordained by William Greer, then Bishop of Manchester, to the parish of St Philip, Salford. I had chosen to return to Lancashire partly because I wanted to reconnect with my origins after an education in the south-east, and partly because like several of my friends I believed it was necessary to test my understanding of Christianity against the realities of life in an industrial city.

From that point of view, if from no other, Salford was ideal. Old Salford on the west bank of the Irwell and old Manchester facing it on the east bank together make up the oldest large industrial area in the world. Its population had begun to rocket in the late eighteenth century, reaching 100,000 by 1800, and rising again to 500,000 by 1850. The young Friedrich Engels and his Mary knew it intimately, and he drew on it for a good deal of the most horrific material in his early book on *The Condition of the Working Class in England in 1844*.

At the time when St Philip's was built in 1825 the vast population of this area had inevitably largely lost touch with the Church. There were two rather genteel town churches of Queen Anne date, St Ann, Manchester, and Sacred Trinity, Salford, full of rented pews, and there was the old Manchester Parish Church (today the Cathedral) where the legendary

Joss Brooks held sway as Chaplain. A rough, eccentric character, his ministry is chiefly remembered for – and cannot have consisted of much more than – the conducting of astonishingly large and chaotic mass baptisms and weddings.

The government recognised that in the new manufacturing towns a population was developing which was quite without religion, and it voted two large grants of public money for the provision of churches as a thank-offering for the victory at Waterloo. St Philip's, a formidable pile erected in 1824 by Sir Robert Smirke in the Grecian style then fashionable, is one of the 'Waterloo churches'. Inside, it is evident that this is a building designed to seat as many people as possible for the money. Upstairs in the gallery, the tightly-packed cheap seating for the poor can still be seen. Downstairs there were originally rented pews for the middle classes, who in those days before commuting still lived along the main streets of the new industrial towns. Their pew-rents, like today's Steward-ship Schemes, helped to finance the church, but it was difficult not to be reminded of Jesus' criticism of the Pharisees for monopolising the chief seats in the synagogues.

Still, in the early nineteenth century the community did at least attempt to provide seating in church for the new industrial proletariat. Between 1801 and 1851, 2529 new Anglican churches were built up and down the country. If they had all been large like St Philip's, so that they averaged 750 seats each, then they would have provided just under two million seats.

Unfortunately, even this was nowhere near enough. The population had risen in the same period from 8 to 18 million. As a result, by the mid-century in the great manufacturing towns there were enough seats in church for only about one-third of the population, half of these seats being in parish churches, and the other half being in Chapels and Roman Catholic churches.

It is clear then that even if everyone in the great towns had wanted to go to church, there were never enough seats for them all to gather as a community in the traditional village fashion. And did they want to go? It seems not. The Census of 1851 (whose figures include an element of guesswork, but are the best we have) claimed that 42% of the England-and-Wales population had attended church on the day of the count. But Horace Mann, who organised the religious census, was well aware, and pointed out, that the percentage was higher than 42 among the upper and middle classes and among country people, and much lower in the industrial areas. It was lower still in the worst slum parishes – about 10% – and lowest of all among low-paid working men in the prime of life.

These men had been cured of their traditional deference, and they no longer accepted either the existing social order or the Church that was allied to it. There is a chilling account of their views in a letter written in 1843 by W.F. Hook, the Vicar of Leeds. Hook was no firebrand, but a solid Oxford High Churchman, an historian and a weighty and respected figure.

> In the manufacturing districts [the Church] is an object of detestation to the working classes. Among this class I have many friends, zealous and enlightened Churchmen; and from them, and the persecutions they endure, I know the feeling which exists. The working classes consider themselves to be oppressed people. They think that they can only obtain the right and importance they desire by exhibiting their strength . . . .

Hook goes on to say that the workers despise upper-class philanthropists like Lord Shaftesbury. They, the workers, regard themselves as a new Party or class in the State, and

> . . . many of them are noble and enthusiastic lovers of their Party. They place Party in the stead of the Church; and they consider the Church to belong to the Party of their oppressors; hence they hate it, and consider a man of the working-classes who is a Churchman to be a traitor to his Party or Order, – he is outlawed in the society in which he moves. Paupers and persons in need may go to church on the principle of living on the enemy; but woe to the young man in health or strength who proclaims himself a Churchman.

Thus wrote Hook in 1843, just a few years before the 'year of revolutions', 1848, the year of Chartism and the Communist Manifesto. 'They place Party in the stead of the Church', he says, indicating that a new and secularised social group has appeared. They are secularised because for them the political struggle to advance the cause of the working class in the present world (*saeculum*, in Latin) has replaced religion as life's highest imperative. In the next few years a cluster of new ideas entered the English language: *secularism* (1846), *secularist* (1851), and *secularisation* in the sense of changing education, morality and practical living so as to make them purely this-worldly in their reference (1863). So far as I can discover, it is only much more recently that we have commonly used *secularisation* in the further sense of the progressive extension of instrumental or utilitarian ways of thinking to more and more areas of life, so that the influence of religion in society and in individual thinking gradually contracts until eventually the sacred vanishes by having been wholly absorbed into the profane. But though the word is new, the reality it stands for was clearly present in the nineteenth century, a period of such rapid change and population-growth that there was plenty of room within it for both massive church expansion and a steady process of secularisation to be happening simultaneously.

The 1840s were critical years. Some notable foreign thinkers, such as the philosophers Ludwig Feuerbach and Auguste Comte, were openly making the switch from God to man, from the next life to this, and from religion to humanism, and they were influencing the many leading English writers who were losing their faith in that decade. But the bulk of the English middle class did not lose their religion until somewhere between Darwin and Bloomsbury, whereas the workers began to lose their faith much earlier. For some generations they continued to respect Jesus and religion; but they felt the Church was not for them.

Why was this? There is a great deal that can be said. The Poles, the Irish, the Romanians, the Greeks and others have folk churches, in which the complete identification of the people with their church was forged by centuries of hard struggle against foreign domination. A folk church seems strong enough to survive industrialism, at least for some time. But in England we never quite had a folk church. Religious change always began with the King and the Court, who then simply imposed the new order on the country. So it had been with King Ethelbert of Kent in 597, with William I and his detested Norman bishops and abbots, and so (most notoriously) it had repeatedly been with the Tudors and Stuarts. As a result the English have a long tradition of resenting, or at least being mildly sceptical about, a religious order imposed upon them from above by grandees. The men who burnt down the Bishop's palace at Bristol in 1831 were expressing sentiments familiar from the ballads of Robin Hood, and even long before that. English religion has always been easier to repudiate insofar as it has been perceived as laid on by the government, like poor St Philip's church which, much though I love it, does not look as if it was built by the people to express their faith. It looks like a preaching-hall put there by the government to civilise the people, which indeed is why it was originally built.

Yet though there might be occasional riots and revolts, England probably remained a land of majority religious practice until 1800. I say practice, rather than belief, because we have so little evidence as to what the common people actually believed before modern times. The picture of 'The Ages of Faith' is a picture created for us from the evidence left us by the tiny minorities of those who could write and the powerful whom they served. But historians now exploring the records of local Church courts turn up evidence suggesting that among the people there was a far wider range both of speculation and of superstition than the authorities liked to admit.

However, levels of orthodox practice must have been high. In medieval times the population fluctuated considerably, but in late thirteenth-
century England there were around 10,000 parish churches for 3,000,000
people. A land that, in spite of being very poor by modern standards, sets
out to provide a rich and costly church for every 300 or so people is
clearly very devout. Tudor and Stuart London was less devout, but it had
perhaps 80 churches for 80,000 people. Religion remained very important:
consider for example the very ample provision of new churches in the
rebuilding after the fire of London. The pagan self-assertion of the
Renaissance, the free-thinking of the Deists, the licence of the Restoration,
and the scepticism of the Age of Reason – movements such as these still
affected only very small élites. So if one seeks a simple answer to the
question, when did most people stop going to church?, then the best reply
that can be given is that, in England at least, permanent mass defection
from the Church began in the early industrial towns.

And why did some leaders of the industrial working class forsake
religion for politics? They had suffered an extreme dislocation of their
lives, so that they had become like refugees. They had left behind an
agricultural society in which the human social order had been bound into
and adapted to the natural order, and in which the whole scheme of
things had claimed the authority of God and tradition. That old order
had also been harsh and had provoked rebellion, and yet they had
understood it and it had more or less successfully held their allegiance.
But in the new industrial areas the old social controls that had held
people to the Church broke down, and the bigger the town the worse the
breakdown. The Church appeared to neglect or disdain the industrial
areas. People found themselves thrust into a new man-made world,
whose organisation no longer witnessed effectively to any overarching
divine order. Nature, the created order, appeared only in the form of raw
materials and physical energies harnessed and directed by man. There
was no superhuman Power any more. The conditions of life of the poor
were imposed not by God but by the managers and stockholders who had
set up and who controlled the new order. The traditional religious quest
for salvation from the power of evil must be reformulated. It must be
translated into political struggle to overthrow capitalism and establish a
just society on earth.

Here then, among the *déclassés* of the Industrial Revolution, modern
secularism emerges in its clearest and most uncompromising form, as
feelings and energies that had formerly expressed themselves in religious
and other-worldly terms come to be redirected towards this-worldly and
political ends. In the process a certain messianism enters the language

of politics. The nation-state takes over something of the special sense of corporate identity, historic mission, and veneration for its saints and martyrs that had once belonged to the Church alone. The brotherhood of believers takes a secularised form as working-class solidarity. Continuing an old tradition, the suffering proletarian may be seen as a Christ-figure. The dedicated Party worker has many of the qualities of a devoted Church worker.

Behind these changes, questions arise. If the Industrial Revolution was based on a new secularised conception of the natural world and natural forces, then where had this come from? We will consider the question in our next chapter. And, more immediately, if there was ever a holistic, total Christian scheme of things in which everything was immediately related to God, then what *is* the secular, and how did it ever come to birth at all?

The spread of secular ways of thinking

To secularise something means to transfer it from the sacred to the secular realm. On the large scale the process of secularisation implies the progressive transfer of Church functions, rights and privileges to non-religious agencies.

However, that implies that the sacred is being methodically stripped and in the end completely swallowed by a confident, well-organised and self-conscious secular power. This makes us want to know how a secular power strong enough to do such a thing ever developed in the first place.

Christianity began as an eschatological religion of redemption. This meant that in a backhanded way it already acknowledged that there was a secular realm, with which it had nothing to do precisely because the secular – everything belonging to this present world-order – was evil, under God's judgment, and shortly to be brought to an end. The Christian had to die to the world, flee from it and all its works, and look for the speedy arrival of a supernatural deliverance at the End of All Things. The secular was everything evil and transient, everything that the faithful had to repudiate.

Unexpectedly, the End was delayed, and it became clear that many believers would spend their entire lives in this present world without ever seeing the consummation that they all hoped and prayed for. A conception of the whole of human life as being spent in a state of exile developed. This world was a dangerous obstacle-course, a pilgrimage fraught with perils on every hand towards a homeland that would be entered only on the far side of death. The believer looked neither to his right nor to his left, but soldiered on with his eyes fixed on his goal. In church, he

27

contemplated images of earlier travellers who had already completed their courses and were now safely established in the heavenly world – Christ, Mary, the saints and martyrs. *Every* image in church was an image either of a denizen of heaven or of the way to heaven through the font, the altar and the Cross.

When Christianity became the established faith of the later Roman Empire, images of the living first appeared, in the shape of royal persons who manifested on earth something of the blessedness and a good deal of the authority of heaven. Socially, now, as well as metaphysically, believers looked up, rather than either forwards or sideways, to see the realisation of their ideals. The Church was pleased to see the Emperor legislate along lines that were in accord with its teaching, but its prime interest was still not in social administration during the present era, and it was content to leave large areas of political and social life in other hands, without attempting to take them over.

The Church's continuing low esteem for this present life, with the consequent decay of public spirit, was blamed by Gibbon for the eventual fall of the Empire. Alternatively one might argue that it was precisely because the Church was not too heavily invested in the Empire that it could survive its collapse and help to build a new order afterwards. Perhaps Christianity owes its unique flexibility and power of renewal to the fact that it can never put all its eggs in one basket; but however that may be, a precedent had been created. A secular realm independent of Church control and with its own distinctive ways of thinking could exist, and could reappear when more stable and prosperous times returned in the Middle Ages.

We can detect a turning point in the twelfth century, with the hesitant rise of a warm interest in human love and of naturalism in art. Here we find the first beginnings of a favourable attitude to sexuality and to women, among the writers of romances and the courtly lovers of France. In the Cistercian house at Rievaulx in Yorkshire we find a positive evaluation of 'particular friendships' between monks. In the leaves carved on the capitals of Southwell Minster are some of the earliest examples of naturalism in European art.

These are certainly significant developments. After centuries of hard struggle and strict discipline, both military and religious, society is becoming more prosperous and beginning to relax. The barbarian virtues recede a little, and the softer, more feminine virtues of a high civilisation begin to come forward. There are more signs of devotion to Christ's humanity and especially to his sufferings, as in the devotions to his Wounds and Precious Blood. There is more interest in the merely human affections and more attention to earthly beauty. All sorts of new things, like realistic portraits, perspective and landscape will in due course follow.

Another development, however, is still more important for the emergence of a conscious and organised secular sphere of life, and that is the secularisation of the monarchy and the state. In the early Middle Ages the King had been a sacred, anointed and priestly figure, as he always remained in Byzantium. But in Western Christianity the clergy have tended to arrogate all sacredness to themselves, to see themselves as an élite Church within the Church, and so to regard as merely secular everything that falls outside the sphere of their own exclusive control. Ironically, in the high Middle Ages after 1100, as the clergy themselves became stronger, more organised and more privileged, so they desacralised the King, his functions of government, and the laity. 'The King is a layman, nothing more', they said, not realising that they were creating a potential rival. For clerical supremacy, in declaring the King and the State purely secular, was actually setting up a very strong alternative power-centre from which there might one day come a militantly secularising backlash against itself.

During the later Middle Ages the royal power and influence over the Church slowly increased. When the Protestant Reformation came to England, Henry VIII perceived that the historical moment had arrived when the King could assert his sole rights within his own domain. Under the Tudors the clergy began to forfeit their exclusive control even within their own sphere, as well as losing much of their influence in the law, politics and the exchequer. The Church courts began their long decline.

In the seventeenth century Dissent won at least the right to exist. Not every citizen needed to be of just the same religion as the sovereign, a vital step in the development of a more plural, tolerant and ultimately sceptical society. In the nineteenth century the forces of Dissent and of Secularism allied with each other to attack the traditional privileges of the Established Church. It was especially difficult to defend those privileges after the 1851 census had made it clear that only about half the country's worshipping Christians supported the Anglican Church. So the Church lost her special privileges in relation to membership of Parliament, the magistracy, the universities, the officer-class in the armed forces, the teaching profession, marriage and so on. Soon there appeared civil registration of births, state education, civil marriage, divorce and municipal burial-grounds. In effect the non-religious were gaining parity all along the line; and in the twentieth century this process was taken still further as the secular realm gained the moral confidence to expropriate from the clergy even their pastoral functions and their role as local community leaders and inspirers of philanthropic and charitable activity.

The last is a sign of the increasing moral autonomy of secular man. He has no hesitation in simply appropriating many Christian virtues, such as concern for prisoners, the sick, the hungry and the oppressed. At the same time he sharply criticises many traditional Christian doctrines and teachings such as those to do with original sin and the disciplining of children, the subjection of women, and the prohibitions against nakedness, homosexuality and contraception. In other areas, such as fasting and abstinence, he has cheerfully abandoned and forgotten the traditional religious disciplines and has independently invented new and secular equivalents such as sponsored mortifications for charity. So modern secular man invents his own autonomous ethic and is no longer accustomed to allowing religious authority to prescribe his morality to him.

More important even than any of this is the vast proliferation of non-religious and autonomous trades and professions, forms of expertise and branches of knowledge in modern times. This proliferation over the centuries has developed so far that it now goes without saying that most people in their daily lives are not obliged to take any cognizance at all of religion.

The form of secularism that we now have owes a good deal to engineering metaphors. It is chiefly concerned with efficiency, or what in the current jargon is called optimisation. Human activities and institutions at all levels are subject to the imperative: 'Resources ought to be managed and human affairs ought to be administered in such a way as to maximise overall human well-being!' It is not a form of rationality that can understand either art or worship, but it has become dominant. It is a world-view in which science has replaced theology, and interest has shifted from religion and morals to politics and economics.

There has been a complicated change in the way people understand themselves and the world around them. Instead of seeing the world in terms of poetry, myth and symbol – always seeing one thing in terms of another, and almost everything in terms of stories and human imagery – we have come to see the world in terms of mathematical frameworks and structural regularities. Instead of explaining things by reference to occult spiritual powers, we explain them by reference to a built-in law-abiding-ness. In the process our knowledge has multiplied so enormously that our ancestors seem to us to have been like men living in a dream. They explained from above, we explain from below. To understand things we take them to pieces and reassemble them to find out how they work, as a boy does with his motorcycle. Galileo called this 'the method of resolution and composition'. We now see everything, including even human beings themselves, as having been built up by slow degrees from simpler fore-runners. Pre-scientific people saw everything the other way round. They explained from above, estimating everything in its relation to the ideal and heavenly order of things. We see human beings in terms of the animal background from which they have risen; they saw human beings as having fallen from original perfection. The moral and religious ideal was very vivid, and gave to pre-scientific man the yardstick by which he measured and assessed everything around him.

The shift, then, is from myths to maths, from animism to mechanism, and from explanation down from above to explanation up from below. As the change from the old world-view to the new takes place, people feel less and less need to refer to the religious realm. It no longer seems so urgently necessary to secure the favour of spirit-beings behind the scenes. We no longer instinctively look for supernatural admonitions in the small reverses of fortune that happen to us every day. Those people who do think they are receiving little messages all the time seem to be superstitious or even mad. The explanatory utility of religious ideas thus fades away. Myth begins to get a bad name and to be equated with untruth. Religion seems to be evacuated of its descriptive content, that is, its capacity to inform us about how things are and how the world works. Few people still think that some one religion gives the only correct account of what there is out there in the universe. The job of describing the universe seems nowadays to be done much more adequately by science. So religion comes to be seen as concerned rather with inspiration than explanation. It expresses itself inwardly as piety, outwardly as ethical striving to realise its ideals.

The persistence of religion
The process of secularisation has been going on very slowly for a very long time. Its beginning, at the height of Christian civilisation in the twelfth century, seems to be connected with the fact that Christianity makes a sharper distinction than other faiths between the clergy and the laity, and between the sacred and the secular. The faith itself tended to push political and economic man away, out into a non-religious realm. In time, that secular realm of politics, economics, science and technology outgrew and overwhelmed the sacred. Religion lost its influence in public life, and in the past century or so has even lost much of its influence in private life as well.

As early as Galileo and Descartes a new view of the universe and a new intellectual outlook was developing which had little in common with the older Christian outlook. With the industrial revolution and the subsequent development of modern civilisation whole classes of society altogether lost touch with traditional faith. Today, a second industrial revolution is beginning which during the next century will probably eliminate most of what is left of traditional societies and traditional ways of thinking. There are plenty of disillusioned conservatives about who do not like modern secular rationality and who deplore the loss of the old values, but how can they stop what is happening? They cannot actually prove the truth of their supernatural beliefs. On the contrary, the whole development of modern society has, for a very long time now, been unfriendly to such beliefs.

We started by asking why people do not go to church, but it is also worth asking why it is that in spite of everything so many people still do go to church. If the whole climate of thought has been so inimical to religion for so long, how does religion survive?

It survives, surely, because the progressive weakening of religious institutions and religious thought does not alter the fact that at the deepest level religious needs and impulses are as great as ever. Some of the traditional functions of religion have now been taken over by other agencies, and it would be foolish nowadays to look to religious action to cure disease or to ensure a good harvest. But other and more serious motives to religion remain unchanged. We are still prompted to religious dread and longing by the thought of our own death, our own littleness, and the precariousness of human values in the face of Nature's vast indifference. What immense epochs there were before us and will be after us, of which we know nothing and that know nothing of us! How frail the human is, how wretched most men's lives, and how threatened our happiness is by evil within us and about us! It is still the task of religion to generate an order of meanings and values for us to live by, an order which can give moral weight and purpose to individual and social life. Human society will always need such an order as a gyroscope that keeps the moral life properly poised between commitment and non-attachment, pursuit of the active social virtues and inner disinterestedness and freedom.

Traditional religion, then, survives for the very good reason that it still works – as religion. Unbelievers may rightly point to the intellectual difficulties of the theology, but believers are more impressed by the fact that the old faith still has power and still delivers the goods.

Here is a puzzle. The believers say, 'The faith works, so the theology must be true.' The sceptics retort, 'The theology can't be literally true, so how can the religion work?', and the familiar arguments between believers and sceptics begin, arguments which everyone feels have by now become inconclusive and profitless. The match has been drawn by repetition of moves, and the spectators have drifted away in boredom.

Twenty years ago in Salford I first began to see that the reason why the disputes were so futile was that both sides shared a common misconception about the nature of religious belief. In the face of sceptical attacks, the believers were mistakenly trying to defend positions to which in their hearts they were not really committed. I was acting as a hospital chaplain. Patients under stress would often revert to traditional ways of thinking, and then the striking thing was that I myself would be aghast and would try to talk them out of it.

There was a woman who had had a handicapped child. She was desperate, blaming herself. She must have offended God in some way, to be punished like this. What sin had she committed and how could she put things right?

That certainly was once the correct religious response to the birth of a handicapped child. Indeed, until quite recent times a monstrous birth was a major portent and a sign of really serious divine displeasure. But I could not bring myself to endorse that view. I had to insist that the handicap had natural causes. I said, 'Don't blame yourself. God is not punishing you.' I, minister of the Gospel, felt I had to deny her religious response as being too crude, and instead put forward a secular interpretation of her child's handicap. Wouldn't you?

The same thing happened with a man dying of cancer. 'Why is this happening to me? What have I done to deserve this?' He gave out the bitter, familiar complaint of a man struck down and dying in his prime. Now there was no doubt about the line I ought to take, because the Book of Common Prayer lays it down expressly. I must tell him that his cancer was sent him by God, and he must repent. The Prayer Book says, 'Whatsoever your sickness is, know you certainly, that it is God's visitation . . . render unto him humble thanks for his fatherly visitation, submitting yourself wholly unto his will [and] it shall turn to your profit.' So I had to tell this fellow that he must thank God for the cancer, and must repent and submit.

I could not do it. As in the other case, I felt impelled to say that cancer has natural causes, and I could not honestly see it as directly sent by God. But I tried to suggest to this man, as to the woman earlier, that we can conquer affliction by turning to God. We have to escape from our small, suffering, narrow consciousness and surrender ourselves out into the infinite divine consciousness. 'Think of a river, flowing out into the sea,' I murmured, the best I could do.

At the time, being young and foolish, I did not fully work out the implications of what I was saying. I could not stomach the idea that calamities like a baby's deformity or a man's cancer were directly caused by God. If I sincerely believed that about some evil that had happened to me, I believe I might go mad. A malignant God might send any number of further agonies at any moment and I could do nothing at all to ward them off. I clearly felt the scientific view of things to be a blessed release from that kind of terrorism. The world is a continuous natural process, and we should not think that natural events bear little occult messages to us. That is nowadays a kind of insanity. We ought to love natural science for its power to free us from superstition and fear, and science is a jealous wife who rightly demands complete fidelity. You must be consistent. You cannot hold the scientific attitude part-time.

Yet I still wanted to recommend religious values and attitudes to patients. I remained convinced of the value of prayer and worship and the urgent need to develop in oneself the inner religious resources to triumph over evil and suffering. I wanted to invoke the resources of faith, not in order to explain events, but in order to call up the strength to face events. By 'rock-like' faith we surely mean faith that gives just that sort of inner strength. God is a refuge, not a theory.

The implication of this is that we can and should dispense with signs and wonders, and cease to look for objective proofs of faith. In the modern period we have come more and more to explain events in this world in this-worldly terms. We no longer seem to require the old idea that there is an invisible world of supernatural beings lying behind this world. By and large, people have found that scientific explanations are better explanations than the old explanations in terms of spirit-agencies. This great cultural change does not mean the end of religion, but it does mean giving up some obsolete religious ideas.

One night there was a man who had a brain tumour and was not expected to live. An operation had just been performed and he lay unconscious, surrounded by relatives. At their request I prayed with them and stayed some time. Two nights later he had made a remarkable recovery, and was indeed eventually discharged. The relatives all thought there had been a miracle and crowded round me alarmingly. I was confounded. 'Thank the doctors. Thank God! Forget me, forget miracles,' I said, and did not mention the matter to my colleagues. In later years I have recalled the incident as a joke against myself, the sceptical Anglican who disapproves of religious enthusiasm. But now I no longer see it as comical. No, my instinct was correct. One ought always to discourage belief in miracles – as Jesus reportedly did.

I think I was at that time approaching the view that religion does not explain the causes of events in the world, and religion does not offer an auxiliary technology to be introduced when science has failed. Religious things must be done for their own sakes, and entirely disinterestedly. I came nearest to this conclusion one night at about 3 a.m., after I had left a death-bed. The patient had been quite unconscious and no relatives had come to sit by him as he died. I did not hold the magical view that giving him the last rites would actually alter his eternal destiny from what it would otherwise have been. So nobody knew I had been there and even I did not think I had achieved anything measurable; and yet I still thought it had been worthwhile. Why? My thought was mythological. I said, 'On the day of Judgment it will be the case that somebody cared, somebody turned up. I hope somebody else does the same for me when my time comes, and that is all there is to it.' Mythological thinking is not clear thinking, but that was the best I could do at that moment. Now I can put it a little more plainly and say that a religious act like praying has to be done for its own sake and because it is intrinsically good to do it, and not for the sake of some kind of subsequent pay-off. Religion is a way of responding to life, shaping life, giving ultimate meaning and value to life.

Ah, but this is only the crudest preliminary indication. We have a long way to travel before the picture can become clearer.

Chapter 2
THE MECHANICAL UNIVERSE

Modern secularism, I have suggested, largely consists in the diffusion of 'technological rationality' (i.e., instrumental, utilitarian or 'engineering' ways of thinking) through more and more areas of our lives. Behind secularism stands the Machine Age; and behind the machine there stands the mechanistic view of the universe. The reason is that the machine is itself drawn from nature, made from natural materials and harnessing natural forces. Thus the theory of the machine has to be a special case of an already-existing general theory of nature as a whole.

Because in this way the theory of how men make things work is grounded in a theory of how the world itself works, the very first technologists in primitive times thought that there must also be craftsman-gods, and saw their own skills as having come down from heaven. They thought of the technical processes that they were using as being simply speeded-up versions of natural processes. Those who first extracted metals, for example, saw themselves as copying the process by which metals are formed naturally in the womb of Mother Earth, and indeed the smelting-ovens of traditional Africa remain womb-shaped to this day.

The general idea, then, is that human engineering presupposes cosmic engineering; human technical activity is grounded in some greater pre-existing cosmic activity. But in that case what vision of nature underlies the Industrial Revolution, and in particular that extraordinary thing, the fully powered mass-production machine? The key point is that when we design a machine to be efficient – more efficient when designed in just this way than it would be if it were designed some other way – then we must be using applied mathematics. We must be thinking of the force that the machine harnesses as an almost abstract mathematical quantity, non-sacred, regular, predictable and controllable. And since this power we have harnessed is a natural force, we must have the same conception of the way those forces operate in nature at large.

That is what is new. In traditional societies manifestations of non-human power and non-biological movements in nature tend to be associated with supernatural Powers. Almost any event that is not caused by men or animals, but which is important or unexpected or awesome, is seen as caused by a spirit – and spirits are precisely *not* abstract, measurable, impersonal and controllable. Early civilised man had of course harnessed wind, water and fire, but they still remained unpredictable, capricious and a little awesome or numinous. There remained a tendency to animism, to seeing all winds, rivers, storms, fires and so forth as manifestations of sacred Power. As the first Greek philosopher said, 'Everything is full of gods.'

So mankind begins by seeing natural forces as Powers in the religious sense, and not as power in the modern engineer's sense. If an industrial revolution is to occur there must first take place a revolution in people's understanding of nature. They must come to see natural energies as impersonal, measurable, law-governed and controllable. Hence the importance of the scientific revolution.

The medieval world

Even today relics of pre-scientific thinking are still abundantly present in our language and symbolism, and they help us to understand what the old world-view was like. We still speak of famous entertainers as 'stars', as if there is an analogy between their exalted, shining social condition and the heavenly bodies. The people are seen in terms of the cosmic objects, and the cosmic objects in terms of the people. Stars in both senses become ideals that we look up to for guidance and inspiration.

In the old cosmology such a way of thinking was everywhere dominant. People saw the universe through cultural spectacles; that is, in terms of elaborate patterns of symbolism and religious belief. The effect was to generate a perceived harmony between the cosmic order and the social order that integrated mankind into the universe. Even people's experience of space and time was ordered by religious ideas.

An old parish church provides a concrete example of the principles involved. We approach it from the profane, neutral, public world of the street. As we come to the churchyard gate we recall that every arch, gate or doorway is important because it marks the transition from one region of space to another. We undergo a change of state when passing through it, and must be careful. Demons lurked by thresholds, and foundation-sacrifices were once offered when gates were set up.

Many churchyards have a lych-gate. 'Lych' means corpse, and the lych-gate was the place where the corpse rested, waiting for the funeral service which would complete its transition from the world of the living to the world of the dead. In Christian terms all doors and gates symbolise the passage from the profane world to the sacred world, from this life to the next life, and from judgment to salvation.

In the churchyard the dead lie sleeping and waiting for the Lord's coming. The church building itself, in Western Christendom, is an image both of the cosmos and of Christ's body on the cross. The west door of the church marks another entrance, this time to the community of Christ's body. Near to it is usually placed the font, which is symbolically both a grave and a womb, a place of death and rebirth.

Within the 'nave' of the church – a word that itself recalls a ship, the ark of salvation – the people congregated for worship are arranged rather as if they were in procession, on their pilgrimage through life to heaven.

The chancel arch, which we come to next, is yet another symbol of the passage from the earthly to the heavenly worlds. It is often screened, with a Rood – a crucifixion scene – mounted on top of the screen. Sometimes there is a Doom painting on the east wall of the nave, high above. Thus death, the sacrifice of Christ, and the Last Judgment must be passed through on the way from the profane world below to the heavenly world above. Within the chancel the various ministers who lead worship, the clergy and choir, are clad in the white of heaven.

A feeling of sacred awe becomes more intense as we come to the railed-off sanctuary. Rising steps indicate increasing degrees of exaltation and holiness. There may be a Bishop's throne, which symbolises the authority of God; but the chief focus is the altar or table which represents the only way to God, Christ's sacrifice, the communication of God's grace to men, and the communion of the Church with God through Christ.

Walking up through the church, we have experienced the religious organisation of space into a series of increasingly sacred zones. In the Church's year, time is similarly organised, with ferial days, fasts, black-letter days, red-letter days and major feasts. Religion thus presents space and time to us, not as the abstract mathematical quantities of modern man with his rulers and clocks, but as symbolically ordered and richly structured. We have encountered rising degrees of rank, interconnected and overlapping symbols, sacred powers and influences. If we can imagine a society in which such ideas were so powerful that they governed the way people perceived everything in the human and natural worlds, then we have an inkling of what the medieval outlook was like. Where we see the world in terms of mathematics, mechanisms and natural causes, they saw it in mythical and religious terms. For us, external reality is inert and only given meaning insofar as it is ordered by human creative activity, naming it, classifying it, imposing theories on it and harnessing it. In effect, we think of ourselves as having to make our own order to live by, our own society, science and art. But their universe was already saturated with pre-established divine order and meaning. In a far richer sense than can be the case for us, it was a real *cosmos*. Everything – not only Christ, but everything – ultimately descended from the heavenly world. From the supernatural world above radiated a sacred organising power which structured all their experience of space and time, of the world and society and the individual's life-history.

The sources of the old Christian culture were not purely biblical, but included a large element of Greek philosophy and cosmology. Indeed, the cosmology came almost wholly from Plato, his pupil Eudoxus, Aristotle and Ptolemy. The physical universe was finite and spherical, being something over 100 million miles across. It consisted of a series of concentric glassy shells, one inside another, made of an incorruptible material called the quintessence and having embedded in them the fixed stars and the various wandering planets. They all rotated, and the entire system was powered from above, motive energy descending from God through his angels and the various planetary heavens down ultimately to influence events on the corruptible Earth, fixed and stationary at the centre of the universe.

Each of the planetary heavens could be seen as being linked with one of the virtues and as having its own population of angels and departed souls. Each planet was also linked with one of the metals on Earth, and influenced some part of the human body. It was an astrological world, in which the signs of the zodiac in the starry heaven influenced human life through the planets. Thus Leo through the Sun influenced the heart and made people sanguine, Aries through Mars influenced the head and face, and so on. Surprisingly to a modern Christian, Christ was often portrayed at the centre of the zodiac, his power radiating out through its signs.

The Earth was the only part of the universe which was changeable and corruptible, and therefore could have a history. It was made of four elements, earth, water, air and fire, each of which had its natural place. Earth is lowest, for it sinks in water, whereas water issues forth from the earth and rests on its surface. Air-bubbles rise through water, so around and above the Earth is the natural place for a spherical envelope of air. Flames rise in air, so that beyond the atmosphere there must be a fiery sphere, filling out the rest of the sublunary realm. Thus everything tends to rise or fall in a straight line as it seeks out its proper level in the scheme of things. The Earth and the Heavens were not only made of different materials, but different physical laws applied; heavenly motions are naturally circular or orbital, whereas on Earth natural motions are linear.

Meanwhile, within the Earth itself is the underworld of Hell, also a hierarchy but inverted with its various circles descending step by step to Satan who lies wedged at the very centre, at the opposite pole of the universe from God.

In this way the universe incorporated a value-scale, everything good, eternal and perfect being ranged rank upon rank above men up to the feet of God. All authority and power thus came down from above, while conversely everything disruptive, disorderly and evil came up like volcanoes and earthquakes from below.

Thus too everything about him revolved around man on Earth, and had a hidden meaning for him. He was the microcosm of Creation, the little world. The macrocosm, the great Cosmos itself, was an intricate system of symbols enclosing man. It was like a sacred text, full of signs and hidden meanings that called for interpretation, and the person best qualified to explain its inner meaning for you in the way most important to you was not the engineer or mathematician but the preacher, the interpreter of scripture, and the theologian. This was a culture in which religion was the most powerful explainer of the way things are going. Everything that was or that happened, existed or happened for a purpose, and all explanation was teleological – that is, all things were explained in terms of the divinely appointed purpose they tended to fulfil.

More than that, the old medieval view of the world had harmonised Greek science and philosophy in a way that had the useful side-effect of backing up social and ecclesiastical authority. One very influential early medieval writer, known as Dionysius, divided up the nine choirs of angels into three orders in the celestial hierarchy, and then showed how on earth there was a corresponding ecclesiastical hierarchy in the shape of the threefold ministry of bishops, priests and deacons. Later schemes became much more elaborate, but running through them all was the idea that the authorities on earth reflect and are continuous with the cosmic powers.

The principles involved in all this were not specifically Christian, but were common to virtually all ancient societies. If human beings are to flourish, their way of life must be adapted to and interwoven with the natural order. Whereas we, looking back with eyes influenced by Marx, tend to see the analogy between the social order and the cosmic order as an ideology of domination, it did not seem so to them at the time. It would simply never have occurred to them that things could or should be otherwise. Also, because religious thought is very much more flexible and loose-knit than scientific thinking, their outlook was less totalitarian and systematic, much more varied and internally diverse, than our short summary has suggested.

However, there were certainly power-interests involved, whether or not people were conscious of their nature. Through the years of the Renaissance and the Reformation the Catholic Church in the West remained on the whole committed to the defence of Aristotle's natural philosophy and the traditional world-view, and sometimes all the more determinedly committed when it perceived an implicit challenge to its own authority. For the old scheme did back up the Church's authority: because everything in the universe was ultimately dependent upon and energised by the power of God, nature was not autonomous. For its daily working it depended on God – and therefore science depended on theology, and all branches of knowledge were subject to Church control. Because truth and social authority were bound together, knowledge was politics. Any challenge to the traditional world-view was implicitly a challenge to those who held power in society, and so inevitably involved a power-struggle. In our own century a major revolution in physics is not immediately perceived as a threat to the very foundations of society, but things were different in Galileo's time.

Galileo

The revolution in men's understanding of the universe that came about between Copernicus and Newton is an oft-told tale, and one in which there is a whole line of great figures, but of them all it is Galileo Galilei (1564–1642) who has perhaps the strongest claim to be reckoned the father of modern science, and whose career and fate have the greatest significance for us.

Galileo was born in the same year as Shakespeare, and spent his working life in the neighbourhood of Pisa, Padua and Florence. Behind him stood a line of distinguished Paduan mathematicians, and the great Renaissance traditions in drawing and in the mechanical arts. It was natural for men in his period to see themselves as following in the tradition of one or other of the ancient Greeks, and Galileo's own patron was not a metaphysician like Plato or Aristotle but the engineer and mathematician, Archimedes. Galileo was himself a good craftsman, and his universe was not the old sacred universe of myth and symbolism but an engineer's world.

How is Galileo's peculiar originality to be described? One way of putting it is to say that instead of setting out to explain events in terms of their *final* causes (the purposes that they were appointed to fulfil), he explains them in terms of *efficient* causes, by showing that they follow in a regular way from preceding events. Thus events are seen as mechanically pushed from behind, rather than as goal-seeking. But profounder still in its implications was the importance Galileo attached to applied mathematics. What swept the world clean was his conviction that the great Book of Nature was written solely in the language of mathematics. All natural events could be resolved into local motions of material bodies in accordance with mathematical laws that could be experimentally demonstrated – and this analysis constituted the only path to a true understanding of nature.

So, in the famous experiment with the inclined plane, Galileo demonstrated the nature of acceleration:

A piece of wooden moulding or scantling, about 12 cubits long, half a cubit wide, and three finger-breadths thick, was taken; on its edge was cut a channel a little more than one finger in breadth; having made this groove very straight, smooth, and polished, and having lined it with parchment, also as smooth and polished as possible, we rolled along it a hard, smooth, and very round bronze ball. Having placed this board in a sloping position, by lifting one end some one or two cubits above the other, we rolled the ball along the channel, noting, in a manner presently to be described, the time required to make the descent. We repeated this experiment more than once in order to measure the time with an accuracy such that the deviation between two observations never exceeded one-tenth of a pulse-beat. Having performed this operation and having assured ourselves of its reliability, we now rolled the ball only one-quarter the length of the channel; and having measured the time of its descent, we found it precisely one-half of the former. Next we tried other distances, comparing the time for the whole length with that for the half, or with that for two-thirds, or three-fourths, or indeed for any fraction; in such experiments, repeated a full hundred times, we always found that the spaces traversed were to each other as the squares of the times, and this was true for all inclinations of the plane, i.e., of the channel, along which we rolled the ball. We also observed that the times of descent, for various inclinations of the plane, bore to one another precisely that ratio which, as we shall see later, the Author had predicted and demonstrated for them.

For the measurement of time, we employed a large vessel of water placed in an elevated position; to the bottom of this vessel was soldered a pipe of small diameter giving a thin jet of water, which we collected in a small glass during the time of each descent, whether for the whole length of the channel or for a part of its length; the water thus collected was weighed after each descent, on a very accurate balance; the differences and ratios of these weights gave us the differences and ratios of the times, and this with such accuracy that although the operation was repeated many, many times, there was no appreciable discrepancy in the results.

For his experiment Galileo has attempted to set up an ideal situation in which the only variables that matter are speed, time and distance. So far as the techniques available to him allow, he tries to eliminate factors like friction; and he shows that the precise angle of his sloping plane does not matter by proving that it can be varied without affecting the essential point, which is that the velocity of a falling body is proportionate to the time it has been falling. He then draws a graph to illustrate the mathematical relationships involved.

By simplifying the situation, by repeated trials and careful measurements, and by mathematical analysis, Galileo has begun to discover unvarying laws of local motion. And he has shown Aristotle to be mistaken in one important matter, for Aristotle had had no proper concept of acceleration. He merely supposed that the velocity with which a body falls is constant and is directly proportional to its weight. But as Galileo already knew, when a large ball of lead and a small ball of lead are dropped simultaneously they strike the ground simultaneously. Now he had the mathematical model which would correctly describe their accelerating movement.

Galileo was convinced of the truth of the mechanistic view of nature, and of the power of mathematics to unlock Nature's secrets. By working on those assumptions he had got significant results, and felt himself vindicated. The next stage was to use his accumulated results and observations as polemical weapons in a determined onslaught against the remains of the old Aristotelian philosophy of nature. Rivals had to be driven from the field without compunction, for only when people adopted Galileo's set of assumptions would science make real progress.

Here is Galileo at his most revolutionary; not merely the discoverer of new scientific facts and theories, but the man who deliberately set out to overthrow the prevailing set of basic assumptions (or paradigm, as it is today often called) on which scientific work was done, and replace it by a new paradigm.

Galileo was a loyal Catholic who believed that his new paradigm (his mechanistic philosophy of nature and his mathematical and experimental method of enquiry) was just as compatible with the Catholic faith as the old one had been. Yet there were some obvious difficulties. In the dynamical view of the world now gradually taking shape, motion is seen as built into the universe and as being perpetual. Bodies remain in motion unless something arrests them; and then action and reaction are equal and opposite. Motion is conserved, and the universe no longer needs continual fresh injections of energy coming down ultimately from God the Prime Mover. As the universe thus tends to become automobile, the old argument from motion to God as the Prime Mover breaks down. The new mechanics can analyse and explain the way the physical world works without any necessity to refer to God in order to tell the full story. Physical science thus begins to become autonomous – logically independent of religious control – with an implied threat to the Church's truth-power, her hegemony over all branches of knowledge.

At the time, all this was latent rather than patent. Of more immediate significance was Galileo's work in astronomy. The Copernican astronomers of Galileo's time were imbued with platonic and semi-mystical ideas. Galileo wanted none of such notions. He took the essentials of Copernicanism and adapted them to his own preoccupations – his mechanistic philosophy and his war against the Aristotelians. Hearing about the possibilities of lining up a series of lenses, he made his first astronomical telescope, turned it on the heavens and (being what he was) immediately began to see fresh arguments against Aristotle. He saw, or thought he saw, not the closed, Earth-centred universe of the Middle Ages, but the universe of Copernicus with countless stars scattered across immeasurable space. The moons of Jupiter also became an instant argument against Aristotle, for they seemed to show that there could be no crystalline spheres; and the way they orbited their planet was a visible proof that there could indeed exist in nature just the sort of solar-system configuration of bodies that Copernicus had postulated. If Jupiter could carry satellites with it without leaving them behind, then the Earth might similarly be able to carry the Moon along with it.

Galileo hastened to publicise his discoveries in a small work called *The Message from the Stars* (1610), which had a great success. The conflict with the Church began to develop soon afterwards, but it still needs to be stressed that it was not Galileo's discoveries as such which caused offence. Nor was he in any way anti-Christian: indeed, his outlook was rather conservative, for he still distinguished celestial mechanics from terrestrial mechanics. In the heavens God has ordained that bodies shall naturally move in circular orbits, whereas on earth their motions can be analysed into combinations of linear motions. No, the real cause of offence was Galileo's passionate hostility to Aristotle and his dogmatic insistence on the truth of Copernicanism. He argued that if Scripture seemed to rule out Copernicanism, then it must be speaking merely metaphorically.

Friends in high places in the Church advised Galileo to move more slowly. The Church would surely accept Copernicanism, given enough time, and a clear demonstration of its truth. But events moved too quickly. In 1616 Consultors to the Holy Office advised that it was revealed truth that the sun moves. Galileo's teaching was therefore heretical, and he must abandon it. On 26 February a representative of the Holy Office, probably exceeding his powers, summoned Galileo

> . . . and did order him to relinquish altogether the said opinion, namely, that the sun is in the centre of the universe and that the earth moves; nor henceforth to hold, teach or defend it in any way, either verbally or in writing. Otherwise, proceedings would be taken against him by the Holy Office. The said Galileo acquiesced in this ruling and promised to obey it.

The document from which this passage is taken is faulty in form, and we cannot be quite sure that Galileo really accepted quite so strict a ban or, even if he did, whether he needed to consider himself bound by it. What is sure, though, is that next month the Holy Office condemned attempts to reconcile Copernicanism with Scripture, and suspended Copernicus's book. It remained in suspension till 1757.

Galileo was, however, a very prominent figure, and he did not lack powerful supporters. The ban, even read strictly and literally, still seems to leave a loophole: the merits of the Copernican theory, as a hypothesis, could perhaps be discussed in a book of Dialogues in which the author's own final opinion was not explicitly stated. So Galileo finally published his *Dialogue on the Two Chief World Systems*, in 1632, having (as he thought) first cleared it with the Church authorities. It bears the proper *Imprimaturs*.

Unfortunately, although Galileo had indeed stuck to dialogue form, his love of polemics had got the better of him. The Copernican spokesman scored too overwhelming a victory, and was too mocking in his treatment of the Aristotelian spokesman, who appeared as little better than a simpleton. He was even called Simplicio, and Pope Urban VIII, who had long been friendly to Galileo, was mortified when it was pointed out to him how brutally some of his own arguments, put into Simplicio's mouth, were being mocked. Besides, if the decree of the Holy Office against Copernicanism could be treated so cavalierly in this case, then its authority in other matters would be undermined. So the wheels were set in motion. The book was referred to a Commission, and they reported unfavourably to the Holy Office. The sale and publication of the book were stopped, and Galileo was summoned to Rome. An old man now, and in failing health, he reached Rome a few days before his sixty-ninth birthday. The hearings began on 12 April 1633. He defended himself, and there were those who still hoped for leniency. But the fact that, when seeking the *Imprimatur* for his book, he had failed to warn the censor about

45

the old (but dubious) ban of 1616 on his propagating Copernicanism told against him. After receiving a report on the progress of the hearings, the Pope ruled that Galileo must be obliged 'even with the threat of torture' to give satisfactory answers. When he had given them he must formally abjure his book and must suffer imprisonment, and the book itself must be prohibited.

A few days later the celebrated recantation took place, and thereafter Galileo was treated relatively mildly, being allowed to return to his villa at Arcetri. Apart from a short period when he was permitted to move to Florence for medical treatment, he stayed in Arcetri for the remainder of his life. In spite of his various handicaps and restrictions he continued to work, receiving visitors, teaching, dictating, and arranging for the publication of his writings in towns like Strasburg and Leyden which were beyond the effective jurisdiction of the Holy Office.

The condemnation of Galileo has been endlessly discussed and inevitably mythicised, with Galileo personifying the spirit of free enquiry, reason and enlightenment, and the Church being portrayed as oppressive and obscurantist. Others say with breezy confidence that it was all an unhappy accident: if the Church had accepted Copernicanism there need never have been any conflict between science and religion, and the subsequent history of Europe would have been very different.

Such views are superficial. Very great issues were and still are at stake, although it is in the nature of such cases that the antagonists at the time are never fully aware of them. For example, it is clear in retrospect that the revolution in cosmology whose success Galileo ensured was to have enormous social implications, because from now on great institutions like kingship, religion and the moral order could no longer claim the sort of cosmic backing that they had always had in previous societies. In the long run people would begin to perceive authority and order as coming up from below rather than down from above, from within the human community rather than from a higher world above; and it is a significant fact that the first successful democratic revolution in modern history was actually getting under way in England during the last years of Galileo's life. But at the time nobody either could or did formulate this thought clearly. It was too new, and people were not to become conscious of it for some generations yet. But gradually the leading political philosophers abandon the model of a king who by divine right exercises absolute rule over his subjects, and begin to replace it with a new social-contract model of the State. Finally, when the ideas of a citizen-state and representative government are established, it becomes possible for people to look back and see clearly how very differently political authority was validated in earlier times – and it at last becomes apparent that a revolution in world view has led to a profound social transformation, even though Galileo himself could have had no inkling of any such thing.

Equally significant in the long run was Galileo's reductive treatment of the forces, powers and influences that are at work in nature. His new paradigm recognises only those forces that work in a regular, testable and mathematically describable way. All the old mystic correspondences and hidden influences are swept aside as vain fancies. Astrological influences seemed to be intelligible within the context of the old way of thinking, but after Galileo anyone who has had a scientific education finds the very idea of astrological influence not so much false as simply unintelligible. We cannot imagine the mechanisms; we cannot think what the mystic bond that links a twelfth of the human population with a zodiacal sign is supposed to *be*, or just *how* the stars and the planets are thought to control events in human social life. With Galileo new standards of clarity and distinctness begin to be set, and by those standards the problem with astrology is not that it is false, but that it is too hopelessly vague and confused to be able to attain even the dignity of falsehood.

The vagueness in question here is not like the vagueness of weather forecasting. Meteorologists make definite measurements, from which with the help of clear mechanistic theories they deduce definite predictions. Because the global weather-machine is very complex the predictions can be mistaken, and no doubt often are. But nobody doubts that the weather has intelligible natural causes, and that meteorology is a genuine science in which progress can be and is being made. As more data are gathered and processed faster, the forecasts get steadily better. But astrology's vagueness is of a quite different and altogether more serious kind. The forces it postulates are apparently not detectable with scientific instruments, and there are not clear, testable mechanistic theories connecting in detail the relative positions of heavenly bodies with details of human character and behaviour. Astrology cannot attract serious interest, even if specific forecasts are successful, and significant correlations are established, unless and until it comes up with more definite and testable theories to link them.

More seriously, what is true of astrology is also true of other and more weighty ideas of hidden powers and influences at work in the world. What about divine providence, the causal efficacy of prayer, the operation of divine Grace, the activity of the Holy Spirit, and so forth? Can these ideas be brought up to the standards of clarity and precision set by mechanistic science, and if not, why not? If, as most people are agreed, the idea of testing religious beliefs by the scientific method is inappropriate, the question will still remain, 'Do they then suffer from the same sort of incurable woolliness as astrology, or is there at least some non-scientific way in which they can be made clearer and more definite, so that we can understand just what is being claimed by them?'

People reply that modern science is no longer mechanistic in the sense in which it was in the days of Galileo and Descartes. This is true enough, if you have a clanking, materialistic, one-thing-pushing-another image of mechanism in your mind; for mechanical models in that sense have indeed been largely replaced in physics by subtler mathematical models. But the newer models are still proposing detailed and repeatable, publicly specifiable and publicly testable regular patterns of connection between events. They are still mechanistic, in a non-materialistic sense, and the requirement of precision and testability is as inexorable as ever.

So Galileo's new paradigm for science puts a great many religious ideas on the spot. It makes the philosophy of religion, which attempts to define the precise status of religious ideas, an important subject. But, again, Galileo himself did not see how radical were the implications of his own view of nature. He was content to say that God the Creator had written two Books, the Book of Nature and the Book of Scripture. In nature God was revealed simply as an engineer and mathematician, for the Book of Nature was written solely in the language of mathematics. The Scriptural revelation, by contrast, was written in a human language of words, metaphors and symbols. For generations afterwards this served as a politically convenient way of distinguishing the provinces of science and religion and minimising conflict between them, and Galileo did not enquire too closely into just how the providence, the miracles, the guidances, the interventions and the answers to prayer of which Scripture tells were to be fitted into the world of nature as he saw it. All that was for the future.

Pascal

The condemnation of Galileo did not altogether crush the spirit of Italian science, but it certainly increased the attractions of lands further north where scientific publication was easier, such as Holland and England. In France a very intense Catholic revival was in progress and it was necessary to be discreet, but the men of learning who crowded the meetings of the many informal scientific societies and academies succeeded on the whole in avoiding conflict with the authorities. One of them, Blaise Pascal (1623–1662), was both a gifted mathematician and experimenter and a man of passionately intense piety. He more than anyone else was the first to grasp something of the implications for faith of the 'New Philosophy'.

Pascal was the son of a high-ranking civil servant of Clermont-Ferrand. His mother died when he was only four, and he was raised to be a prodigy by his gifted and cultivated father. As has often happened in such cases, he grew up highly cerebral, puritanical and liable to depression. He once censured his married sister for caressing her own children, and in his *Pensées* (published posthumously in 1670) declares that it would be morally wrong for him ever to attract love because he could not reciprocate it. All his feelings went into his thought, his faith and his writing. Not surprisingly, men of Enlightenment principles from Voltaire right through to Nietzsche saw in him a textbook case of the pathological side of Western Christian religious psychology in its most tragic form. Subsequently, though, he has been rehabilitated, and we moderns are likelier to be thankful that his personal sufferings were turned to posterity's gain by his pen.

Pascal was brilliant: he published his first work, on the conic sections, at seventeen. In a classical series of experiments he demonstrated the mechanical principles of the barometer, helping to make it into a scientific instrument for measuring atmospheric pressure (and incidentally hammering another nail into Aristotle's coffin by confirming the existence of the vacuum, whose possibility Aristotle had denied). He invented mechanical computers which work and are still to be seen in the Musée du Conservatoire des Arts et Métiers in Paris, and he laid the foundations of modern probability theory. He even organised a horse-drawn omnibus service in Paris.

By the end of the 1630s Pascal senior was taking his young son to meetings of Paris scientific societies. One of the most remarkable of these groups met in the Place Royale, in the cell of the Minim Father Marin Mersenne, where René Descartes would attend when he visited Paris. Pascal met him there.

Descartes (1596–1650: see also pp. 131–33) was the leading theorist of the new mechanistic science, an uncompromising rationalist, and also (purportedly, at least) a loyal and orthodox Catholic; but the real interest guiding his philosophy was the justification of scientific knowledge. Starting, as everyone knows, from nothing but the method of thoroughgoing doubt and his intuition of his own existence as a thinking subject, Descartes aimed to establish a basic metaphysical framework by pure speculative argument. In his system there were three entities: the thinking and observing human mind as a spiritual substance; the mechanistic universe of bodies in motion; and God, who guaranteed both the existence of the physical universe and the power of human reason to attain to an accurate fundamental science of nature. The system sounded orthodox – did not Descartes believe in God, the world and the human soul? – but from another point of view it looked rather as if Descartes was merely using God to underwrite something else which was much more important to him, namely the capacity of human reason to generate from its own resources a complete science of nature.

Now Pascal had one thing in common with Descartes, for in both of them the individual human subject has a certain primacy. In the older medieval tradition the cosmos came first. Man was integrated into nature; it was as if the human psyche was spread out over nature, which was thus perceived as full of value, meaning and purpose. But the mechanistic philosophy had purged nature, secularised it, swept it bare; and the effect was that the human psyche was so to say drawn back into itself. The mind became vividly conscious of itself as being quite different in kind from the natural world which it contemplated. Descartes even defined matter and mind as opposites, the former being essentially spatially-extended and unthinking, the latter non-spatial and thinking. Alienation between the mind and the world became a common theme of the period. In literature, therefore, we find a heightened self-consciousness and an interest in psychological exploration.

The difference between Descartes and Pascal is that Descartes took the human mind out of the world of nature in order to make it exempt from natural law and able to observe nature from outside, from the theoretical standpoint of a pure scientist. Descartes does not *complain* about a sense of alienation in the way that Pascal does; he quite deliberately *creates* the alienation so as to provide the physicist with the required standpoint for doing physics.

However, the alienation of the mind from the world, which Descartes finds so desirable from the point of view of doing physics, is terrifying to Pascal from the religious point of view. That is the difference: in the end Descartes cares most about physics, whereas Pascal cares most about God, and he finds Descartes's coolly instrumental use of God revolting:

> I cannot forgive Descartes: in his whole philosophy he would like to do without God; but he could not help allowing him a flick of the fingers to set the world in motion; after that he had no more use for God.

This saying is not at all fair to Descartes's position (and indeed is only attributed to Pascal: we do not have it in his own handwriting), but it does convey something of Pascal's repugnance for what he sees as a deep lack of religious seriousness in Descartes's thought. Pascal does not deny the mechanistic vision of the universe, he does not deny the results of the new science, and he does not even quite deny the formal validity of Descartes's arguments; but he does say that the new world picture and the new view of man's place in nature creates a fearsome religious problem to which the cool God of the philosophers is no sort of answer. The human heart yearns, and in the cold universe now revealed it finds no response to its yearning, but only 'the eternal silence of these infinite spaces'.

Quite independently, Pascal already had a strongly Augustinian or Western Christian religious psychology, with its deep sense of how paradoxical, how inwardly divided, how corrupt and self-deceiving, how full of vanity and wretchedness, anxiety and despair, how great and yet how little, how suspended between angel and beast is human nature; and this sense was intensified still further by the new universe of science. Man was indeed suspended between opposites, the infinity of greatness above him disclosed by the telescope and the infinity of littleness below him disclosed by the microscope, and in all of it he could find nothing that met his heart's need. Like some later existentialist, Pascal sees a large part of human life as consisting in various attempts to escape by diverting oneself from the insoluble and tormenting questions of life. Hence his interest in gambling as an expression of boredom, despair and the need to seek out distractions: his famous Wager argument is more than just a sophistry or an *ad hominem* attempt to exploit the gambler's interest in calculating odds. Pascal sees, even shares, the psychic condition that leads people to gamble; and he is in effect saying, 'You are right to despair, right to see that the questions of life have become an insoluble enigma, right to see that you are at the mercy of something unknown to you, and right to see that you must cast yourself on that mercy. In almost every way your own deep self-understanding of your own heart and your own predicament are so nearly correct. Only, see now that it makes sense that you should cast yourself on the Mercy, not of chance, but of God, for the void in your heart is one that only God can fill. If this gamble comes off, then you gain everything; and even if it does not, at least you cannot be any more lost than you are now.'

If we interpret Pascal's Wager along these lines then we see how strong is his sympathetic self-alignment with the audience of aristocratic 'libertines' he has in mind, and how existential is his thinking. It becomes clear that the God on whom we are to bet is not the God of reason, but the God of the Bible who as Pascal sees it can alone satisfy the human heart. And by the God of the Bible Pascal of course means the God revealed in Jesus Christ. As creation, the world of nature, has become destitute of any perceivable religious meaning and value there is no longer any way to God through the physical world. Pascal's religious thought therefore becomes heavily concentrated upon the human realm. God must reveal himself in and through the human: that is, through Christ.

Here in Pascal we can see an early stage in a highly important shift in religious thought which was deeply to affect both Protestantism and Catholicism. It becomes more internalised, more man-centred and more Christ-centred. The older style of religious thought was more God-centred, and went through the cosmos and the social order: believers prayed to God through the cosmic Christ. But in the seventeenth century we find the beginnings of a tendency to see God only in the human Christ. Hymns and devotions addressed simply to Jesus become really common for the first time. A kind of humanism appears which sees in Jesus a friend, an elder brother, an accessible focus of devotion and an ideal of human piety. Religious thought focuses on the psychological, on conversion and grace and the believer's inner life, rather than on the older cosmological themes. Here is the seed of later movements such as pietism, methodism and evangelicalism which are still influential today, and it is the clue to the interpretation of Pascal's amulet, the piece of parchment which after his death was found sewn into his clothing:

> The year of grace 1654.
> Monday, 23 November, feast of Saint Clement, Pope and Martyr, and of others in the Martyrology.
> Eve of Saint Chrysogonus, Martyr and others.
> From about half past ten in the evening until half past midnight.
> Fire
> 'God of Abraham, God of Isaac, God of Jacob,' not of philosophers and scholars.
> Certainty, certainty, heartfelt, joy, peace.
> God of Jesus Christ.
> God of Jesus Christ.
> My God and your God.
> 'Thy God shall be my God.'
> The world forgotten, and everything except God.
> He can only be found by the ways taught in the Gospels.
> Greatness of the human soul.
> 'O righteous Father, the world has not known thee, but I have known thee.'
> Joy, joy, joy, tears of joy.
> I have cut myself off from him.
> 'They have forsaken me, the fountain of living waters.'
> 'My God wilt thou forsake me?'
> Let me not be cut off from him for ever!

'And this is life eternal, that they might know thee, the only true God,
and Jesus Christ whom thou hast sent.'
Jesus Christ.
Jesus Christ.
I have cut myself off from him, shunned him, denied him, crucified him.
Let me never be cut off from him!
He can only be kept by the ways taught in the Gospel.
Sweet and total renunciation.
Total submission to Jesus Christ and my director.
Everlasting joy in return for one day's effort on earth.
'I will not forget thy word.' Amen.

'This is faith', says Pascal, 'God felt by the heart, not by the reason.'
Arguments and proofs can produce no more than a temporary and
superficial assent; and even if there were a valid argument from the world
to God, it would end merely in the god of the Epicureans, a being of no
religious interest. The true God is found only through Christ and by the
way of the heart.

Many people are content with this. They feel that by his profound
analysis of the human condition, by his demonstration of our need for
saving faith, by his own leap to faith, by his personal testimony and by
his doctrine of 'the heart' Pascal has sufficiently vindicated his Christianity. What more need be said? Unfortunately, the real questions have
only just begun. Galileo had already taught, by his doctrine of the Two
Books, a clear distinction between scientific and religious truth – though
he of course held, even if he did not prove, that the two books have but
one Author. Now, in Pascal, there is a very sharp distinction between
faith and reason, which makes it difficult if not impossible to say what is
the precise status of his faith-assertions.

Consider a Shakespearean hero, strutting and ranting as he unburdens
himself of a long speech. Do we expect the speech to be *about* anything, as
Max Beerbohm once implied he did when he said disrespectfully that
Shakespeare's speeches when examined did not seem to mean very
much? No we do not, and Beerbohm was (perhaps deliberately) missing
the point; for the great Shakespearean speeches are almost entirely
expressive rather than descriptive. That is to say, their function is to
express the thoughts, feelings and intentions of their speakers in magnificent metaphors and rhetorical tropes. To suppose that a Shakespearean
speech needs to be checked item by item against things out there in
reality in order to have meaning is to miss its point. The meaning it
expresses is the speaker's own meaning, not something out there that he
means to speak about; and the truth it expresses is the truth of authentic
and powerful expression, not the truth of correspondence with indepen-

dent facts. The human mind has a natural tendency to realism, the doctrine that our words must designate things and that all truth is correspondence with external fact. But a great many of the most important kinds of human utterance are not really descriptive at all, but expressive.

So is Pascal's faith then just expressive, true simply in the sense of being an authentic expression of human religious feeling clothed in standard Christian metaphors? Or does he suppose that there are real invisible objects out there, such as God and Christ, which answer to his language? To use a terminology I have recently been trying to introduce, is Pascal in religion a realist who thinks that there exist special religious objects corresponding to religious ideas, or is he a non-realist? The answer is that Pascal's rejection of metaphysical reason as a way to God leaves him with no way of knowing for sure what the objective position is; and therefore it presumably does not matter to him. His view that metaphysics is irrelevant to religion entails that in order to gain an authentic faith he has to move to a standpoint from which he cannot tell whether his own faith-language is descriptive or expressive. To gain the kind of *saving* faith that he seeks as being alone worth having – faith in a *hidden* God – Pascal has had to go beyond worries about objectivity. In this context 'hidden' means 'non-objective'.

Such is the inner meaning of every kind of faith that rejects metaphysical support, or recognises that it can no longer be had; and it highlights a neat ironical contrast between Pascal and Descartes. Descartes has in his metaphysics an objective God. Descartes is 'orthodox' – but quite non-religious, for his professed Catholicism makes no serious difference to his real life and activity as thinker and scientist. By contrast, Pascal has religious seriousness and is a passionate Christian whose whole life is invested in his faith – but he does not have objectivity.

In the contrast here between Pascal and Descartes we see a striking early example of a puzzle that crops up repeatedly in later years: the claims of theological realism and of religious seriousness now pull in opposite directions. Either you can claim to have an objective God, like Descartes, or you can have an authentic Christian faith, like Pascal. It is one or the other: take your pick.

The point is not an easy one to grasp, and anyone who tries to make it too explicitly is liable to bring down the furies upon his own head. Unreflective people are natural realists in theology, just as they are in all other matters. But because any way to faith that has perceived the religious inadequacy of metaphysics is implicitly non-realist, and because since the rise of science our religious language is no longer fully integrated with our knowledge of the world about us, the issue of realism versus non-realism is the great undiscussed question underlying the whole development of modern religious thought. This book will be the first survey to keep it constantly in mind.

Chapter 3
THE HISTORICAL ANIMAL

The biblical world-view

Because they learnt it in earliest childhood, most people even today probably remain more familiar with the Genesis account of the creation of the world than they are with the scientific story that has officially replaced it. It pictures God as beginning, apparently, with the primal chaos and then setting it in order by imposing a series of distinctions upon it, until it becomes a complete and perfect creation, very good in his eyes and a fit habitation for mankind. We gather that the world was created all at once, relatively recently, and that it is coeval with the human race for which it was made. Mankind was specially created by God to be only a little lower than the angels, at the pinnacle of things visible, and given dominion over all lower-ranking creatures. Evil and suffering have entered the world only since the Fall of Man.

We can amplify this picture with the help of other Old Testament passages, so as to reconstruct how the ancient Jews saw their world. It is an archaic, earth-centred universe. The dry land is a huge flat disc, with the seas gathered into oceans around and upon it. Round the rim of the earth-disc are the pillars supporting the firmament, and the earth itself also rests on pillars that run down indefinitely.

Above the earth the heavenly bodies move like lanterns across the underside of the glassy sapphire dome of the firmament. In the firmament itself are trapdoors, the windows of heaven, which God can open to let out the snows, the hail and the rains. So there must be waters above the firmament, stored away in special chambers or treasuries in the space between the lower and the highest heavens. There are also chambers of the winds.

Heaven is not very high, for there is a story in Exodus of men ascending to it by climbing a mountain and then stepping out upon its sapphire pavement. Up there is the Throne of God, who is able to look down and watch all that we are doing. Earth is called his footstool.

Below the firmament, as well as the waters that were gathered into seas by God at the time of creation, there are also abyssal waters under the earth that rise in 'the fountains of the great Abyss', wells and springs. Also beneath the earth is Sheol, the Pit, the abode of the dead. The Underworld of the ancient Israelite was in fact much the same as the one Homer describes in Book XI of the *Odyssey*.

This view of the world was like that of many other tribal peoples in being based on casual observation with the naked eye, eked out with a few everyday analogies. Rain falls down, so there must be waters above the sky and the blue dome of Heaven must be like an inverted colander. We bury our dead, so perhaps they whisper to each other down there below ground, as the prophet Isaiah says. It is a view of the universe fantastically remote from that to which we have become accustomed since Copernicus and Galileo.

But the gap is much bigger than I have so far suggested. The Bible knows of no science and no scientists, and the ancient Jews had no idea of framing a general sketch or diagram of the cosmos. The nearest they get is the Genesis creation-story, which is really theology and not science, for it is intended to show the power and sovereignty of God rather than the structure of the cosmos. My picture of their world-view was a modern commentator's abstraction, untrue to their ways of thinking. They had no organised factual knowledge or science, so that they had no idea of the universe as an organic unity with its own independent existence and its own principles of change. That idea of Nature as a whole, which we owe to the Greeks, they simply lacked. Where we see a natural world they saw effects of the activity of God. They saw a range of diverse phenomena which all in different ways expressed and revealed God's power, wisdom, glory and good pleasure. To use a biblical image, all things revealed God, as drapery reveals the movement and activity of the body inside it.

Thus they saw everything in its relation to God, and for them nothing existed quite apart from God. There was no secular realm and there were no autonomous branches of knowledge. The world was a theatre for the manifestation of sacred power. There was a hierarchy of lesser powers leading up to God, the supreme sacred power, the Lord of Lords who overruled and activated all subordinate agencies.

However, I have still not reached the most fundamental contrast between their outlook and ours, which is that their whole world-view was not so much indicative as imperative, concerned with showing you how you must live. They lacked the stock of theoretical concepts that we have inherited from the Greeks, so that their language did not have terms for religion, morality, experience, conscience, personality, virtue, history, nature, or indeed for theory itself. Instead, the Bible speaks of God's word, command, law, truth, knowledge, justice, mercy, righteousness, holiness and glory.

All their uses of language were very much more ethical and imperative than ours are. What we in English call the Ten Commandments are in Hebrew just the Ten *Words*, because words themselves were seen as being like forces that shape events and guide behaviour. *Thinking* is ethical deliberation, deciding in one's heart what to do, *truth* is moral constancy and reliability, and *knowledge* is *ac*knowledgement, discriminating between good and evil, and cleaving to and communing with that which one has chosen. Through and through, biblical thought is practical and religious. There are very few, if any, quite neutral facts and therefore there is no Greek-type theoretical knowledge of God or of any other religious object or event. To use a later terminology, the Bible's outlook is voluntarist rather than realist, for it stresses the primacy of the will rather than of being.

The effect of all this is that in ancient Jewish thought a religious belief was not a sort of explanatory theory. Rather, it was a demand for obedience and a claim on one's allegiance. Knowing God is simply equated with doing righteousness. Hence to this day Jewish faith still remains a matter of practice and of community loyalty, rather than of doctrine, about which Judaism has always been tolerant.

We have seen that biblical cosmology, so far as there is such a thing, is primitive, earth-centred and pre-scientific. One might expect, then, that those people who today believe the Bible to be the inerrant Word of God would be flat-earthers. In fact they are not: they reserve their wrath for the unfortunate Charles Darwin. Religion was more badly shaken when the universe went historical in the nineteenth century than it had been when the universe went mechanical in the seventeenth century.

One factor is this: at the beginning of the nineteenth century a good deal of early modern science was still in some respects religious. It had a static view of nature, and still tended to invoke God as the original establisher of the cosmic order. Though nature was now officially mech-,anical it was still seen as revealing God's attributes, and works of natural history still sermonised. One of the best-known of these books was *The Wisdom of God manifested in the Works of Creation* (1691) by John Ray, 'the Aristotle of England' and Fellow of Trinity College, Cambridge. It continued to be reprinted and read with enthusiasm right into Darwin's time, for it typified a compromise between science and religion that seemed so satisfactory that the biblicists were willing for its sake to overlook the gulf between the Bible and Sir Isaac Newton.

The basic idea was an extension of the theory of the Two Books. Mechanistic science was allowed to explain the structure and workings of physical nature without restriction. But who had designed this beautiful world-machine and set it going in the first place? Only Scripture could answer that question. So science dealt with the everyday tick-tock of the cosmic clockwork, and religion dealt with the ultimates: first beginnings and last ends, God and the soul. This demarcation of the provinces of scientific and theological explanations had the authority not only of Galileo but also of Sir Francis Bacon behind it.

It was a happy compromise while it lasted. Science actively promoted the cause of religion by showing the beautiful workmanship of the world. No mechanistic theory seemed able to account for the origin of life and the adaptation of organisms to their ways of life. Only a wise and good Creator could have originally made ducks' feet and bills to be just the shape they would need for their survival. It was a good God who had thought of putting the mountains in the right places to precipitate rain from the clouds and give us fresh water to drink. Such is the old Argument from Design, and if it seems quaint to us now, it once seemed cogent and did a good job by shifting people's eyes away from seeing God at work in the freakish and fearful to admiring his wisdom and workmanship in the ordinary course of things. Religion became less nervous and superstitious, more calm and rational. Belief in witchcraft and evil spirits, omens and portents, and little particular judgments and providences gradually faded. People ceased to think that God was sending occult messages to them all the time. Faith became milder and cooler. The typical believer was a man like Gilbert White of Selborne, the most sensible sort of saint that any religion has ever produced.

But there was a fatal flaw in the synthesis. Religious ideas were being used to plug the gaps in scientific theory. Science could not yet explain how animals and plants had originated and had become so wonderfully adapted to their environment – so that was handed over to religion. People still made a sharp soul-body distinction, and the soul fell beyond the scope of science – so everything to do with human inwardness and personal and social behaviour remained the province of the preacher and moralist.

Religious ideas thus came to be understood in an excessively realist and quasi-scientific way, because they were being used to make up for the deficiencies of current science. But when science began to produce historical and developmental explanations of how the cosmic order had taken shape, it inevitably displaced the religious ideas that had been used as stop-gaps. So there was conflict.

The first science to become historical was geology. The story is a long one, because even as early as the seventeenth century men like Robert Hooke and Nils Steensen (Steno, of Denmark) were already casting a speculative eye at fossils and landscape. But the very idea of an immense pre-human history of the earth was difficult to get hold of until the successive stages of that history had been clearly fixed. A crucial advance here was made by an amateur.

William Smith

William Smith (1769–1839) was a drainage engineer and mineral surveyor. Born the son of a blacksmith at Churchill in Oxfordshire, he got his only formal education at the village school before being apprenticed to a surveyor at Stow-on-the-Wold. He set up in business on his own and took lodgings at Rugborne Farm, High Littleton, near Bath, while supervising the construction of a canal to serve the North Somerset coalfields. Even as a boy Smith had already begun picking up rocks and fossils, but now he was keeping systematic geological notes and forming his own ideas. He himself was later to call Rugborne Farm 'the birthplace of geology'.

The canal project succeeded, and soon Smith was in demand all over the country in connection with mining, drainage, surveying, canal-building and similar work. Wherever the ground was cut open, there was Smith, noting the succession of strata and collecting the fossils of each layer. As his collections and records grew, he was singlehandedly un-ravelling the geology of almost the whole of England and Wales.

Smith did not regard himself as a scientist. As he saw it, the information he was gathering was simply useful to him in his own line of business, and he neither belonged to the Geological Society of London nor knew anything of the controversies then raging among geologists. But he had collected and organised the facts far more thoroughly than any of the academics, and from 1815 he began to publish them in detail, beginning with his huge *Map of the Strata of England and Wales*, 8 feet 9 inches by 6 feet 2 inches, five miles to the inch, price 5 guineas, boxed in sheets. In the following years he issued books, plates of fossils, maps and sections through the landscape, until his money was gone and he was forced to sell his house to pay his debts.

What had Smith achieved? He had invented methods of geological mapping and technical terms that are still in use today. He had effectively shown that the Earth's surface is a buckled and worn-down layer-cake. Not all the layers are present everywhere, but such layers as are present are always in the standard succession from granite (the oldest) to London clay (the youngest). Although the chemical composition of a stratum may vary from one place to another, its fossils remain constant, and Smith was the first to realise that the unvarying sequence of the fossils provides the geologist with his best signposts, his chapter-titles in the history of the earth. A descent below ground is a descent, not into the mythic Underworld, but into the Earth's own remote history. Smith saw that that history could be reconstructed. As he put it, the orderly and legible succession of strata, each with its characteristic fossils, 'must readily convince every scientific or discerning person, that the earth is formed as well as governed, like the other works of its great Creator, according to regular and immutable laws, which are discoverable by human industry and observation. . . .' He realised the implications of the fact that there is a succession not only of rocks, but of living things:

> large portions of the earth once teemed with animation, and . . . the animals and plants thus finely preserved in the solid parts of the earth's interior, are so materially different from those now in existence, that they may be considered as a new creation . . . They are chiefly submarine, and as they vary generally from the present inhabitants of the sea, so at separate periods of the earth's formation they vary as much from each other; insomuch that each layer of these fossil organized bodies must be considered as a separate creation; or how could the earth be formed *stratum super stratum*, and each abundantly stored with a different race of animals and plants?

It is good to report that Smith lived long enough to win the scientific acclaim he deserved and to see geology securely launched by Charles Lyell, in his *Principles of Geology* (1830–33), as the first historical science of nature – a science that explains, not merely how some area of nature works today, but how it has developed. Religious stories about how the world-order was first constituted here begin to be replaced by well-founded scientific accounts of its gradual evolution through the steady working of natural causes.

It was a crucial moment in the history of religion, yet Smith had no idea whatever of being a revolutionary. Unspeculative, he betrays no sign of anxiety about breaking with the Genesis account of how the world began. Like many of his contemporaries, he seems to accept something like the Frenchman Buffon's idea that each day of creation in the Bible must correspond to a whole geological epoch. Also like many of his contemporaries, Smith thinks that God works through natural laws. The suggestion that all things were created finished and complete in a series of miraculous flashes would clearly leave no room for any stage-by-stage scientific explanation of how they came to be, which would be very unsatisfying to an enquiring mind. So for a long time there was a compromise: God makes things, but he does so through natural laws which scientists can discover. God was like a constitutional monarch whose acts, being in accordance with rules and so predictable, are fully explicable.

The upshot is that Smith sees each geological stratum with its characteristic life-forms as a distinct nomothetic creation (that is, as having been made by God through the working of regular laws of his own action in nature). There must have been several such acts over an immense period, so that God's work of Creation comes to be seen not as all-at-once and supernatural but as a temporally-extended process, in which God works through laws.

In the geology of the early decades of the nineteenth century God was still about and directing the world process, though in a more behind-the-scenes way than formerly. The older catastrophic and immediate irruptions of God's activity in the world-process were defended vigorously, but they gradually faded as natural explanations of geological phenomena became more satisfactory. Eventually the law-governed natural process came to be described simply on its own terms, with no obvious remaining need to refer to its rubber-stamping by the constitutional Monarch of the universe. So by degrees geology became autonomous, secular and positive, as God's part in it came to seem of less and less explanatory significance.

In the rock sequence is embedded the fossil sequence. Would biology go the same way as geology? Not necessarily – or so at least it was claimed – because although the fossil record undeniably displays historical succession and progression, it does not follow that it displays evolution. God might have specially created the succession of forms. Many felt that although mechanistic types of explanation might be able to explain all the features of inorganic nature, it strained credulity too much to suppose either that 'chance collocations of atoms' could have brought the first living things into being, or that mere natural process could have given rise to the whole subsequent succession of living organisms. Deeper still, there was an ancient religious connection between the ideas of life, the breath of life, and the activity of Spirit. Life was a mystery: there was something very special about it. It could only have been brought into being by a supernatural agent.

If many people felt that there had to be something special about the origin of life, they felt even more strongly that there could not be a naturalistic explanation of the origin of man, with his moral and religious capacities. Man transcended nature: to embed him completely within it would destroy the very foundations of religion and morality. A writer who had a very large public in Britain only a decade or so before *The Origin of Species* reveals how strongly these anxieties were felt.

Hugh Miller

> The low thunder of every railway, and the snort of every steam-engine, and the whistle of the wind amid the wires of every electric telegraph serve to publish the fact . . . that it is in the department of physics, not of metaphysics, that the greater minds of the age are engaged.

Thus wrote the celebrated Scottish geologist Hugh Miller (1802–1856), the stonemason from Cromarty, by way of warning the Churches that the chief challenge to their faith was nowadays coming not from philosophy but rather from the natural sciences. Miller was writing in his very popular book *Foot-Prints of the Creator* (1847), trying to refute evolution and prove that the fossil record and the latest scientific knowledge were still in accord with the book of Genesis.

Miller was not of course attacking Darwin, but an earlier and altogether less formidable evolutionist, Robert Chambers, author of *Vestiges of the Natural History of Creation* (1844). The *Vestiges* is a rather preposterous book, but it did teach the progressive transmutation of species, and against it Miller wrote a veritable dinosaur of a book, the last major work of biblical geology, blending scientific and scriptural thought in a way that would soon come to seem incongruous. Miller says that the author of the Bible and the author of Nature are one and the same. If so, then the patterns of action ascribed to God in the Bible must have analogies in the natural order, and Miller actually tried to prove from the fossil record that the fish and the reptiles had followed the biblical pattern of original perfection followed by a decline and fall. The reptiles began great and splendid, until God cut them down to size and humbled them, and gave their kingdom to the mammals. The once up-standing saurians declined into such degenerates as snakes. Early fish are nobly-fashioned, and it is only later in the fossil record that we find the degraded and distorted shapes of flatfish. So, trumpets Miller, it is simply not true that the fossil record supports atheistic philosophies of secular progress and natural advance. The book was loudly applauded and went into seventeen editions.

Hugh Miller was a strange man. Clever, canting, eloquent and with a sure sense of public taste, he was the only geologist who ever wrote best sellers. Yet there is no reason to doubt his sincerity, and it really did seem

63

to him that if human beings had risen progressively from animal forebears then the entire Christian scheme foundered. To start with, it would mean that the doctrines of Original Righteousness and the Fall were untrue. Man was naturally a rising being rather than a fallen one, getting nobler all the time rather than degraded and in desperate need of supernatural deliverance. In addition, the naturalistic and this-worldly outlook of evolutionism denied any qualitative difference between men and beasts, and so must lead to the loss of belief in life after death. People would cease to think of themselves as immortal souls with an eternal destiny and subject to the authority of a transcendent moral Judge. Like other writers of his time, Miller was clear what the consequences would be:

> The development doctrines are doing much harm on both sides of the Atlantic, especially among intelligent mechanics, and a class of young men engaged in the subordinate departments of trade and the law. . . . When persons in these walks become materialists, they become turbulent subjects and bad men.

You cannot put it plainer than that. By weakening the credibility of the religious deterrent, evolutionism would be subversive of the social order. The implication was that Miller's own geology, by endorsing the Christian scheme of Fall and Redemption, would support the social order.

For Miller the days of Creation are vast epochs, and the paleontologist studies the works of God on the fourth, fifth and sixth days, namely the Paleozoic, the Secondary and the Tertiary, linked with the kingdoms of the fish, the reptiles and the mammals. With the emergence of man late on the sixth day the creation is complete, and God's work moves into its redemption phase. But since the Redeemer is the Creator, Miller believes – as pre-scientific ages had believed – that there must be analogies and correspondence between Scripture and Nature, between the gospel of redemption and the facts of science. Hence his – to us, surprising – belief that the fossil record of fish and reptiles ought to and does embody themes from Christian theology.

The public loved this, but Miller's line of thought was already becoming outmoded, and his books which were once so hugely successful now lie forgotten. However much people might dislike Darwin's ideas, a serious scientist of the 1860s could no longer present a theory like Miller's as an alternative to them.

Charles Darwin (1809–1882)

The Origin of Species (1859) has been called the last great work of science in which the theological ideas play an important part, but in spite of – or is it because of? – the masses of evidence, there is still disagreement about Darwin's private religious views. Yet, as he himself was the first to insist, there was nothing very remarkable about his opinions. They were very much what might have been expected in a scientist of his period and temperament.

First, quite early in life – in the late 1830s – he lost belief in the Bible as a divine revelation. Only a few years before, things had been rather different. 'Whilst on board the Beagle', he recalled, 'I was quite orthodox, and I remember being heartily laughed at by several of the officers (though themselves orthodox) for quoting the Bible as an unanswerable authority. . . .' But soon afterwards he had come to see 'that the Old Testament was no more to be trusted than the sacred books of the Hindoos'. All his life he was sensitive to suffering and evil and (like many other Victorians) he was shocked by the cruel massacres that are ordained by God in the Bible, as well as finding much else in the Old Testament that he simply could not believe. Reading the Gospels led Darwin to think what a strange world they come from: 'the more we know of the fixed laws of nature the more incredible do miracles become, – men at that time were ignorant and credulous to a degree almost incomprehensible by us . . . many false religions have spread over large portions of the earth like wildfire. . . .' Such considerations led him to lose faith in the Christian revelation.

Secondly, Darwin was all his life a traditional scientific mechanist, inclined to materialism. He thought science should explain phenomena in terms of causal laws and mechanisms and not in terms of reasons and purposes. He did not believe that God acted immediately in the world. If there was a God, then he acted only through laws. Darwin taught the world how to see animals and plants as products of natural selection working on variations, a way of looking at them which excludes the Argument from Design. So, for Darwin, if there is any God at all, then God is very remote.

Yet Darwin was reluctant entirely to give up belief in God. In the *Origin* itself he speaks of 'the laws impressed on matter by the Creator', and of the Creator as having breathed life into the very first living things. All through his later life, in reply to questions from correspondents, he speaks of

> . . . the extreme difficulty or rather impossibility of conceiving this immense and wonderful universe, including man with his capacity of looking far backwards and far into futurity, as the result of blind chance or necessity. When thus reflecting, I feel compelled to look to a First Cause having an intelligent mind in some degree analogous to that of

man; and I deserve to be called a Theist. This conclusion was strong in my mind about the time , as far as I can remember, when I wrote the *Origin of Species*, and it is since that time that it has very gradually, and with many fluctuations, become weaker. But then arises the doubt – can the mind of man, which has, as I fully believe, been developed from a mind as low as that possessed by the lowest animals, be trusted when it draws such grand conclusions?

I cannot pretend to throw the least light on such abstruse problems. The mystery of the beginning of all things is insoluble by us, and I for one must be content to remain an Agnostic.

That is Darwin writing in 1876, near the end of his life, and rather more agnostic than he had been when he wrote *The Origin*. He was indeed typical of his age, and typical of a curious misunderstanding which underlay the general loss of faith.

Like many of his contemporaries Darwin saw religious beliefs as being of basically the same kind as scientific hypotheses. He and T. H. Huxley always assumed that Natural Selection and Special Creation by God were two rival hypotheses to account for the facts of biological adaptation. If Natural Selection had won the argument, then God had lost it and must beat a retreat. Religion was a kind of primitive science, steadily withdrawing as modern science took over and redeveloped its territory on more up-to-date lines.

No doubt it was the continuing influence of the post-Newtonian compromise that led Darwin to think in this way. In retrospect it now seems obvious that in the controversies too many people were clinging obstinately, not so much to false religious beliefs, as rather to a false and indefensible quasi-scientific conception of what religious beliefs are. It is a fact that deep assumptions about the nature of religious beliefs are often more strongly held than the beliefs themselves.

However, there is still the question of what Darwin's age called 'man's moral and religious capacities'. In the past the definition of human nature had been largely in the hands of preachers, moralists and philosophers, with dramatists (and more recently, novelists) also playing a part. A few philosophers, Hume and Schopenhauer for example, had pioneered more or less thoroughgoing naturalistic doctrines of man. But in general the human being had been defined in terms of his relation to non-naturalistic standards – ethical standards, religious standards, standards of rationality. We (so to say) assessed ourselves from a nature-transcending viewpoint; the truth of what we are appeared as we measured ourselves against timeless norms, exalted above the flux of nature.

On almost the last page of *The Origin*, Darwin had already hinted that evolutionary ideas could and would be applied to psychology. In

The Descent of Man (1871) and *The Expression of the Emotions* (1872), he developed this theme, suggesting that human behaviour and human mental capacities have the same sort of historically and biologically explicable structure as the human body. He even suggested that ethical standards, by binding human groups together in mutual sympathy, respect and co-operation, might themselves have had selective advantages in very early times, much as a trained and disciplined army may be expected to prevail over a rabble. Religious ideas too may have been valuable for the same reason, in that they embody publicly and impress upon each individual the claims of society and its standards.

These are only hints, but they are very significant hints. They suggest that it might be possible to see morality and religion as made for man, rather than the other way round; and that a naturalistic and 'genealogical' interpretation of the social function and the development of morality and religion could enable them to be seen in a new way. Above all, there was evidently scope for a Darwin of the mind to work out a new theory of human personality *from below*, in which the basic concepts would be the biological drives, the economy of the emotions, and the mechanisms by which in us nature has been turned into culture, and sentience into self-consciousness.

Sigmund Freud

Darwin was not a genius in the all-round Germanic sense, but he was a biological theorist of such astonishing power that to this day he still dominates large areas of his subject. For some reason great theoretical thinkers are very rare in biology, and Darwin was able to effect a revolution in our view of ourselves and our place in nature of enormous historical significance. The question arises, how did it come about that his ideas were accepted so quickly? Basically, because their time had come, and people were ready for them.

> In endless space countless luminous spheres, round each of which some dozen smaller spheres revolve, hot at the core and covered over with a hard cold crust; on this crust a mouldy film has produced living, knowing beings. . . .

That is from Schopenhauer's *The World as Will and as Idea* (1818; second enlarged edition, 1844), and was written many years before *The Origin of Species*. In Schopenhauer's great work the ideas of a universal pressing towards life and struggle for existence, of the conscious self as resting upon a far greater unconscious basis, and of the primacy of the sex-drive in human nature are already prominent:

Consciousness is the mere surface of the mind, of which, as of the earth, we do not know the inside, but only the crust.

The affirmation of the will is the persistent willing itself, undisturbed by knowledge, as it fills the life of man. . . The genitals are the focus of the will. . . In the sexual act is expressed the most decided affirmation of the will to live beyond the individual life.

Here Schopenhauer has rejected the idea that there is a distinct human rational soul, an immortal substance that transcends nature. On the contrary, we are like corks bobbing on the ocean, and our consciousness is a temporal by-product and the mere tool of an eternal and irresistible striving force that he calls 'the will'. Evidently the ideas of men like Darwin and Freud were not just novel and unexpected scientific discoveries that dropped into a culture quite unprepared for them, but were themselves products of a tradition that had long been moving in their direction. It was not Freud who invented sex but Schopenhauer, almost a century before him.

In spite of the widespread impression that the nineteenth century was an optimistic age of progress and expansion, the new naturalistic understanding of man could easily lead to pessimism on the part of those who felt that human beings were locked into nature and the prisoners of natural forces. Schopenhauer himself was a pessimist who saw man as 'a squirrel in a cage'. Since for him there is no question of our being able to modify in any way the implacable natural force whose playthings we are, he rejected entirely the Christian belief that the human person is capable of salvation and perfect happiness in his bodily existence. Instead his religious outlook was ascetic, for he held that it is possible in oneself to turn the will back upon itself and extinguish it. One can thus enter into the impersonal bliss of Nirvana. But this final state of salvation is indescribable. From the point of view of the natural man who lives in the world, it cannot be distinguished from nothingness. Nevertheless, Schopenhauer did affirm this ineffable ultimate state, so that although he rejected God and was strongly naturalistic in his philosophy, he is still in an important sense a religious thinker.

Sigmund Freud (1856–1939) was not. He rejected even Schopenhauer's minimal escape route. At the age of six Freud was shown by his mother a lesson that many Jewish mothers have taught their children: she rubbed her palms briskly together and pointed out the little black twists of grime that appeared: 'See, we are made of earth, as the Bible says.' Dust thou art, and unto dust shalt thou return; a certain tough-minded realism about the human lot thus reached Freud through the Jewish tradition. In later years he recalled the deep impression that this incident made upon him: 'I slowly acquiesced in the idea I was later to hear expressed in the words, "Thou owest nature a death."' For the mature Freud the highest spiritual state a human being can attain is stoic fortitude and a sober, unflinching acceptance of reality without the need for protective illusions. Because the drives that power us are not only insatiable and unconquerable, but also conflict both with each other and with what external reality will permit, no perfect inner harmony and happiness is possible in this life. Nor is there any other life: Freud has no sympathy either for Schopenhauer's asceticism or for his tenuous concept of salvation. Few thinkers before Freud – Hobbes and Hume are among those exceptions – had so starkly rejected all forms of belief in a *summum bonum*, the highest good and state of perfect blessedness that had traditionally been regarded as the ultimate goal of human life. In Freud's psychoanalytic theory and practice nothing more was offered to his patients than a modest reduction of their unhappiness, just enough to make life endurable.

At this point, though, we do hear a few faint echoes of religion. During the nineteenth century people who had once taken their sins to priests were beginning to take their problems to physicians, and Freud was himself conscious of the analogy between the modern analyst and such earlier practitioners as exorcists and confessors. As a long, guided passage through suffering to self-knowledge, the experience of analysis could be seen as a modern version of the ancient mythological descent into the underworld. However, although the understanding gained in the journey freed the patient from the domination of disabling illusions, it delivered him only into a clearer recognition and acceptance of the necessities of the human condition. In no sense did it promise any emancipation from those necessities.

The key to interpreting Freud's hostility to religion is therefore his rejection of any doctrine of supernatural salvation. Seen from any other starting-point, Freud's thought about religion appears too often to be confusing and of poor quality. Notoriously, he sets aside speculative religious thought as irrelevant and concentrates all his fire on the emotional dynamics of religion. The real God is not the philosopher's abstraction but the overwhelming jealous Father, the 'bloody mountain deity', 'the mighty personality of religious doctrine'. But why the objection? Freud himself, as is well known, was highly patriarchal and believed in strong fathers. He fully acknowledged the vital role that religion had played in the past in reconciling human beings to the demands of social life. He insisted that man is always a horde-animal rather than a herd-animal, in that all human groups are bound together in common subjection to a dominant leader-figure upon whom they project their emotions. And he recognised that the indwelling heavenly Father, being more rational, infallible and universal in his requirements, is the natural successor in us of the mortal and fallible human father. Put all these points together, and one might have expected that on his own premises Freud would have seen that belief in a Father-God who personifies *to* the individual the demands of culture and conscience *upon* the individual is likely to remain a permanent social and psychological necessity. Since nobody has done more than Freud to insist upon the historicity of the self and the inescapable persistence and power of the child within us, it ill becomes Freud to disparage religious belief as childish. To cite a parallel example which Freud did recognise, an adult human male who fails to recognise the importance of the child within himself in his relations with women is himself immature. Equally shallow is Freud's analogy between the practices of religion and those of obsessional neurotics. Almost all of human social life is ritualistic. The mere observation that the Church is ritualistic no more justifies a reductive analysis of its faith than the mere observation that the ancient university I serve is ritualistic justifies scepticism about its contributions to knowledge. Naturally academics are finicky and precisionist. So what?

Freud's reply to these criticisms of his attack on God shows his resemblance to Darwin. He thinks that if religious belief in its crudest and most literal form is shown to be no longer tenable, then the refined forms must break down as well. He felt that by exposing the natural human emotional mechanisms involved in belief in God he had taken the heart out of it. Henceforth, anyone who understands him and yet continues to defend religion will be able to defend it only as a desirable illusion for other people to hold. The growth of critical awareness has indeed shown how and why belief in God was once so vital, but has shown it in such a way that it cannot now regain its old authority. Those who still commend belief as useful and desirable can do so only because they know in their hearts that the battle is lost.

In this way Freud, like so many unbelievers, opens his argument by insisting disarmingly that the heart of the matter lies in an extremely literal or 'conservative' view of religious *meanings* – and then exploits it in order to arrive at an extremely sceptical view of religious *truths*.

He dealt in the same way with the social function of religion, by starting from religion in its most established and authoritarian form. He correctly points out that the great demand-systems by which in the past human nature was disciplined and socialised are now too harsh for the modern psyche to bear. Traditional religion was a system of domination which exacerbated anxiety and guilt quite as much as it relieved them, and whose promises and consolations are now, he says, perceived to have been illusory. In future it must yield up its throne to the milder and more rational rule of science and utilitarian ethics. At first there would be some sense of loss as people learned to live without the traditional comforts of religion, but in time the gains would be seen to outweigh the losses.

Freud was at this point too optimistic about the prospects for societies based entirely on scientific rationality, and neglects to examine the true role of religion in modern societies. He sees only the old kind of religion, religion used as a tool by society to persuade or coerce the individual into accepting the demands of culture, and fails to see that in modern conditions religion often plays a quite different role, as the strongest single weapon available to us in the struggle against totalitarianism. Religion in this new role is liberating precisely because it sets up a scale of values distinct from and at many points in conflict with civic values. So important is this value-conflict that in Christianity most of the key exemplars of faith (the Baptist, Jesus, almost all the Apostles, the Martyrs and Confessors) are commemorated as victims of the very same state-power for which Christians have always prayed. In this way *religion itself expresses a tragic vision* and, being tragic, is liberating precisely because it opposes any neat totalitarian systematisation of the moral life.

This recognition of the importance of moral tragedy is very recent. In the Church, it has been brought about by her changed relationship to the State and civil society. In moral philosophy, it has taken the form of a revolt against the very idea of a coherent system of morality. Its chief source is Nietzsche, whose writings Freud knew well.

Yet Freud was surely right to think that a clearer view of the psychological dynamics of faith in God would have a powerful demyth-ologising effect. It would show people that religion really is human and historical, and reveal how much of projection, of illusion, of domination and of guilt-induction there has been in religion. At the very least, it would force religious change; but Freud himself goes further than that, in demanding the outright abolition of religion. He doggedly insists that all mysticism is desire to return to the womb, sainthood is impossible and ritual obsessional. Dismissing philosophical theology as worthless, he rules out the possibility that a demythologised form of religion might be able to conserve certain essential and irreplaceable religious values. For him, there is nothing in religion that merits preservation.

Underlying his whole discussion is his rejection of the concept of salvation. The very idea that religion might make a valuable contribution to psychic growth was ruled out, because Freud's system left so little room for any psychic growth in adulthood. From Freud's strictly Darwinian starting-point we exist only to transmit our genes, and after we have done that, nature can have no further use for us. So Freud's system provides a most elaborate theory of psychological development up to the attainment of full sexual maturity, and he allows for some subsequent repair-work. Otherwise nothing.

There was also a lurking anomaly in Freud's lifelong passion for the archaic. He built up a cherished collection of statuettes, at first mainly classical, and then increasingly oriental and primitive. They so filled his study that patients complained that it looked more like a museum than a doctor's consulting room. He loved them because of the affinity between the archaic and the unconscious. There was an analogy: as the vast unconscious mind has developed a thin skin of rationality on its top, so in human cultural history modern Western rationality has been super-imposed upon the millions of previous years of archaic thinking. Yet how could Freud reconcile his passion for the archaic, which he knew still bulks so large in our minds, with his scientism when the statuettes in his room were daily pointing out to him that the archaic is magical and religious through and through?

There were possibilities here for a return to religion, if the unconscious could come to be seen as not merely biological but also historical; as a repository of the religious history of the race. Someone who felt that scientific rationalism by itself is too narrow and deforming could argue that it was necessary to mediate between the conscious rational surface of the mind and its magico-religious depths. In this way there might be opened up possibilities of psychic growth and integration that Freud had neglected. He had an associate who took just this route.

C. G. Jung

Like some other great figures who have lived in our century, Jung suffered a certain diminishment by publicity in his last years. The first to whom it happened was Tolstoy; others have included Albert Schweitzer and (to a lesser degree, perhaps) Einstein, Freud and Picasso. In each case the man has tended to become fixed in the public mind as he was in his old age rather than as he was in his prime, and in Jung's case this is particularly misleading because the mystic sage of Bollingen had evolved so far from the busy young psychiatrist of the Burghölzli mental hospital in Zürich sixty years earlier.

Although C. G. Jung (1875–1961) was nineteen years younger than Freud, he was the faster developer of the two. By the time they first met in 1907 he had already done original work at the Burghölzli. Using association tests he had noticed, and had demonstrated physiologically, the way in which a cluster of words could have strong emotional associations of which the patient was unaware. This led him to introduce the term 'complex' into psychology and to take an interest, rare at such an early date, in the work of Freud. He had read *The Interpretation of Dreams* when it first appeared in 1900, and it seemed natural to ask whether Freud's ideas about how to interpret dreams and neurotic symptoms could be used to gain insight into full insanity, especially the delusions of schizophrenics. Some progress was made, but a number of other themes of a less Freudian kind also began to emerge. From the complex and from the well-known phenomena of multiple personality, Jung was led to the idea that fragments of the mind can take on the appearance of distinct and autonomous personalities. He also noticed that the delusions of schizophrenics often resemble theologies: they are like private religions, or personal myths which the psyche seems to have generated by way of explaining its present condition and adapting itself to the world. Often there were surprising resemblances between the myths and symbols produced by the schizophrenics, and those with which Jung was familiar from his studies in mythology and comparative religion. The idea that there is an affinity between religion and madness is very old. At this stage in his career Jung was not yet favourably disposed towards religion, so it led him to think less highly of religion rather than more highly of madness.

In 1906 Jung sent Freud a copy of his pioneering book on *The Psychology of Dementia Praecox*. Although he was already fifty years old Freud was still struggling, and much pleased by any signs of serious international interest in his work. Next year a very successful meeting took place, and the two men were close allies from 1907 to 1912. It is misleading, however, to picture Jung merely as a disciple who became an apostate. He was already a figure of considerable physical presence, social gifts and intellectual brilliance, who was developing ideas of his own. Far from being overawed by Freud, he behaved in some ways more like a potential rival for the leadership of the psychoanalytical movement. He soon gained the presidency of the International Association and the editorship of its journal, posts he did not hasten to relinquish as the split developed. When Jung finally did break away at the age of thirty-seven, it seems reasonable to surmise that he did so because he sensed that he could and would become something on his own account. By 1909 he had already resigned from the Burghölzli in order to develop the growing private practice that he conducted from his handsome new house at Kusnacht, and in 1913 the final breach was marked by the publication of *The Psychology of the Unconscious* (later called *Symbols of Transformation*), which announces Jung's arrival at a point of view decidedly different from Freud's.

All seemed set fair for Jung but, as it turned out, the break with Freud was followed by a long period of mental turmoil which lasted from 1913 to 1917. To put it in ironically mild terms, the experience from within of states of mind that he had previously theorised about only from the outside greatly accelerated the development of his thought.

Jung was influenced both by modern Romantic and by very archaic ideas of possession and inspiration. To the Romantics a creative thinker is the barometer of his age, one through whose spiritual struggles new insights and life-possibilities come to birth. In primitive thought, the shaman and the prophet must pass through spectacular ordeals of initiation in order to emerge on the far side with spiritual authority and wisdom. Put these two ideas together, and one can see why Jung came to see his own private mental breakdown as having a constructive and even a public significance. His sense of the correspondence between the inner and outer worlds even led him to see his 1913 visions of world destruction as prophetic of the World War. His own inner storm ran parallel to the great political upheaval going on around him in Europe. He listened attentively to the personifications that rose in his mind and spoke to him, treating them as if they were oracles, like biblical angels telling of things to come. He began drawing mandalas, mythological diagrams of his inner world of the type used in Himalayan Buddhism as aids to meditation. In his mandalas the various conflicting factors in Jung's unconscious are represented by symbols balanced against each other on opposite sides of the diagram, the whole moving inwards towards a central focus. The mandala thus expressed and assisted the soul's movement through spiritual conflict towards synthesis and integration. Jung was beginning to see so-called mental 'illness' as being in reality an unusually speeded-up and dramatic process of psychic transformation and growth.

As a child Jung had begun a lifelong practice of fashioning talismans, private objects or fetishes that expressed and symbolised facets of his inner self. He did not claim any personal artistic ability but his talismans, his carvings and his paintings suggested to him an expressive theory of art. In its spontaneous striving towards integration, the psyche seeks symbolic expression. In our craftwork we allow it to express itself and then, by looking at what we have made, become more conscious of what we are and what we are becoming. A completed series of objects that we have produced can be seen as an objectified spiritual biography, and the work of producing them has itself been therapeutic, for it has helped the psychic process along. The source of artistic creativity thus lies in the psyche's spontaneous urge continually to develop itself by expressing itself in symbol and story.

This reminds us of Coleridge's claim to have composed *Kubla Khan* 'in a profound sleep'; and certainly Jung himself became very good at lowering his inhibitions and letting the psyche rip. The brilliant and heterodox book *Answer to Job* (1952), written in his seventies, is sufficient witness to that. But there is a price to be paid. Much of Jung's writing is too rambling, rhapsodical and diffuse, and compares very unfavourably with that of Freud, the apostle of rationalism and a strong ego, who expounded his own thought with great clarity. At his best Jung is marvellously stimulating; but the fact is that real art requires not only Jungian inspiration but also rigorous rational control and self-criticism. Coleridge's claims are now known to be untrue; he was, shall we say, romancing.

Similarly, in the field of religion, Jung's method of self-abandonment to the unconscious differs by only a hairsbreadth from passive and self-indulgent reverie. Jung was in fact a very active and hardworking man who as an introvert used solitude to recharge his batteries. He always stressed how violent is the confrontation with the unconscious, and how painful is the requirement that the little self must die to allow the greater Self to be realised. He himself should probably not be blamed for the fact that the religion of his later years appeals all too much to the very well-to-do.

Jung may underestimate the importance of the will in religion, but his account has other and very great merits. He sees the psyche as a self-regulating organism that seeks inner and outer harmony. Its products are not, as with Freud, merely the effects of past causes but are teleological, looking forward to goals yet to be attained. More than any other post-Darwinian thinker, Jung has given meaning to the second half of human life by showing how through art and religion the psyche can move towards fulfilment in old age. He also suggests at least the outlines of a new way of looking at religion, as being admittedly a many-sided expression of universal human nature, but none the less valuable for that. Beneath the personal unconscious, in his scheme, lies the collective unconscious which is common to the whole race. In it are to be found the archetypes – not specific symbols, but innate propensities to generate patterns of myth and symbolism – from which the whole marvellous variety of religion, myth and art has arisen.

The objective side of religion, its institutions, dogmas, myths and rituals, is interpreted as a psychic projection, and is thereby made available to us as a vast body of resources to be used by us in the service of a modern spirituality. Jung's anthropocentric view of religion suggests that all the variety of the world's religions is the expression of a deep common human nature in which we all participate, and so inspires the historian of religions to believe that his subject when approached in a receptive and sympathetic spirit will become intelligible, and will be genuinely useful to his secular contemporaries.

Though a pastor's son, Jung became dissatisfied with orthodox Christianity at an early age. In philosophy he was a follower of Kant, who held that we can know only phenomena and not things in themselves. So he was always agnostic about the objective or metaphysical truth of religious beliefs. Sometimes he called himself an empiricist, someone who deals only with facts of experience, which in effect means that as a student of psychology and religion he deals only with what human beings have thought and felt and done about religion. If he commends religious belief, he commends it only as 'psychologically true', or instrumentally valuable in helping to produce an integrated personality. The objective side of religion was either inaccessible or even irrelevant, for Jung often speaks as if the real referents of all religious beliefs are psychic, the objective God 'out there' being merely a projection of the true God, who is the God-image in the psyche.

Jung was thus a consistent non-realist in his philosophy of religion. What makes his thought interesting is that he fully accepts the projection-theory of religion developed by atheists like Feuerbach and Marx, and then unexpectedly turns it around and derives from it a new set of arguments for taking religion very seriously indeed after all.

In doing so he relies on the idea of internalisation. In the Middle Ages men's psychic life had been projected out upon the world. The outer and inner worlds were fused in a single sacred vision and, except in the case of a few mystics, levels of individual self-awareness were rather low. You scarcely needed to explore your inner self when it was all out there, spread across the sky and painted on the walls of your parish church. Today though, when science has secularised external reality, religious meaning and value have been sucked back into the psyche. People feel spiritually starved. To modern secular man who feels that his life lacks meaning Jung says that it is all still there, inside you. Your dreams and fantasies and spiritual discontents are symptoms of its clamour for recognition. The impoverishment of the external world has necessarily been accompanied by a parallel enrichment of the inner world. The old religious imperative to look within and to seek self-knowledge, and the old religious doctrines that God is within the heart and that the felt need to seek him is itself evidence that we already have him, thus take on new meaning.

Jung very neatly turns the flank of the Darwinian criticism of religion. Challenged to come to terms with the fact that we human beings are wholly products of nature, with our biological history written into every cell of our bodies and into the structure of our personalities, he can retort, 'In that case we must also come to terms with our cultural and religious evolution, because that *also* has left its residues in our psyches. If our biological prehistory is in some measure reflected in our growth as embryos in the womb, by the same token our religious evolution is in equal measure reflected in our early childhood development, as we grow from the magico-religious thinking of infancy through the mythical-dogmatic thinking of the junior school to the autonomous and internalised faith of adulthood.' Jung can accept the challenge of naturalism by pointing out that our religious expressions are also part of the totality of nature, human nature and history.

A doubt remains. Since Jung claims to be a scientist, it has to be asked how far his doctrines of the psyche, the collective unconscious and the archetypes can be tested by scientific method. Are these doctrines in some sense factual, or do they merely provide a mythical justification for the much less contentious proposition that since all religions are human social products, and modern knowledge now ranges so widely, there is nothing to stop us from browsing where we wish and drawing nourishment from many sources? Is Jung really saying any more than that?

The answer is that, in spite of structuralism and other movements since Jung's time, we do not yet know the answer.

Chapter 4
GOING BY THE BOOK

Scriptures

All the great faiths are scriptural: Jews and Christians have their Bible: Hindus have the Vedas, including especially the *Upaniṣads* and the *Gita*; Sikhs have the Granth and Buddhists the Pali canon; Muslims the Qu'ran; the Chinese have Confucius and the Taoist scriptures – and so on. In each tradition, education largely consisted in learning to read so as to be able to steep yourself in the scriptures. The scriptures and commentaries were thought of as providing a complete course in holy and saving knowledge, and immersion in them filled you with divine wisdom and happiness. The study of the scriptures was itself an important act of religious devotion, and what was learnt from them was a large part of the stock of knowledge that society lived by, for until the modern period began there was not very much formal secular education. Indeed, there was not by today's standards very much secular knowledge to impart. By 'knowledge' people mostly meant moral and religious knowledge, not scientific knowledge; and religious knowledge was entirely different in character from scientific knowledge. Religious knowledge is a personal condition of inner strength, wisdom and peace of mind that you get by being deeply schooled in the scriptures, the devotion and the practice of your own tradition of faith. Religious knowledge is *received*, and is always thought of as something divine and eternal that comes down from heaven. So the Hebrew Torah and the Muslim Qu'ran were thought of as books eternally laid up in heaven that had been dictated to Moses and Muhammad. Although the Holy Book had appeared at a point in time, it was really an everlasting and heavenly thing. This effectively concealed the human and historical character of the Holy Scriptures, for it was supposed that God had dotted the last *i* and crossed the last *t* in eternity, before the Book ever appeared in history.

By contrast, scientific knowledge is not linked to any particular tradition of faith. It is morally neutral. It does not profess to change us inwardly or to give us eternal happiness. It is man-made, provisional, ever-changing and fast-growing. It is directed towards understanding and controlling the world about us, and in that role it is prodigiously powerful.

Scientific knowledge is so different from religious knowledge that it might seem that the two could easily co-exist without coming into conflict. However, in practice, as everyone knows, conflict does occur at many different levels. Science-based culture is activist and progressive, tending to see change as a good thing, and from its standpoint religion often appears to be obscurantist and morally backward. By contrast religion often sets its golden age in the past and tends to regard any change as being for the worse. The goals of secular and progressive science-based social development are regarded by the religious as unsatisfying, un-spiritual and shallow.

Because religious knowledge claims completeness, finality and eternal validity it becomes involved with cosmology. Religion commonly furnishes the community with a general characterisation of the cosmos and of their own history. It offers an account of human origins and destiny, and provides interpretations and remedies for disease, famine and other contingencies of life. But these are just the territories that modern science has particularly made its own. Its power has proved so great that in every society nowadays the intellectual authority of scientific medicine, agri-culture and astronomy is acknowledged as soon as they are understood. In these areas, religion must simply withdraw.

More generally, religion promotes an accepting and acquiescent temper of mind, whereas science promotes and requires analytical and critical habits of mind. Science teaches one always and systematically to question received theories and try to improve on them, to seek out difficulties and anomalies, and to pick things to pieces and check them over bit by bit. From the point of view of traditional religion, the scientific and critical temper of mind is presumptuous, awkward, trouble-some and rebellious.

During the second half of the seventeenth century scientific and critical ways of thinking became established. Inevitably people began to apply these new ways of thinking to the content and the sources of religious knowledge. This transformed the conflict between the traditional-religious and the critical-scientific ways of thinking into a conflict within religion itself, a conflict which has continued for three centuries without even approaching a solution. On the one side are those to whom the traditional conception of religious knowledge gives a sense of reality both timeless and immediate, so weighty and solid that they cannot imagine how it could be given up. On the other side stand those for whom the old conception has become plainly untenable, and who think that faith must now be seen as a continual quest rather than as a guaranteed deposit in our present possession.

The argument between the two points of view becomes fierce when the Bible is the topic at issue. For the traditionalists the Bible is a divine and holy book, whose author is God himself. It is his Word to men. The only fitting way to read it, and the only way to unlock its secrets, is to read it with the traditional receptive devotion. The critical attitude must be unsuitable because it is question-begging, assuming in advance that the Bible is not God's Word but a merely human book.

To this the biblical critic replies that there are many religions and many sacred books. We cannot just assume dogmatically that one of them is authentic and ignore the others. Holy books must be read critically, to appraise the religious and moral values they teach and the historical information they give. Besides, the Christian Bible is clearly a human historical document, tied to certain past times and places. If we are to use it as a source of information, we must obviously ask of it the same questions as we put to other historical documents. Unlike some sacred books, the Bible has a very mixed literary character. Its writings were not scriptural from the first. They began as occasional writings, which were preserved, won wide esteem, and were eventually *made* scriptural by decision of the Church. Thus the conception of 'the Bible' as scripture is not original, but a secondary historical development. The Epistle to the Romans is, on the face of it, presented to us as having been written by Paul to some people in Rome. It does not even purport to be addressed timelessly by God to mankind. So the biblical critic says, My method of reading the Bible is the natural one, not yours!

The argument has raged and raged. Here are some typical episodes from it.

Pusey burns his fingers

In 1825 Dr Lloyd, the Regius Professor of Divinity at Oxford, said to the young Edward Pusey, 'I wish you would learn something about those German critics.' Word had reached Oxford that the new German theology was important and ought to be studied. A Cambridge man, Hugh James Rose, had recently returned from the Continent and had preached sermons, later to be published in a book, denouncing the new ideas. Some catching-up evidently needed to be done, but there was a difficulty, for it

Top Victorian industrial Britain, Manchester *c.*1850;
below Matthew Arnold

René Descartes,
by Franz Hals

Blaise Pascal,
after Quesnel

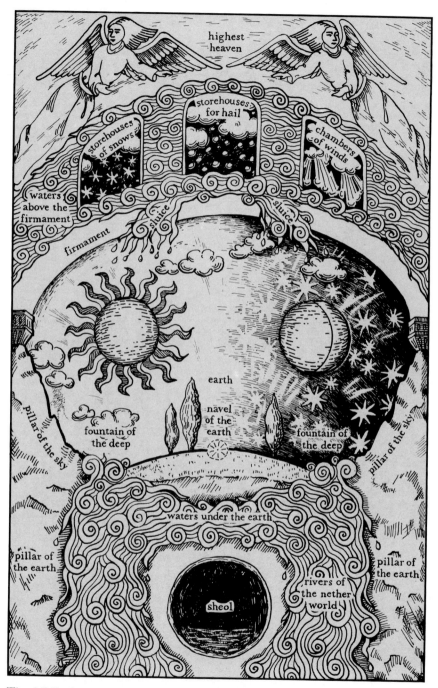

The biblical conception of the world (adapted from *Ancient Cosmologies* by Carmen Blacker and Michael Loewe)

Top   William Smith's geological section from Bath to Southampton, showing the succession of strata;
below   William Smith, 'the Father of Geology'

Darwin at the time of
the *Beagle* voyage

The later Darwin as
seen by a cartoonist
at the time of the
publication of
The Descent of Man

Top Freud in 1906; *below* part of Freud's collection of classical, oriental and tribal statuettes, kept in his consulting room

Top Jung at Bollingen, 1958;
below David Friedrich Strauss, about 1860

Above William Robertson Smith in 1877, from the portrait by Sir George Reid at Christ's College, Cambridge;

right Albert Schweitzer in his student days, in the 1890s

seemed that only two people in all Oxford knew the German language. Dr Lloyd, whilst not going so far as to think that he himself ought perhaps to become the third, evidently felt that the subject was one with which a rising young man might decently concern himself.

Edward Pusey (1800–1882) was certainly rising, being highminded and serious of purpose to a degree noteworthy even by the standards of his own strenuous generation. He took Lloyd's hint and began to study German. In June he left for Germany, and settled in Göttingen. By August he was attending the lectures of the great Eichhorn on the Five Books of Moses.

At that time the cultural gap between Britain and Germany was wide. Pusey was himself the product of an aristocratic family background of unbending Tory principles, and of Eton in the days of the notorious flogger Keate. English culture was, frankly, backward. Germany had been far more deeply affected by the spirit of the Enlightenment and it boasted universal education, a great number of universities, and a galaxy of brilliant thinkers and scholars.

John Gottfried Eichhorn, already seventy-three years old, was one of the best known of these scholars, still lecturing and in the Indian summer of his career. He was one of the great exponents of biblical criticism, treating the Bible just as he would treat any other ancient literary work. His conclusions were not particularly radical by the standards of later times, but there was enough in them to startle a foreigner from a more innocent world. In an anonymous work of 1779 Eichhorn had argued that the tales in Genesis about the Creation of the world, the first human beings, the Flood and so forth were of the same kind as the many similar stories in classical literature. The idea may not seem surprising today, but in holding it then Eichhorn broke down a traditional line of demarcation. Every Englishman who had learnt Latin knew that the Roman poet Ovid has a Creation-story and a Flood-story, but the influence of religion inhibited people from seeing that the Latin Creation and Flood were legends or myths of much the same status as the Hebrew Creation and Flood. Somehow the biblical Creation and Flood were regarded as revealed truths, and all non-biblical Creation and Flood stories were merely heathen fables. After Eichhorn it became increasingly common to use the word 'myth' of both, myth being (according to him) the style of thinking found among all peoples in the earliest stages of their history.

Eichhorn, then, was the first to begin to apply the term 'myth' in biblical studies, but this was only part of a larger change of attitude. In the old religious way of reading the Bible, you picked up the book and God spoke to you directly out of its pages. By contrast, scholars like

Eichhorn regarded the Bible as a human historical document and everything in it as a human product. A biblical story of God appearing and
speaking was not for him actually a case of God's appearing and speaking,
but merely evidence of a fascinating period in the early development of
human consciousness when people had thought in such terms. In this way
God himself was swallowed whole by the historical outlook: like everything else in the Bible, God was a product of human thought in a particular period of human history.

The old way of thinking was a kind of unhistorical religious immediacy. People would have defended it by saying that God is unchangeable.
The God who spoke to Abraham is identical with the God who speaks to
us, and God uses for our present guidance today the old narrative of his
dealings with Abraham. The 4000 years that have intervened are neither
here nor there, for God is not subject to historical change. We do not read
the Bible primarily to learn history, but in order to be taught by a God
who is not historical but eternal and who always deals with people in just
the same way. There is no difficulty in supposing that God speaks to me
today in and through the way he spoke to Abraham then.

Such was the old way of thinking, but in Eichhorn it is plainly
beginning to be replaced by the new historical and man-centred way of
handling religious ideas. One can imagine its traumatic effect on Pusey.
Able and intelligent, he could not but be excited by the new vistas
opening before his mind, but at the same time his deep religious conservatism and seriousness were affronted by much of what he was hearing.
Fifty years later he recalled:

> I can remember the room in Göttingen in which I was sitting when the
> real condition of religious thought in Germany flashed upon me. I said to
> myself, 'This will all come upon us in England; and how utterly unpre-
> pared for it we are!'

In his detailed critical judgments, Eichhorn recognised that in the book
of Genesis there are two interwoven narratives, one in which God is
called Yahweh, 'the LORD', and one in which he is called Elohim, or
'God'. He saw that the law in Deuteronomy is different in character from
that in Exodus, Leviticus and Numbers; and he tended to be a 'rationalist', in the sense of one who gave rationalistic explanations of miracle-
stories. Pusey recalled long afterwards his sense of shock at the levity with
which Eichhorn treated the story of Balaam's talking ass:

> Eichhorn had then a great reputation for acuteness, but was profane. I
> asked a theological student whether he was going down, the term being
> nearly over. He said no; he should wait till the history of Balaam came

on, because it was such fun. This I heard with my own ears; and I heard the lecture. I heard a titter going through all the room, and I saw only one person who was grave.

Even more comical – and significant – was Pusey's later recollection of the preaching in the local Lutheran parish church, as described by his biographer, H.P. Liddon:

> The preacher of the day was a Rationalist, and was engaged in showing – but in language which the educated only would understand – the general untenableness of some portion of the Gospel history. In doing this he had occasion, of course, constantly to mention the Holy Name of Jesus. The church was full of country-people or simple townsfolk, and each time our Lord's Name was mentioned they bowed their heads reverently: 'evidently making each mention of our Saviour the occasion of an act of devotion to Him'. Of the drift of the sermon to which they were listening they had no idea; to them it was edifying on account of the frequent mention of our Saviour's Name. Pusey would frequently refer to this when insisting that God overrules human error so completely as, at times, to make the teachers of error the unintentional servants and friends of truth.

The story is no doubt amusing for the way it describes the earnest liberal preacher, going far above his congregation's heads and wrestling courageously on their behalf with difficulties that have never occurred to them. Yet, as told, the story is also disconcerting in the complete assurance with which the later Pusey and his biographer assume they know better. Just how do they know that the poor rationalist preacher is a fool? Whence comes their superior insight?

All this, however, is somewhat to anticipate. Pusey in Göttingen, twenty-five years old and studying fourteen hours a day, was undoubtedly interested in and attracted by the new German theology. He moved on to Berlin, where he managed to meet a number of the leading figures of the time, including the liberal theologian Schleiermacher and even the great Hegel. Over the next two or three years he acquired a thorough knowledge of German theology and especially of Old Testament and Semitic studies. His findings were communicated to the British public in a book on the theology of Germany which came out in two volumes, in 1828 and 1830. It sought to correct the over-simplified and polemical account previously given by the Cambridge visitor to Germany, Hugh James Rose.

All went well for Pusey on his return to Britain. In a few short months in 1828, he was appointed to the Regius Professorship of Hebrew at Oxford, married, and was ordained deacon and priest by the same Dr Lloyd, now Bishop of Oxford. Professionally, Pusey had arrived and was secure; but there was a fly in the ointment. Hugh James Rose had publicly attacked his book on the theology of Germany, and there was just a whiff of doubt about his orthodoxy.

Pusey made a show, for a time, of defending his very mildly liberal views on biblical inspiration and such topics – but that was only while covering his inglorious retreat into the rigid ultra-orthodoxy of his later years. In the end he disowned his German theology book and produced instead works of such appalling dullness that not even professional theologians can now bear to read them. England was not yet ready for biblical criticism.

The tragedy of D.F. Strauss

In 1825, as Pusey arrived to study at Göttingen, the young D.F. Strauss (1808–1874) entered the Tübingen Stift. This famous college is a mixture of high school and Lutheran seminary and is linked with the Protestant theological faculty of the University.

Tübingen, founded just before the Reformation, is the state university of Württemberg and has long been one of the chief intellectual centres of Europe. It was the university of Melanchthon and Kepler, and more recently the idealist philosophers G.W.F. Hegel and Friedrich Schelling had passed through the Stift. In 1817 a Catholic theological faculty was added to the venerable Protestant faculty, and by Strauss's time religious thought at Tübingen had begun to move into one of its great creative periods.

However, as the recent case of Professor Hans Küng has shown, Tübingen theologians are tugged in various directions. Because the faculties are training the clergy of the future there is inevitably a demand for their teaching to conform to current standards of orthodoxy. At the same time, Tübingen is a state university ultimately controlled by a State Education Minister. Finally, Tübingen religious thought has often been avant-garde, stressing historical change and the need for reformulation of the faith. So the intellectual tradition calls for adventurousness, but the State authorities want no trouble and the Church for its part naturally asks that the young should not be led astray by the latest academic fashion, but be taught an authentic and preachable faith.

At the Stift Strauss and his friends became immersed in Romanticism and mysticism. In 1828 they began to study together the great book of the age, Hegel's *Phenomenology of Spirit* (1807). This awesome if obscure work offers a vision of the whole of world history as the progressive evolution of a single infinite spiritual Life, all previous religions, philosophies and phases of consciousness being but aspects of the development of Spirit. In effect, God is seen as immanent and historical, being identified with *Geist*, the Mind that is unfolding in the history of all humanity. Christian theology was a symbolic and local anticipation of the universal truth that Hegel had now disclosed. For example, its doctrine of the divinity of Christ foreshadowed the real truth that the evolving human totality is indeed an Incarnation of God, inasmuch as it is the emergent self-expression of Spirit. The doctrine about Christ is really a doctrine about everyone, and the great supernatural mysteries and miracles that surround Christ are really mythic pictures of moments in the spiritual life of everyone. So Christianity is explained and taken up into a larger synthesis.

A theological student who has picked up ideas like these is in a potentially awkward position. In that same year of 1828, when he was twenty years old, Strauss wrote a prize essay of which he afterwards said:

> I proved exegetically and by the philosophy of nature the resurrection of the dead, with complete conviction, and as I dotted the last *i* it was clear to me that there is nothing to the entire story.

Three years later Strauss was acting as a curate in a small country parish, and he and his friend Christian Märklin, who was in the same position, wrote to each other about the intellectual dilemma they faced. Hegel had taught them that popular Christianity is only a set of particular symbols of a higher universal truth; but you could not preach that from the pulpit, for the parishioners would not accept it. When Strauss and his friend were preaching they found they had to speak as if the Christian symbols stood for supernatural historical facts. They had to talk as if the Virgin Birth, the Incarnation, the miracles, the Resurrection and Ascension and so on had actually taken place as unique miraculous events, and this naturally gave them a bad conscience. What were they to do? They could not go back to the old theology, but nor could they simply preach the higher spiritual truth, for that would destroy the faith of ordinary people. Yet it also seemed wrong to leave the ministry and leave the Church to the traditionalists, for part of the problem was the fact that Strauss and his friend were good pastors with real vocations to the ministry and to theology. Strauss thought it best to stay in the ministry, for Hegel had after all shown that the inner content of Christian imagery is indeed true. You could, for example, preach the Resurrection and attempt gradually to coax people away from the crude popular idea of it as a past event to the truth – already taught by St Paul – that the resurrection is really the new life upon which believers are entering.

In 1832 Strauss was appointed to an assistant lectureship at the Tübingen Stift. There he was happy, and a successful teacher. But his success caused some jealousy and in his third year, having temporarily given up lecturing, he took up the project of a life of Jesus.

The stimulus came when a Berlin journal rejected an article he had written outlining some of his own ideas, on the ground that although the piece was good it was too bold for publication. Strauss was indignant: 'It is time that an end was made of this deceitful concealment of views!' For just over a year he sat writing in the bay window of the junior lecturers' room overlooking the gateway-arch. *The Life of Jesus Critically Examined* came out in two big volumes totalling over 1500 pages, in June and October 1835.

The book had a tremendous success. It made him famous and destroyed his career, at the age of only twenty-seven. He never fully recovered from the blow.

The chief idea of the book is simple. The Christian Gospels are strange works whose contents call for interpretation. Two main schools of thought were current in Strauss's day. The supernaturalists accepted the idea of miracle and supposed that the events reported in the Gospels had happened just as described, having been brought about by supernatural powers – whether the power of demons, or the power of God acting in and through Jesus. Such was the theory of the traditional dogmatic orthodoxy. The other party, the rationalists, were religious liberals who did not accept the notion of supernatural interventions, and preferred instead to give natural explanations of events that in their view had been misinterpreted as miraculous.

Strauss's book gives very detailed refutations of both these theories, playing them off against each other. In their place he provides a new and comprehensive mythological interpretation of the Gospels. The supernaturalists were too credulous and the rationalists too unsympathetic, and both were too uncritical about the historicity of the Gospels. What Strauss shows is that Jesus was a Jewish teacher and martyr, imbued with apocalyptic ideas, whose followers accepted his claim to messiahship. In accordance with their general outlook, they retrospectively clothed his figure with supernatural attributes derived from the Old Testament. Given the thought-world of the time, no deception was involved: it was understandable that the figure of Jesus had been mythicised by the religious imagination of the early Christians in order to express their beliefs about him. Thus the whole of the supernatural in the Gospels is not history but religious symbolism, of which a full literary explanation can be given by tracing its Old Testament sources.

Most students of the Gospels today would concede that Strauss was basically correct in his views, although nowadays the point is more likely to be made by saying that the Gospels are works of theology rather than of simple history. It was a marvellous book for a man so young. Furthermore, Strauss at the time of writing it was still a sincere Christian, albeit of the Hegelian sort that spiritualises the dogma and makes it universal. Yet the book caused an almost unparalleled uproar. Strauss had set aside the Gospel of John as largely unhistorical, had ended with a merely human Jesus who seemed insufficient to sustain the traditional dogma, and – perhaps worst of all – had shown that precious mysteries long thought of as divine revelations were in fact no more than creations of the human mythopoeic imagination. But if this was shocking to the faithful, it was also very uncomfortable for the liberal theologians. They were put on the spot. They had to ask themselves if they were moving in the same direction as Strauss, and if so whether they were willing to share his unpopularity and to forfeit their jobs like him. Or were they going to surrender their integrity and avoid offending the orthodoxy that paid their salaries?

Strauss had himself described the dilemma at the end of his book. What is the modern theologian to do? People think he is a hypocrite. As Strauss very simply and clearly puts it, 'by the Church the evangelical narratives are received as history: by the critical theologian they are regarded for the most part as mere myths.' If that is the position, then how can the theologian continue to preach in the Church? Strauss's answer recalls his debate with his fellow-student Märklin a few years before. He cannot expect to convert the Church to his point of view, nor himself to the Church's. But nor can he simply leave theology at the very moment when he has discovered the truth and penetrated into the deepest mysteries of the subject: that would be impossible. No, he has no choice but to stay with the problem and try as best he can to bridge the gulf between the consciousness of the theologian and the consciousness of the Church. The collision has not arisen merely because of the rash curiosity of one individual; on the contrary, 'it is necessarily introduced by the progress of time and the development of Christian theology; it surprises and masters the individual, without his being able to guard himself against it.'

In the closing sentences of the whole book Strauss betrays some dawning unease about its likely reception. His later career as an exile from faith was sad, and his treatment remains a dire warning. Other theologians since him have suffered some part of his fate as rebel and exile. It is good to think of him as their flawed, unofficial patron saint.

95

THE SEA OF FAITH

The system of terrorism

Strauss's *Life of Jesus*, perhaps the most important single theological book of the nineteenth century, caused a sensation in Germany and cost its author his career, but in Britain at that time the outlook for biblical criticism – or indeed for any kind of openly professed religious liberalism – was if anything still worse. Strauss's book could only be sold in England as an anti-religious work. Its publication was financed by a small group who hoped to further the cause of social reform by weakening the grip of Anglican orthodoxy on public opinion. After delays, the famous translation by George Eliot at last appeared in 1846.

There were however a few theological liberals, though they had to be circumspect. On 15 August 1858 one of them, the Reverend Benjamin Jowett of Balliol College, Oxford wrote to another, Canon A.P. Stanley of Canterbury, to tell him that a small group was planning to publish a collection of essays:

> We do not wish to do anything rash or irritating to the public or the University, but we are determined not to submit to this abominable system of terrorism, which prevents the statement of the plainest facts, and makes true theology or theological education impossible.

Stanley, a prudent man with sensitive antennae, declined to join the project, and the book appeared without him. It was called *Essays and Reviews* and it came out in February 1860. Nobody could call it an exciting book today, but it caused a greater brouhaha than any other English theological book of the period.

Essays and Reviews is a mild plea for religious liberalism by a predominantly academic group. Frederick Temple, the Headmaster of Rugby School, advocated free biblical criticism; Rowland Williams of Lampeter described the work of a well-known German amateur biblical critic; H.B. Wilson cautiously expressed the hope that in the end all men might be saved, and claimed (to Pusey's especial annoyance) that it was permissible to regard biblical prodigies like Balaam's talking ass as legendary; Charles Goodwin ridiculed Hugh Miller and others, and exposed the error of treating Genesis as a source of scientific information; and Jowett himself argued that Scripture 'is to be interpreted like other books'.

At first there was little fuss, but then on 1 October a leading freethinker published an article against the book. The jurist Frederic Harrison denounced 'Neo-Christianity' because as an atheist he did not wish to see Christianity liberalised. So, as has happened since, he managed to provoke churchpeople into injuring their own cause, by turning them against the liberals within their own ranks. 'Soapy Sam' Wilberforce, the

96

Bishop of Oxford who had attacked Darwin a couple of years before, duly rose to the bait and wrote a violent article accusing the Essayists of 'moral dishonesty' in continuing as clergymen while holding liberal views. After this the hunt was up. In February 1861 the Archbishops of Canterbury and York and twenty-four other Bishops issued a letter describing the pain the book had caused them and the measures they were contemplating against it, and Convocation took the first steps towards officially condemning it.

In the agitations of the next three years most of the seven essayists suffered. Charles Goodwin was a layman and could not be prosecuted, Baden Powell died, and Mark Pattison, the Rector of Lincoln College, Oxford, maintained the pose of ironical and impregnable detachment he had shown in his essay. The other four were less fortunate. The two beneficed clergymen, Williams and Wilson, were pursued in the Church courts. They were condemned in 1862 and then acquitted on appeal to the Privy Council in 1864; but they never recovered from the strain. Frederick Temple was given a bad time at Rugby, but managed to live it down so successfully that in his old age he even became Archbishop of Canterbury. Finally, Jowett, as an Oxford don, was best pursued through University channels, so Pusey persuaded two other theology professors to join him in prosecuting Jowett before the Vice-Chancellor's Court. Fortunately the Vice-Chancellor's Assessor appointed to hear the case wisely refused to admit it, saying that he doubted if he had jurisdiction. So Jowett survived to become the legendary Master of Balliol, but the affair had so scarred him that he never again spoke his mind in public on a religious question. Thus, in spite of his boast of 1858, he did in the end 'submit to this abominable system of terrorism'.

The legal actions arising from *Essays and Reviews* had hurt everyone involved, but in the end they had failed. Still Pusey did not give up. In the spring of 1864 signatures were being collected for a Declaration. The great majority of Anglican clergymen – some eleven or twelve thousand of them – signed it, affirming the Church's faith in the authority of the Bible and the everlastingness of Hell-punishment. At the same time 137,000 lay people signed an address to the Archbishops, who themselves issued Pastoral Letters denouncing the book. Convocation finally condemned it in June 1864.

The hysteria had lasted three whole years, in an atmosphere that at moments resembled a witch-hunt. The theologian F.D. Maurice complained that the Oxford Declaration had been taken round the younger clergymen like a loyalty test so that they were in effect signing it under duress. 'Sign or we will starve you!' was how Maurice saw the threat, and he did not care for it: 'This is what is called signing "for the love of God",' he complained. But however much one dislikes the unscrupulous tactics employed against *Essays and Reviews* by Pusey, Wilberforce and others, they were fighting with every weapon they could lay their hands on for something infinitely precious to them, namely the divine authorship of the Bible and the traditional conception of religious truth. They thought the liberals had cut themselves loose from the Rock of the true faith, and were adrift upon the open sea. Who could tell where they might be cast ashore?

The bitterness of the nineteenth-century controversies is only comprehensible if we first recognise the greatness of the issues involved. Once the old straightforward view of the Bible had been abandoned, things would surely never be quite the same again.

The trial of Robertson Smith

Scotland's moment of truth, the trial of Robertson Smith, is a possible exception to the generalisation just made, for in that gruelling struggle Smith steadfastly defended his claim that he could combine advanced critical views with a faith of the strictest Calvinist orthodoxy.

William Robertson Smith (1846–1894) was a gifted child of the manse who became a minister of the Free Church of Scotland. In his student years he swept the board in mathematics as well as in theology. He learnt German and made the necessary intellectual pilgrimages, to Bonn in 1867 and to Göttingen in 1869. In 1870, when still only twenty-four, he was appointed Professor of Old Testament in the Free Church College at Aberdeen. During the next few years he alternated teaching with visits to Germany to study with the leading Old Testament scholars and orientalists.

In the 1870s a ninth edition of *Encyclopaedia Britannica* was being prepared, and in spite of his youth Smith was asked to contribute many articles to do with biblical topics. The idea was that Smith both knew the latest scholarship thoroughly and also – as a trainer of ministers in the hyper-orthodox Free Church – could presumably be relied upon to take a solidly-learned and responsible line. The volume containing Smith's article 'Bible' appeared in 1875. It was the chief cause of his later troubles.

The leading ideas of the article were new to most British readers. According to tradition rather than to any express declaration in their text, the first five books of the Bible, called by Jews the Torah or the Law, were wholly written down by Moses at the dictation of God, and so have been the basis of Jewish religion ever since Moses' own time. The five books of Moses therefore come first in the Bible in date of authorship as well as in their authority under the Old Covenant, having been penned complete in about the fourteenth century BC. First the Law, and then the Prophets: first God lays down through Moses the perfect pattern for Jewish religion, and then much later the prophets come along to recall the people to it.

By Smith's time it had become clear to the leading scholars that this account must be wrong, for if you scan the historical books of Judges, Samuel and Kings, covering the long period from the first Israelite settlement in Canaan through to the Babylonian Exile, you do not there find the law of Moses functioning as the basis of Israelite religious life. However, towards the end of the period there is an episode in which a law-book is found in the Temple in 621 BC. King Josiah was reportedly inspired by this discovery to change Judah's religious constitution along the lines called for in the central chapters of the book of Deuteronomy. Furthermore the historical books themselves, and also some of the prophets, appear to have been edited in the style of Deuteronomy. So it looks very much as if the theology of Deuteronomy, and a school of writers and teachers who propagated it, appeared only at the end of the Monarchy-period. Finally, the book of Nehemiah contains an account, dated well after the Exile, of the Law of Moses being solemnly proclaimed. It is read out to the people with commentary, and they accept it as the basis of Judaism henceforth.

From these and other facts it seems that we must reverse the traditional order of the Law and the Prophets. The originators, the creative prophetic teachers, come first and the codifiers come second. In our experience that is surely the usual sequence of events. The Law of Moses undoubtedly incorporates many very old traditions and sums up the legacy of the prophets, story-tellers and priests of pre-exilic times, but it only reached its present form and it only became the basic Scripture of Judaism after the Exile that had lasted from 587–538 BC. And if the prophets thus come first, they grow in significance. They are not merely the restorers of Mosaic ethical monotheism, but rather its founding fathers.

Why then did the Torah come to be attributed to Moses? It is typical of ancient thought that it blends together different orders of meaning. The five books of the fully-codified Law are seen as first in importance, they are set first in the order of books in the Hebrew Bible, and they deal with the earliest times and the most sacred matters. But it was Moses who according to ancient tradition had led Israel out of Egypt, had established the Covenant, and had been pre-eminent as prophet and priest. Naturally he becomes the central figure in the Torah, and being seen as the ultimate source of Israel's Law he is equally naturally regarded as its author. In the context of traditional thought-patterns, there is no misrepresentation in attributing the Torah to Moses.

In 1875, however, this revolution in the the way we see the Old Testament was neither accepted nor even understood by the general public. Only the most well-informed had heard about it, and even they were likely to regard it as extreme.

The issue was this: given that Robertson Smith held these critical opinions, were they in conflict with the Church's faith in 'the immediate inspiration, infallible truth and divine authority of the Holy Scriptures', to which Smith was also committed?

In his reply Smith argued that you must not simply identify the Word of God with the letter of the Bible. The Bible *contains* the Word of God. The Bible is a human, historical product and it describes human historical events. As such it is subject to the ordinary canons of historical criticism. Yet after you have done all that, after the historical reconstruction is complete, you can still hold as firmly as ever the faith of a Christian that in and through this stretch of human history, and this series of ancient writings in Hebrew and Greek, there has taken place an immediate revelation of God's infallible Word to men.

Though Smith's opponents kept reformulating the charges against him, they could not convict him and in the end he was dismissed by a simple resolution of the General Assembly of the Free Kirk in June 1881. There was an element of political compromise in this outcome. The sacrifice of Smith the individual appeased his opponents, while the fact that his critical views had not been expressly condemned left room for them to continue to be held – and in due course they became standard teaching. Yet it was strange to see a Christian body acting on the precept of Caiaphas.

Smith was not ruined. The 1880s were not the 1860s, still less the 1830s. He immediately became joint editor of *Britannica*, and then moved to Cambridge as Professor of Arabic, as a Fellow of Christ's College, and eventually as University Librarian. But he died too young after a wretched illness, and had given too much of his strength to the controversies of 1875–1881. On his deathbed, in his final delirium, he relived the agony of the long heresy proceedings. His career and his health had been badly affected, and although he left two or three classics, his literary legacy is smaller than it might have been.

The Assembly of the Free Church of Scotland, it is fair to say, did not condemn Robertson Smith unanimously but only by 394 votes to 231.

Who is to say what was in the minds of the majority? Perhaps we may guess that one factor was a suspicion that for all his brilliance there remained something fishy in Smith's claim to combine avant-garde critical opinions with fully-orthodox faith in the Bible's inspiration and authority. If Smith was right, it sounded as if orthodox faith could be maintained almost whatever conclusions the critics might reach. What were the limits? At what point would Smith be finally forced to admit that he must now revise his beliefs?

There was also a problem about the ordinary minister's preaching of the Bible and the ordinary layperson's reading of it. It was part of traditional Protestant faith that anyone can understand God's Word. It is not opaque: God's Spirit interprets Scripture to the honest reader, however humble he or she may be. But modern biblical criticism seems to suggest that we will be misled if we take the Bible at face value. Just as in the Middle Ages it was thought that the believer needs the Church to interpret the Bible to him, so today he seems to need the advice of the scholars. To Scottish Presbyterians, with their ideal of the family Bible in every crofter's cottage, this was impossible to accept.

More generally, the churches have not found it easy to adjust to even the most widely-accepted results of biblical criticism. The points it makes are too sophisticated. For example, the critics say that in each Gospel the beliefs of the Evangelist shape the words he ascribes to Jesus, so we can never quote Jesus absolutely; we can only quote the Jesus of a particular Evangelist. And certainly we should not suppose that Jesus himself actually said any of the things John's Jesus says.

These assertions may be true – I think they are – but they have not proved easy to put into practice, and claims that the churches are coming to terms with biblical criticism seem premature. In practice people go on quoting sayings of Jesus as before, without qualification and without specifying which Evangelist they are quoting. In practice a feast like Christmas, with a vast popular momentum behind it, rolls on without regard to the queasiness of biblical critics. In practice revisions of the liturgy continue to use the language of the old supernatural doctrine, as if our world-view today were the same as that of the early Christians. And there seems no immediate likelihood of a change of direction, when so few people desire it. The majority view probably remains that just as the Church is right to be *ethically* somewhat at odds with the surrounding culture, so also it must be *intellectually* at odds with the world it lives in.

This may explain the one remarkable exception to the general unpopularity of advanced biblical critics. Albert Schweitzer was quite exceptionally radical as a Christian thinker, and he portrayed a Jesus who was at odds not only with his own age but still more with ours. Yet somehow Schweitzer got away with it, because public admiration for the ethical deed he performed in imitation of his Jesus prevailed over suspicions about his orthodoxy.

Albert Schweitzer

Schweitzer was unlucky in living too long. An absurdly inflated personality cult grew up around him, obscuring the real meaning of his life and thought. Eventually the bubble burst, and the man approaching the age of ninety was reviled for being an anachronism. Today he is out of fashion and much in need of reassessment.

Albert Schweitzer (1875–1965) was a Lutheran pastor's son from the Franco-German border country of Alsace, and a kinsman of Sartre. From a very early age he began to play the organ, and became in 1893 first the pupil and then subsequently the friend and colleague of the great Paris organist C.M. Widor. Schweitzer's later musical career continued to be based in Paris, and his book on J.S. Bach was in fact first written in French.

In theology, though, Schweitzer was a German. Being intended for the ministry he entered Strasburg University to study theology and philosophy. Stimulated by the very able New Testament Professor there, H.J. Holtzmann, who had recently argued that Mark is the oldest Gospel and Matthew the next after it, Schweitzer plunged enthusiastically into the study of the Greek Testament.

Even at this early age Schweitzer's attitude to religion was uncommon by today's standards. He was enquiring, undogmatic and remarkably independent-minded. Although he could describe the supernaturalist beliefs of the past with great insight, he seems never to have held them himself. He stood at the end of the great tradition of Protestant rationalism, and all of his life took it for granted that the unreserved pursuit of truth was compatible, was indeed indentical, with a Protestant's loyalty to Christ. Following Kant, he was a metaphysical agnostic who saw religion primarily in terms of ethics and the will. Great though his abilities were, he accordingly regarded himself as destined to be a man of action rather than a pure scholar, and even in his student days had already decided upon the plan of his life: he would devote himself to art and scholarship up to the age of thirty, and would then commit himself to the direct service of humanity. During the 1890s the thinkers who were to mean most to him made their mark on his mind: Goethe, Kant, probably Schopenhauer and certainly Nietzsche. All were highly unorthodox figures, and two were militant atheists, yet Schweitzer's heroic Protestant temper of mind was able to accommodate them readily without the inner conflict and 'doubts' that would be expected of him today. Indeed he never wavered in his loyalty to his village Lutheran background and his singularly tough old father, who continued to work in the parish ministry until the age of ninety-seven.

So Schweitzer took up his Greek Testament. He tells us how his interest in the problem of interpreting the message of Jesus was awakened one day in the village of Guggenheim as he read St Matthew, chapters 10 and 11:

> In Matthew x the mission of the Twelve is narrated. In the discourse with which He sends them out Jesus tells them that they will almost immediately have to undergo severe persecution. But they suffer nothing of the kind.
>
> He tells them also that the appearance of the Son of Man will take place before they have gone through the cities of Israel, which can only mean that the celestial, Messianic Kingdom will be revealed while they are thus engaged. He has, therefore, no expectation of seeing them return.
>
> How comes it that Jesus leads His disciples to expect events about which the remaining portion of the narrative is silent? . . .
>
> The bare text compelled me to assume that Jesus really announced persecutions for the disciples and, as a sequel to them, the immediate appearance of the celestial Son of Man, and that His announcement was shown by subsequent events to be wrong. But how came He to entertain such an expectation, and what must His feelings have been when events turned out otherwise than He had assumed they would?
>
> Matthew xi records the Baptist's question to Jesus, and the answer which Jesus sent back to him . . . Whom does the Baptist mean when he asks Jesus whether He is the 'one who is to come'? (ὁ ἐρχόμενος). Is it then quite certain, I asked myself, that by the Coming One no one can be meant except the Messiah? According to late Jewish Messianic beliefs the coming of the Messiah is to be preceded by that of his Forerunner, Elijah, risen from the dead, and to this previously-expected Elijah Jesus applies the expression the Coming One, when he tells the disciples (Matt.xi.14) that the Baptist himself is Elijah who is to come. Therefore, so I concluded, the Baptist in his question used the expression with that same meaning. He did not send his disciples to Jesus with the question whether He was the Messiah; he wanted to learn from Him, strange as this may seem to us, whether he was the expected Forerunner of the Messiah, Elijah.
>
> I was also driven into new paths of interpretation by Jesus saying to the disciples after the departure of the Baptist's messengers, that of all born of women John was the greatest, but that the least in the Kingdom of Heaven was greater than he (Matt.xi.11).
>
> The usual explanation, that Jesus expressed in these words a criticism of the Baptist and placed him at a lower level than the believers in His teaching who were assembled round Him as adherents of the Kingdom of

God, seemed to me both unsatisfying and crude, for these believers were also born of women. By giving up this explanation I was driven to the assumption that in contrasting the Baptist with members of the Kingdom of God Jesus was taking into account the difference between the natural world and the supernatural, Messianic world. As a man in the condition into which all men enter at birth the Baptist is the greatest of all who have ever lived. But members of the Kingdom of Heaven are no longer natural men; through the dawn of the Messianic Kingdom they have experienced a change which has raised them to a supernatural condition akin to that of the angels. Because they are now supernatural beings the least among them is greater than the greatest man who has ever appeared in the natural world of the age which is now passing away.

Although these chapters of Matthew must have been familiar to Schweitzer since early childhood, their full import had come home to him for the first time. It was evident that Jesus had confidently expected the early arrival of a wholly supernatural Kingdom of God that would transform the conditions of human existence. He was preoccupied with preparing for its coming, which he at first thought would take place within his own lifetime.

This intense apocalyptic expectation had apparently survived Jesus' death. Schweitzer reflected on the fact that in Matthew and Mark Jesus does not instruct the disciples to repeat the Last Supper:

If, I said to myself, the command to repeat the meal is absent from the two oldest Gospels, that means that the disciples did in fact repeat it, with the body of believers, on their own initiative and authority. That, however, they could only do if there was something in the essence of this last meal which made it significant apart from the words and actions of Jesus. But, since no explanation of the Last Supper which has been current hitherto makes it intelligible, how it could be adopted in the primitive community without a command from Jesus to that effect, they all alike, so I had to conclude, leave the problem unsolved. Hence I went on to investigate the question whether the significance which the meal had for Jesus and His disciples were not connected with the expectation of the Messianic feast to be celebrated in the Kingdom of God, which was to appear almost immediately.

The reason why these discoveries were such a shock was that they threatened the whole basis of liberal Protestantism in Schweitzer's time. Throughout the nineteenth century it had been widely thought that Jesus had founded the Kingdom of God as an inward and spiritual reality, a seed growing secretly in the hearts of believers. God reigned within the believer's heart and filled him with the Spirit of Christ, inspiring him to strive to realise the values of Christ in social life. The whole community of believers, spreading the Christian ideal of love and striving for human betterment, would gradually lead mankind toward the goal of history, the establishment of the manifest Kingdom of God on earth. Along these lines nineteenth-century Christian culture harmonised Christian morality with the widespread contemporary belief in progress and social improvement, and the liberal Christian in the modern world could feel confident that his own action was in accord with the original requirement of Jesus.

The Kingdom of God in liberal Christianity thus lay within the present historical order. It was the present dwelling of God in Christ in men's hearts inspiring their actions, and it was the future goal of social development to be brought about by human endeavour. But Schweitzer, together with a number of other scholars of his generation, argued that the original Jesus had been very different from the Jesus of Liberal Protestantism. He had been imbued with the ideas of late ancient Jewish eschatology (teaching about the Last Days) and all his words and deeds were governed by one dominant thought, that an entirely supernatural Kingdom of God would arrive very shortly whether men wished for it or not.

Schweitzer thought that Jesus had been aware of his own exalted destiny. The secret must be kept hidden for the present, but when the Kingdom came Jesus would be revealed in all his glory as the Messiah and Son of Man. Some people objected that if this were so then Jesus must surely have been insane and megalomaniac, but Schweitzer later argued with the help of his medical knowledge that there was no evidence of insanity, and in any case Jesus' hope, astounding though it may seem to us, is quite intelligible in the context of the thought-world of his time.

In ancient Jewish apocalyptic belief the coming of the Kingdom was to be preceded by a period of tribulation, the messianic woes or the birth-pangs of the coming of the Kingdom, of which Jesus often speaks. Finding that the coming of the Kingdom was delayed rather longer than he had at first foreseen, Jesus came to think that it must be his destiny to undergo these woes in his own person in order to hasten the final issue. By thus voluntarily accepting suffering, he would be 'a ransom for many' (Mark 10:45). Hence his decision to go to Jerusalem and allow himself to be delivered into the hands of his enemies. The celebration of the Last Supper was a promise and an anticipation of the Kingdom-feasting which would surely follow his death, as Jesus himself declares in Luke's account of the Last Supper. Repeating the Supper after Jesus' martyrdom, the disciples were continuing to express their confidence that the Kingdom would very speedily arrive: at any celebration, Jesus might join them in his glory.

This interpretation of the beginnings of Christianity was called by Schweitzer, and by the Göttingen theologian Johannes Weiss who had reached similar conclusions a decade earlier, 'consistent eschatology'. It implied that not only the standard dogmatic theology but also liberal theology was wrong, and that the heroic effort of German biblical criticism to define the essence of Christianity by recovering the original Jesus had failed in the moment of its success. It had found him – and he was a figure utterly alien to the modern world.

For Jesus had after all been mistaken. The Kingdom he expected had never come. Schweitzer's Jesus was a tragic hero, a figure of extraordinary nobility and moral grandeur inspired by a sense of destiny, who had taught an ethic of brotherly love and had voluntarily taken it upon himself to endure the tribulations of mankind in the hope of seeing the coming of a new order. It was to this strange new post-orthodox and post-liberal tragic Jesus that Albert Schweitzer gave his life. Although Schweitzer's subsequent thought is in many ways incomplete and unsatisfactory, his historical importance lies in the fact that he was the first post-Christian Christian. As Nietzsche had been the first tragic philosopher, so Schweitzer was (apart perhaps from Kierkegaard, and maybe the Spanish philosopher Unamuno) the first tragic Christian. The later popular conception of him as a soft Franciscan figure is belied by his own words:

> Two perceptions cast their shadow over my existence. One consists in my realisation that the world is inexplicably mysterious and full of suffering; the other in the fact that I have been born into a period of spiritual decadence in mankind. . . .
> I am pessimistic in that I experience in its full weight what we conceive to be the absence of purpose in the course of world-happenings. Only at quite rare moments have I felt really glad to be alive. I could not but feel with a sympathy full of regret all the pain that I saw around me, not only that of men but that of the whole Creation. From this community of suffering I have never tried to withdraw myself. It seemed to me a matter of course that we should all take a share of the burden of pain that lies upon the world. Even while I was a boy at school it was clear to me that no explanation of the evil in the world could ever satisfy me; all explanations, I felt, ended in sophistries, and at bottom had no other object than to make it possible for men to experience the misery around them with less keen feelings.

For Schweitzer, just as much as for atheists like Schopenhauer and Nietzsche, no good purpose is discernibly at work in the course of events in this world. There is no loving heavenly Father looking after everything; on the contrary, the world is a scene of tragic conflict and suffering in which life is alienated from itself. The Christian hero pits against it his own will-to-love, immersing himself in the sufferings of creation, and striving – even though inevitably unsuccessfully – to infuse and transform the amoral will-to-live with the ethical will-to-love. Schweitzer's God is the inspiration of this striving and its ideal goal; in the jargon, his religious thought was voluntaristic, stressing the primacy of the will.

As early as the summer of 1899 Schweitzer reports that he was struck by the thought that 'we are all of us just nothing but "Epigoni"', decadent people of weak will who are rapidly exhausting the moral capital we have inherited from the past. At this point in his thinking Schweitzer is close to Nietzsche: the strength of a culture depends upon the strength of its underlying moral order, and the strength of the moral order depends in turn upon the courage and strength of will with which people affirm their values. In Schweitzer's day that courage was failing. His task was to go back to the beginnings, to descend to the primeval, and by a heroic deed renew the Christian moral order. Although as a follower of Jesus Schweitzer was not introspective, and naturally disclaimed any ideas of heroism or greatness in connection with himself, there can be little doubt that it is in this area that we should seek the real meaning of his decision to go to Africa. In later years people who visited him were shocked to discover how autocratic he was, because they had been led to expect a 'holy soul'. He was of course no such thing: he was a tragic Christian and a man of iron will and determination, wholly unlike the inoffensive weakling that people normally expect a saint to be. The tragic Christian has to be strong.

How strong Schweitzer was became apparent in his early thirties. He was still a busy lecturer, writer and preacher, deeply involved in theological controversy; he was regularly on the train to Paris, where he pursued his career as a concert organist and a writer on organ-building and music; and he was in training as a medical student in the same university in which he was a lecturer. To get through his work he taught himself to do without sleep, sitting up at night at his writing-table with his feet in cold water, drinking black coffee. His fiancée meanwhile underwent training as a nurse so that she could assist him in his future work.

It was not easy to get to Africa: when he first applied in 1905 Schweitzer found the missionary societies suspicious of his theological views, and he was eventually accepted by the Paris Missionary Society to work as a doctor in the Gabon only on the understanding that he would not preach. He would heal, but otherwise would be 'dumb as a fish'. He had to raise the money to build his hospital in the first place, and the burden of fund-raising remained with him for the rest of his life. Eventually the first hospital was built, but the work there was soon brought to an end by the outbreak of the War, in which the Schweitzers as Germans in a French colony found themselves in the position of being enemy aliens.

The rebuilding of the hospital and the resumption of work in Lambaréné was delayed until 1924. Meanwhile the World War had seemed to Schweitzer to confirm his fears about the decline of Western civilisation. He believed that the basis of a vigorous culture must be an ethical affirmation of the world and of life. In the eighteenth century (always Schweitzer's favourite period) that ethical will had been strong, but it had since eroded away into a shallow belief in mere economic and technical progress. He summed up his formula for renewal in the phrase 'Reverence for Life', ethical respect for and affirmation of the will-to-live in oneself and in all other living things.

Schweitzer's formula, and his practice at Lambaréné in the best days of his hospital, suggests that we might see him as a prophet of the new ecological humanism that many people are seeking today. But in fact the ethic of reverence for life was never worked out satisfactorily because Schweitzer could not solve the difficulties with which it faced him.

In the first place, there was a limitation, of which he was quite unconscious, in Schweitzer's own outlook. Wholly European in mentality, a benevolent paternalist who was a generation too old to appreciate the importance of anthropological fieldwork, he never recognised that he had come amongst peoples who had important cultures and art traditions of their own. He gave to Africa, but he did not learn from it.

Secondly, Schweitzer struggled for over fifty years to reconcile his belief that culture must be world-affirming with his passionate allegiance to Jesus, whom he had already shown to be a profoundly world-denying figure. He claimed that it was just an accident of history that Jesus' eternal religion of love had appeared in the context of the eschatological world-view of ancient Judaism; but this ran perilously close to reinstating the same liberal theology that Schweitzer had previously shown to be untenable. The fact was that there was a contradiction between the thesis proposed by him and Weiss, that the original Kingdom proclaimed by Jesus had been wholly supernatural and allowed no place for human action to help it into being, and Schweitzer's own religious voluntarism in which religion was entirely a matter of the human ethical will. In struggling to overcome the contradiction Schweitzer could point out that Jesus had himself required his disciples to practise the ethic of love in preparation for the Kingdom and had himself set his face towards Jerusalem, voluntarily undertaking the messianic woes. Schweitzer argued that the non-arrival of the Kingdom had eventually forced Christianity to turn to this world at the Reformation; and in his last years he saw in the appearance of the atomic bomb a return of something like the original urgency: 'Mankind today must either realise the Kingdom of God or perish.' But the contrast between a supernaturally bestowed Kingdom and one created by human will remains, and gives a tragic flavour to Schweitzer's allegiance to Jesus.

The same note recurs in the ethic of reverence for life: it could not be worked out consistently as a coherent ethical policy:

> The world . . . offers us the horrible drama of Will-to-Live divided against itself. One existence holds its own at the expense of another: one destroys another. Only in the thinking man has the Will-to-Live become conscious of other will-to-live, and desirous of solidarity with it. This solidarity, however, he cannot completely bring about, because man is subject to the puzzling and horrible law of being obliged to live at the cost of other life, and to incur again and again the guilt of destroying and injuring life. But as an ethical being he strives to escape whenever possible from this necessity, and as one who has become enlightened and merciful to put a stop to this self-alienation of the Will-to-Live so far as the influence of his own existence reaches.

Schweitzer's honesty in admitting the difficulties in his own position is admirable, and a reproach to the excessive optimism of modern environmentalists and animal rights campaigners. He seeks to practise the traditional religious virtues of active love, compassion and non-violence, but the universe he lives in is the universe of Schopenhauer and Darwin, competitive and violent through and through. Yet he rejected Schopenhauer's pessimism and resignation as 'pusillanimous' and still insisted on his own ethic of universal active love – even though it was impossible. Karl Barth very shrewdly called the ethic of reverence for life 'an outcry' – an affirmation of the world and of life which was also at a deeper level a cry of protest and of pain.

So Schweitzer's thought remained in the end incomplete. True to his tragic vision of Jesus, he had become the first tragic Christian since Kierkegaard.

The Bible since Schweitzer

Few since Schweitzer have been able to read the New Testament with quite his own peculiar combination of scientific objectivity and religious seriousness. He had expected the religious issue of ultimate importance to him to be decided on grounds of pure scholarship; and he saw that there had after all been something paradoxical about the whole era that he brought to an end. The great tradition of German research into the life of

Jesus had, he said, been 'a uniquely great expression of sincerity, one of the most significant events in the whole mental and spiritual life of humanity'. It had hoped to build up *merely* 'by the increase of historical knowledge a new and vigorous Christianity and set free new spiritual forces'. It had in effect identified faith with critical reason, and it was at just this point that Schweitzer was himself the greatest product of the tradition he ended. If he was almost the first tragic Christian, he was also the most fully truthful one for some time to come, in the sense that he approached the New Testament without any belief in revelation or the supernatural, and yet with an intense personal religious investment in the outcome of what was to be a purely historical enquiry. He was confident that the historical Jesus was recoverable and, whatever he turned out to be like, would be a figure of determinative significance for his (Schweitzer's) own life; and he treated Matthew and Mark in particular in a rather straightforward way as historical sources.

With magnificent consistency, Schweitzer followed his path to the end; but then it was at an end. After him it was no longer possible simply to *identify* faith's approach to scripture with that of critical reason. After him, faith and reason drew apart: it was one thing to study the New Testament in a strictly critical and objective spirit, and it was another thing to make a faith-judgement in response to what you had read.

There were two main reasons for the change of direction. One was that the work of Schweitzer and other New Testament scholars such as Wilhelm Wrede and Alfred Loisy had shown just how great is the culture-gap between the world of the New Testament and the world of the twentieth-century believer. The better we come to understand the thought-world of ancient Palestine, and the more we learn to explain biblical texts in terms of the thought-world from which they come, the more we make biblical research into a branch of the history of ideas. Exegesis becomes the exposition of how they thought then, and an entirely different discipline called hermeneutics will be needed to bridge the gap between then and now. There is no doubt that ancient texts do live on through vast cultural changes and do continue to influence the imaginative and moral life of later generations (think for example of the influence of Plato's *Republic* on later Utopias, Cacotopias and science-fiction visions), but the theory of how this is done is a different matter from the purely historical question of what the text originally meant.

Those who had sought the historical Jesus, up to and including Schweitzer, had somehow assumed that exegesis was hermeneutics; the moment the original Jesus had been found he would at once have an obvious religious significance for the present day. This assumption proved to be mistaken, as Schweitzer acknowledged, because when he found the original Jesus he found a figure utterly alien to the present day. It became apparent that finding the historical Jesus, far from being the whole task, was 'only one of the intellectual preliminaries of the great religious task'.

Worse still, this realisation finally demolished the Bible's old immediate authority. From now on, purely scientific biblical exegesis was a basically secular discipline, an exercise in the history of ideas in antiquity. By itself, it never gets to the present day. As for hermeneutics, it is easy enough to demonstrate the mere fact of reinterpretation: look for example at the different ways in which Shakespeare's plays have been reinterpreted on the British stage in successive centuries since they were written. But how do you distinguish between 'true' and 'false' reinterpretation? You cannot. All you can say is that in dialogue with the text successive generations of actors and producers creatively reinvent Shakespeare in ever new ways. Similarly, the text of the Bible has been fantastically differently perceived both in different centuries and by different interpreters in the same century; and there is no way of deriving from the Bible itself, thus diversely perceived, agreed and time-straddling objective norms to limit the range of future possible reinterpretations of the Bible.

Thus, once the necessity for a clear distinction between exegesis and hermeneutics had been grasped, then exegesis became a mere branch of human historical knowledge, with the usual diversity of opinions; and hermeneutics became an unpredictable and uncontrollable work of human creativity, by which Christianity is continually reinvented and transformed. Christianity comes to be seen more and more as a product of the creative human religious imagination, working within a tradition and in dialogue with its own sources indeed, but no longer constrained by the old fiction of timeless unchanging truths vested in some authority. It becomes a living, ever-changing and diverse organism. This realisation may or may not be seen as liberating, but it is undoubtedly novel.

Furthermore, it has rebounded upon the way we see the New Testament itself. We have come to see that Schweitzer's view of historical knowledge was over-simple. He talked as if it was in principle possible to discover the real Jesus, Jesus as he really was, Jesus independent of the theologising or mythicising process which he underwent in the minds of his followers. But a human being does not exist independently of his social setting and his interaction with other people. Necessarily, the only Jesus the historian can in principle ever hope to reach is Jesus as seen by his contemporaries, Jesus in the context of what he meant to others; in short, a Jesus already highly theologised (for such was the age he lived in), and seen from a variety of points of view. If the various convolutions of Gospel criticism since Schweitzer have led to any agreed result, it is that Matthew, Mark and Luke have each their own theology. Each tells his story and shapes Jesus' utterances in the light of his own distinctive viewpoint. 'Pure' history has become a rainbow's end that vanishes as we search for it. Although many would agree that in broad outline Schweitzer's portrayal of Jesus and his world-view remains more probable than its rivals, they will also insist that it is now very much less historically secure than Schweitzer thought it was.

Where people once thought that the New Testament contains a single coherent communication to men of revealed truth, it now appears that the New Testament contains many distinct human theologies. Where people once thought that a recoverable historical Jesus would step forward as an alternative unifying principle, it is now perceived that we do not have access to Jesus himself, but only to several different portraits of him. In each case the objectively given unifying principle has shrunk, and the diversity of human creative response has grown. It becomes less and less possible to suppose that you can read the New Testament and there find a body of pre-packaged divine truth presented to you for your acceptance. What you are rather presented with is a challenge to religious creativity.

As people come increasingly to feel that purely historical criticism of the Bible is yielding diminishing returns, we may soon see them turning to a more literary approach. There are those who believe that the anthropologists' ways of interpreting myths and symbols, or structuralism and more recent movements in literary criticism, may discover laws that govern the working of the creative imagination and can be used to explain literary texts. If they are right, then we may indeed gain a better understanding of what the biblical writings mean and how they work, but the results will again have naturalistic implications, for they will make it still clearer that the biblical writings are products of human religious psychology functioning under certain historical conditions. The great historical drift towards a man-centred and expressive view of religion will simply have moved on one more stage.

Do we see loss or gain in this process? Loss, if we remain nostalgically committed to older forms of religious understanding; but gain, very great gain, if we are willing to accept the new.

Chapter 5
PROMETHEUS UNBOUND

As both Freud and Jung have pointed out, we sometimes have opposite feelings towards the same object, each demanding expression and each behaving as if unaware of the other's existence. Where this is so, the strange unconscious cunning of the psyche seeks out patterns of action which can both express conflicting feelings and also reconcile them and mediate between them.

The anthropologist Bronislaw Malinowski interpreted funeral rites along these lines, seeing in them an ingenious resolution of our painfully mixed emotions after a death. We are torn between on the one hand grief and dread at the loss of the deceased person and the prospect of having to live without his or her influence and guidance, and on the other hand repugnance and a great need to be rid of that fearsome and anomalous object, the corpse. To solve our problem we distinguish between the dead person's soul, which will continue to watch benignly over us as a venerated ancestor, and his body, which not only may but must be speedily disposed of. At a public gathering we perform rites which secure both points at once and set everything to rest. We do the decent thing by the dead, removing the corpse from our sight to its permanent home just (but definitely) outside the community, while at the same time we comfort each other by reaffirming our common faith and values and memorialising him or her as an exemplar of them, whose memory we will keep forever green.

It comes as a shock to realise that many actions addressed to God are similarly ambiguous; yet there can be no doubt about it, and the feelings involved are intelligible enough. People seek to draw near to their gods, and yet their ulterior motive is to make the gods distant again. For the gods have their place in heaven, upstairs, and we have our place below stairs, on earth; and on the whole it is best that they should keep to their place and we to ours. Relations between the two zones should ideally be formal and correct, we signifying by our behaviour our loyalty and our desire to give good service and to please, and they for their part graciously accepting our service and maintaining the stable running of the cosmic household that supports us. Unduly intimate approaches from either side are suspect. Too close an interest by them in our doings usually means trouble and is not to be welcomed; while, in the other direction, we must always bear in mind how acutely sensitive they are to the least sign of presumption.

Evidently people are here transferring ideas from human social relations to religion. Nor is this surprising, in view of the strength of master-servant imagery in rituals. At any rate, anthropologists emphasise that many religious rituals aim to restore a proper distance between people and their gods. Much religious action is prompted by misfortune. When something unpleasant happens to me I assume that I must have stuck my head above the parapet in some way and attracted attention. So I must perform a ritual to purge my sin and placate the offended deity by reassuring him of my sincere deference at all times. I wish to see his extra attentions cease, and normality restored.

My reactions here imply that I see the gods as touchy and jealous about their own dignity and privileges. They want respect and they hate presumption. If one of their human servants becomes uppity, they will slap him down instantly and ruthlessly.

If you think this analysis implausible then ask yourself why else are people so widely agreed that the very essence of sin is human pride and self-will?

The sin of pride

As if he were trying to steal a march on the Sun, Lucifer the Morning Star – known as the planet Venus – rises in the East an hour or two before dawn. But when the Sun appears in his strength, Lucifer's presumption is rebuked. He vanishes, expelled from Heaven.

Here is the source of various myths that tell of how the Morning Star, arrogant in his beauty, foolishly imagined that he could take the place of the Supreme God. Perhaps the oldest version of the story that we have in writing is found on a tablet from the priest's house next to the temple of Baal in the ancient city of Ugarit. The culture is Canaanite, and the date about 1400 BC. The Morning Star was then called Athtar the Luminous. The great God, the power of nature manifest in the Bull and the Sun, is Baal, whose throne is on top of Mount Saphon. Athtar attempts to replace the absent Baal:

> Thereupon Athtar the Luminous
> Goes up to the crags of Saphon;
> He takes his seat on the throne of Baal the Mighty.
> But his feet do not reach the footstool,
> His head does not reach the top thereof.

Centuries later, in about 539 BC, the prophet Isaiah used the same Canaanite myth in a song ridiculing the fallen King Nabonidus of Babylon and celebrating the collapse of his empire:

> How thou hast fallen from heaven,
> O Bright One, Son of Dawn!
> Thou art cut down to the ground,
> More weak than all peoples.
> 'I will ascend to heaven;
> Above the stars of God
> I will set my throne on high,
> Yea, I will be enthroned on the mount of assembly
> On the highest parts of Saphon:
> I will surmount the tops of the clouds,
> I will be like the Most High'.
> But thou art brought down to Sheol,
> To the depths of the Pit.
> Those who see thee will stare at thee,
> They will ponder over thee:
> Is this the man who made the earth tremble,
> Who shook kingdoms,
> Who made the world like a desert,
> And ruined cities,
> Who did not let his captives go?

Other scraps in the Bible suggested further developments of the story. Jesus has a line in which he declares that he has seen 'Satan fall like lightning from Heaven'. In the Book of Revelation, building on a brief allusion in Daniel, there is vision of the Devil and his angels being defeated in a great battle in Heaven. Michael and his host cast them down to earth, and subsequently they are sealed up in Hell.

In later times Christian Fathers such as Jerome and Augustine, both of whom wrote around AD 400, put together these scraps to make up the great myth of the Fall of Lucifer. It is a story that once gripped the Christian imagination. It inspired both the first and the last Christian epics in English, Caedmon's *Genesis* and Milton's *Paradise Lost* a thousand years later, and it was commonly performed as the first episode in the cycle of miracle plays.

What was the essence of Lucifer/Satan's sin? It was rebellion against the divine order, obdurate self-will and refusal to bow to Christ and to God the Father. The angels are sovereign, eternal beings. As Satan sees it, they do not need to be subject to law; they ought to be free and autonomous. Haranguing his troops, Milton's Satan says:

> Who can in reason then or right assume
> Monarchy over such as live by right
> His equals, if in power and splendour less,
> In freedom equal? or can introduce
> Law and edict on us, who without law
> Err not . . ?

Abdiel, a loyalist angel, argues that all the angels were created through Christ, and that this act of creation imposes a duty of worship. Satan's answer is very interesting and modern-sounding. I did not choose to be created, he says, and I was not a party to any contract; what matters is that I am now autonomous and I see no reason to acknowledge anyone as Lord over me:

> Who saw
> When this creation was? rememberst thou
> Thy making, while the Maker gave thee being?
> We know no time when we were not as now;
> Know none before us, self-begot, self-raised
> By our own quick'ning power . . .

The commentators say that Satan lies and knows that he lies in saying that the angels are 'self-begot', but I believe there is more to it than that. What Satan is saying is that facts about how he came into being are irrelevant to, and cannot diminish, his present consciousness of his own powers and autonomy. Hence he goes on:

> Our puissance is our own, our own right hand
> Shall teach us highest deeds, by proof to try
> Who is our equal . . .

The repeated 'our own, our own' insists upon the point that present autonomous self-possession needs no justification. It simply affirms itself, and no past facts about how Satan came into being can make that self-affirmation mistaken.

At any rate there is no doubt that for traditional Christianity, as for other cultures, this kind of autonomous self-affirmation was the very essence of sin. It was pride, rebellion, disobedience. It was an attempt to transcend the appointed limits of our condition and to enjoy a glory, a power and an independence that are properly God's alone. The Universe in traditional thought is a system of relations of dependency, everything in it being sustained and guided by something else of higher rank. It is a class Universe. We all need our superiors and owe them our allegiance.

God is at the apex of the system, and only God has the absolute freedom of having no one and nothing above him. God alone is a law unto himself. As the Elizabethan theologian Richard Hooker puts it, 'The being of God is a kind of law to his working.' It is sufficient for God simply to act out his own nature for, as Hooker again says, the perfection that God is gives perfection to all that he does, and in the traditional universe only God is perfect enough to be fully self-determining and autonomous. Everything else finds its best fulfilment in obeying God, whose service is perfect freedom. It would be folly to imagine that I know better than God what is good for me, and it would be treason to claim for myself his unique divine prerogative of autonomy.

Within this circle of ideas, curiosity and innovation are naturally seen as evidence of Satan's influence. Consider the contrast between Eve and Mary. Eve is naked and confident. Natural woman, she is inquisitive, inclined to question the divine order, and well able to lead her husband. She is an initiator – and therefore bad. Mary on the other hand is ideal woman; she is virginal, with downcast eyes. The red garment that symbolises her loving nature is well shielded by the full blue cloak of her purity. She is modest, and accepts what comes her way in a spirit of grateful obedience. She joyfully proclaims herself a hand-maid and shows no inclination to step out of line. She is protected against Satan's wiles.

The contrast between Eve and Mary shows that a major revolution in our values must have taken place somewhere along the line, for today Mary looks like the now-rejected traditional ideal of womanhood, and Eve looks more like the modern.

The nature of the revolution is made clearer when we consider how Satan used to work. He gained entry to the soul through the imagination, when the mind wandered, or in sleep. Until about 1700 or so the free play of fantasy was regarded as dangerous and Christians prayed to be protected from it. Art confined itself to reworking older stories and themes. The mind's power to innovate and to generate pure fictions was seen as a source of sin – as the very word 'fiction' (from feigning) itself shows, for feigning is deception and untruth. Saints went out into the desert to do battle against the evil thoughts that rose unbidden in their imaginations. They thought they were combating Satan; but as we now see it, they were in fact fighting only against their own creativity.

Traditional mythology implies an equally severe condemnation of the masculine desire for an increase in scientific knowledge and technical control over nature. It is seen as expressing an overweening pride and ambition, a hubris that must end in disaster.

The classic biblical example was the Tower of Babel, the first sky-scraper, the building that attempts to reach heaven. The story reflects what the nomad fathers of Israel must have felt when they beheld the great ziggurats of Mesopotamia. One of the grandest surviving, at Ur, was built as early as 2240 BC and may already have been partly in ruins at the time when the story arose. In any case, the Israelite response was to assume that God must have been angered by the sight of so great a structure. The builders were getting too big for their boots. God scattered them and confused their language, so that the Tower of Babel remained as art has always portrayed it, unfinished.

Greek mythology has similar stories in which the gods are equally jealous of their rights, though the Greeks typically showed rather more sympathy for the victims of divine wrath. The Athenians revered Prometheus the Titan as the patron of the arts and sciences. It was he who had stolen the technology of fire from heaven and had given it to men. Zeus punished mankind for this by creating another beautiful but inquisitive woman, Pandora, to be Prometheus' sister-in-law. She could not resist opening that Freudian symbol, her vase or box, and so releasing the furies that still torment mankind. As for Prometheus himself, he was chained to Mount Caucasus, where an eagle daily devoured his liver. Each night it regenerated, and each day the torture was renewed. Such is the fate of those who seek to benefit mankind by scientific discovery.

Another technologist was Daedalus, who invented the axe and the saw, and was the first to make images of the gods in human form. He built the Labyrinth for King Minos of Crete, but later was imprisoned in it. To escape, he made wings so that he and his son Icarus could fly to freedom. But Icarus flew too high, too close to the sun. The wax securing his wings melted and he crashed into the sea.

So powerfully attractive is the theme of human technological pride being brought low that new myths have continued to be added until modern times. The Jewish Frankenstein, Rabbi Judah Loew ben Bezabel, who made an artificial man called the Golem, is late-medieval. The Faust story grew concurrently with the scientific revolution, and Frankenstein himself comes from the advanced free-thinking world of Mary Shelley, just after the French Revolution. Even as late as the 1960s there were some who said that the space programme could bring down divine retribution upon America.

The common theme is that there are appointed limits to human freedom, human power and human knowledge. The gods have set bounds which cannot be overstepped with impunity. To rebel against the limits, to overstep the mark or stray from the right path was to court disaster. The myths make an interesting connection between scientific and sexual curiosity that runs in opposite directions in the two sexes. A woman who is too inquisitive, like Eve and Pandora, will become sexually awakened; whereas in men like Faust excessive sexual pride and desire is liable to lead on to an inordinate desire for other kinds of forbidden knowledge and power. The historic subjection of women was primarily sexual, whereas the historic subjection of men was a subjection of their curiosity and creative powers.

For both sexes morality was heteronomous, in being a matter of keeping to a sacred Law imposed upon you by another. This law had been revealed to the Fathers and was enshrined in the Scriptures. It was a preordained and unalterable moral framework for human life.

Such an ethic of tradition, designed to discourage free innovation and social change, has obviously played a very large part in our past. How did we ever come to break out of it?

One factor must be that our tradition is full of paradoxes. Our legacy from the Greeks also includes a purely secular tradition of philosophical ethics, and a strain of radical humanism that saw in man the measure of all things. Still more important, there is a radical humanist strain in Christianity itself. In many of its most central themes the faith seeks to overcome the old dualism between God and man. It focuses around a man in whom God comes to share our humanity in order that through him we might share in his own divinity; a man who has made the old heteronomous law-religion obsolete and in whom we are exalted to a cosmic dignity higher even than Lucifer had before his fall. Thus the faith sets before the believer a whole series of images of human emancipation and perfection – of Christ risen, ascended and glorified, of the saints and so forth – every one of which says, '*You* are to share in this.' It is a faith which was from the first addressed to every human being, and especially to the poor and outcast. It looks for the coming of a new humanity and a perfect society on earth, the Kingdom of God, in which Christ's values and spirit will triumph and there will be no more coercion or oppression. And this revolutionary humanist strain in Christianity is very ancient, being probably older than the conservative, traditionalist strain that was later superimposed on it.

The overlaid repressive and heteronomous strain in Christian religious morality became so dominant that when in modern times European culture turned in the direction of radical humanism it saw itself as rebelling against religion. Yet something of Christian humanism still managed to squeeze through, as we shall see.

The seeds of protest

Among the many sources of the revolution in morals medieval humanism must be mentioned. Its interest in the suffering humanity of Jesus, his naked body upon the Cross, his wounds and his precious blood leads to an emotional reawakening and to interesting cross-fertilisation between religious and secular feeling. Occasionally a murmur of open revolt can be heard.

Aucassin and Nicolette, written in France in about 1200, is nowadays thought to be the most attractive of the medieval love-romances. Aucassin, the son of a Count, loves Nicolette, a maiden of unknown birth who has been purchased from the Saracens by the local Viscount. But he is told he may not marry her because her birth is too obscure, and that he may not make her his mistress because that would be a sin for which he would risk exclusion from Paradise. Aucassin is defiant:

> What would I do in Paradise? I'm not preparing myself to go there. I only want to possess Nicolette, my sweetest companion whom I love so tenderly. In Heaven one finds only . . . those old priests, those old cripples, those wretches who day and night cough before the altars or in the crypts under the churches, those who go around with torn old cloaks and worn old clothes, those who are naked, bare-footed and in pain, those who die of hunger and thirst, of cold and poverty. These are the creatures who enter paradise, and with them I have nothing in common. But to hell instead go handsome nobles, bold knights fallen in tournaments and great wars, strong archers and faithful soldiers. I will go with them. There go also the courteous and beautiful ladies who have two or three friends in addition to their lord husbands. There go gold and all those who are happy on earth. I will go with them, so long as I can have Nicolette, my tender friend, at my side.

This remarkably explicit rejection of Christian values was composed in the central territory of Western Christendom at the height of the ages of faith. It is true that the story is partly comic, and we are doubtless expected to smile at the extravagance of two young lovers whose passion is stronger than the restraints of religion and morality. Yet at the same time there must be an element of identification with them. We expect and we find a happy ending, and Aucassin is in no way punished for his blasphemy.

Aucassin and Nicolette is a *chant-fable*, a unique mixture of song and story. Even if the sentiments in it are strained and highflown, Aucassin is eloquent, and the audience would not have been amused unless they had recognised that a lover might feel as he does. Yet it is surely remarkable that someone in the year 1200 could even imagine attacking Christianity in almost the voice of a Nietzsche, calling it grey and life-denying and

The medieval world-view: around the Earth are the spheres of water, air and fire. Celestial influences rain down upon men, animals and plants. From the *Liber Divinorum Operum* of St Hildegard of Bingen: the Lucca manuscript, *c.*AD 1200

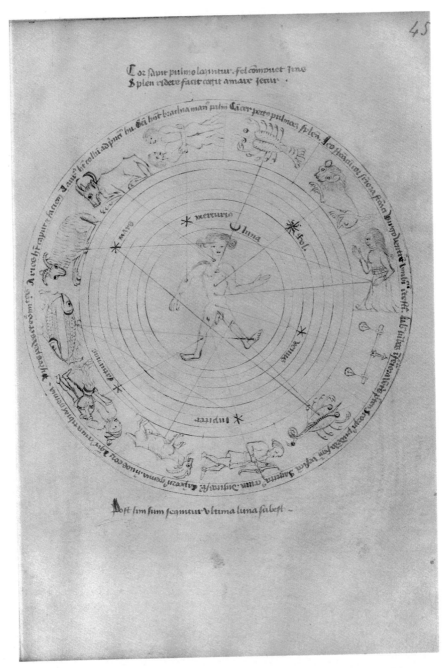

The medieval world-view: the signs of the Zodiac, through the planets, influence various parts of the human body. From a Latin manuscript of *c.*AD 1400 in the Bibliothèque Nationale, Paris

Right   Galileo: portrait
by Joost Sustermans

below   Galileo's study
in his villa at Arcetri,
near Florence,
refurnished for filming

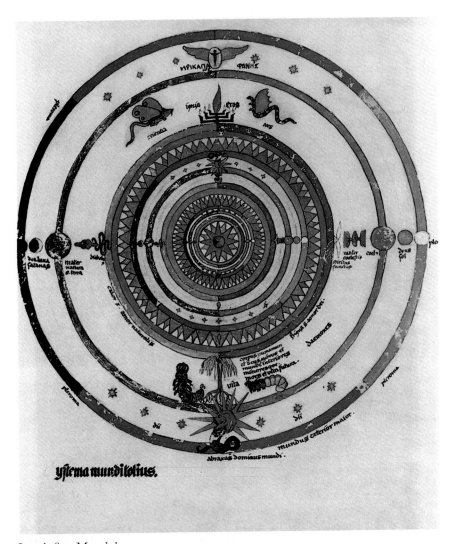

Jung's first Mandala:
note the resemblance
to a cosmological
diagram. The move-
ment of the spiritual life
is from the circumfer-
ence to the still centre.
In the outer circles
opposed principles
within mental life are
balanced against each
other, at top and bot-
tom, left and right

Bollingen: Jung's lakeside 'tower' towards the southern end of the Zürichsee, constructed by him in stages between 1923 and 1955. He saw its plan and development as symbolising his own spiritual life

Images of Christ. *Above* Stanley Spencer's Golgotha is a mound of earth thrown up by workmen in the High Street at Cookham, Berkshire.

In the early Christian period the favoured symbolism was royal and cosmological, as in this example *right* from the 6th century, in the apse of the church of San Vitale, Ravenna

The traditional
Christian types of the
good and the bad
woman. Mary by Fra
Filippo Lippi (detail) is
an obedient
handmaiden with
downcast eyes

Eve by Hugo Van Der
Goes (detail) is
uninhibited and
frank-eyed. But since
the Enlightenment
feminists have
increasingly reversed
the traditional values,
and now look to Eve
rather than to Mary

Above The controversy over Strauss's *Life of Jesus*, as seen by a contemporary caricaturist. Strauss (in German, 'ostrich') helps the labouring man to fell the Cross. The faithful sheep, readers of the Church press, oppose their efforts as Eichhorn (in German, 'squirrel'), the Minister for Education, showers them with decorations taken from a basket held by the King. (From the Schiller National-Museum, Marbach)

Right Marx's office on the groundfloor of 22, rue Vaneau, Paris, refurnished for filming in the original room

extolling instead the lust of the flesh, the lust of the eyes and the pride of life. It shows that even as far back as the Middle Ages there was always the possibility of a revolt of the individual will.

How was it possible? In those days the majority of intellectuals were celibate clerics with a very other-worldly outlook. Yet even among them the old tradition of pagan Latin love-poetry was not quite extinct. The manuscripts survived here and there and could be read, and there is always a certain fascination about a view of life the exact opposite of one's own. If Christianity maintained that to love God perfectly you must give up the world, sensuous immediacy and (above all) sexual love, then it could by its very extremism sometimes tip people over into the opposite point of view, leading them to affirm this world, the senses, the present moment, the individual will and sexual love.

In support of this pagan individualism and humanism the poets rose up to dispute with the clerics. The convention was that the clerics denounced woman as lazy, lascivious and a threat to the salvation of males, whereas the poets praised the goodness of woman and the happiness of sexual love.

The controversy prompted Christine de Pisan to become the first European woman to write in defence of her sex, but the question at issue was not really one of women's liberation. It was a controversy between two views of life, between sacred and profane love, between the next world and this world, between reason and sense, religion and sex, the long-term and the immediate.

The masculine and clerical point of view stressed reason and order, urging us to renounce short-term carnal pleasures in this life for the sake of a better world hereafter. Does this lead to inner conflict? Certainly it may, but if so then that is only to be expected. The cosmos is divided between this world and the better world, and the human being is correspondingly divided between body and soul. Given this general world-picture, it seemed to the clergy inevitable and fitting that in this life we should often be divided personalities in whom the flesh wars against the spirit. They were scholar-priests who owed more to Plato than they did to the Jews. They thought that the present changeable and imperfect world of sense was far inferior to the perfect intellectual world of Heaven that is our true home. What we often forget is that for them Heaven was an intellectual world, and the soul was purely rational. That intellectual world of Heaven is where our souls properly belong. We must fix our minds upon it and not allow our senses to distract us.

The rationalist outlook of the clerics was good for the Church and good for the State. Good for the Church, because if our prime interest is in preparing for a next life of which by ourselves we can know nothing, then we shall be forced to rely heavily upon revelation and Church authority to teach us the saving truths we need to know. Good for the State, because the disciplines of an other-worldly religion which does not expect any great happiness in this life help make good subjects.

How can Aucassin's single squeak of protest hope to make any impact on such a massive coalition of Reason, Church and State? Of course it cannot. To make any progress he has to do various things. First and foremost, he has to shift the focus of reason's gaze from the next world to this present world. He must show that human beings can develop a large body of powerful knowledge of this changing world, can reasonably hope for happiness in this life, and can act autonomously and effectively for their own good in this present era. Natural science, an autonomous ethic and a naturalistic view of man – those are the sort of things Aucassin needs. Until he has made some progress along these lines people will continue to believe that an autonomous affirmation of the human intellect, will and senses and the present life is nothing but the sin of Lucifer and deserves nothing but damnation.

For the present the Church could afford to laugh at Aucassin and even to allow for his point of view. All cultures contain and reconcile internal oppositions, and the two views of life, Christian and pagan, need not necessarily be mortal enemies striving to exterminate each other. On the contrary, they can fit together rather well so long as the Church gets the last word – as surely it must, having as it does the key to the Last Things. You can sow your wild oats all day long, provided that you come home in the evening to Mother Church.

To make it easier, religion has borrowed sexual imagery since biblical times, and the poets of profane love – with great boldness – began to borrow Christian language in medieval France. It became natural for a poet to spend his youth writing erotic verses full of religious imagery and his latter years writing religious poetry full of erotic imagery. When the face of Mary so closely resembled the face of Aphrodite who was to complain if a painter used his mistress as a model for the Virgin? The parallels between the religions of Eros and of the Virgin were lovingly elaborated: the brevity of life, the ardent beseechings, the wounds of love, the extravagant acts of devotion, the sighs and yearnings, the promises and the tears. The symbol of the penitent Mary Magdalen elegantly linked the two cults.

Thus within the culture as a whole, the sensual and profane side of life could be managed, tolerated and even made into a kind of preparation for faith. It was an elegant solution; but it was not to be permanent.

I think, therefore I am

In 1637 Jan Maire of Leyden published a modest-looking anonymous volume. It contained three scientific essays and a long preface called *Discourse on the Method of Rightly Conducting the Reason and Searching for Truth in the Sciences*. More perhaps than any other, this book announces the birth of the modern mind.

Its author was René Descartes (1596–1650), a Frenchman who lived quietly in Holland and was, as we have already seen, an older contemporary of Pascal. It was his first published work. The famous day of solitary reflection in a stove-heated room in South Germany had occurred eighteen years earlier, on 10 November 1619. On that day Descartes had seen in a vision how he could overcome scepticism and establish all the branches of human knowledge on sure foundations; but he had waited all these years for his thoughts to mature.

Especially in France, scepticism was an important force. The great medieval synthesis, a kind of intellectual cathedral, lay ruined but had not yet been satisfactorily replaced. The sceptics thought that the human mind could not get beyond sense-appearances: whatever the underlying reality might be, we could not penetrate to it. Descartes accepted the sceptics' comprehensive criticism of traditional authorities and existing knowledge, but he sought to go right through the fires of scepticism and emerge on the other side with a new defence of knowledge. His plan was to fix the nature of the self and of thinking, and then to show that what really underlay the appearances of things was a set of mathematical laws which the thinking self could grasp.

By 1632 Descartes had a large *Treatise on the Universe* ready to be published, but then he heard of the condemnation of Galileo and suppressed the book. However, Holland was at least more tolerant than Italy, and in 1636 Descartes was forty. If he did not start publishing soon it would be too late. So the *Discourse on the Method* came out, and the gossip of his friends soon obliged Descartes to admit that he was the author. He need not have worried about accusations of heresy, for in spite of some initial rumblings his work soon became very popular and influential.

The main reasons for his success were that he put forward a group of ideas whose time had come, and did so in the most attractive philosophical style since Plato. Furthermore, he retained at least the basic essentials of the Christian world-view – God, the physical world and immaterial human souls – while at the same time being a thoroughgoing exponent of the new mechanical physics.

Descartes contributed as much as anyone to the mood of boundless confidence in the powers of the unaided human reason that marked the next century or so after his death. He was utterly convinced that the individual human mind can attain perspicuously clear knowledge of itself and of the physical world, and he has no room in his thought for any reliance upon the authority of institutions, traditions or ancient authors. In the Middle Ages the truths that had mattered most to men were validated by the Church: social authority was also intellectual authority. But Descartes separates fact from value, and truth from the social order. He will accept nothing as true unless its truth is evident to his own reason with mathematical clarity. To that extent, he is undoubtedly a freethinker; though not in religion.

Descartes's rationalism was supported by the even more significant fact that he was critical. He deliberately sets himself to doubt everything that he can doubt, to review all his convictions and to keep nothing unless it can stand up to searching examination. By his standards traditional culture was a curious ragbag. The old pre-modern sciences – astrology, alchemy, herbal medicine, bestiaries, weather-lore – no doubt did contain some particles of truth, but it was useless as long as it remained so mixed up with errors and superstitions. It was in Descartes's time that people began to grasp the vital point that to make a system of knowledge powerful you must ruthlessly prune out the errors in it. Traditional thought hates pruning and subtracting. It always adds, and so it ends with an untidy mess. Descartes's method of radical doubt as a way to knowledge foreshadows the modern emphasis on experimental falsification as a way of purging and refining our theories.

Another way in which Descartes is modern is that he starts within the individual human subject. Knowledge begins within man. After he had resolved to set aside all his beliefs, reject the testimony of his senses, mistrust the arguments he usually relied on, and even doubt if he was awake, he found that one thing still remained to him: even if he is utterly deceived and even while he doubts everything, he is a thinking subject. Nothing can take that away from him. He cannot doubt that he thinks, for to doubt is already to think.

Now Descartes presses on a stage further. The truth, 'I think therefore I am' has given Descartes his own existence; but what is he? He knows nothing as yet of his own attributes because he has doubted them all. The only truth about himself that he has not been able to reject is that he is a thinker. So he is a spiritual being whose essence is thought. And what makes him so sure of the 'I think, therefore I am'? Nothing but the self-evident clarity of the general proposition that to think it is necessary to be. So, he concludes, what I think clearly and distinctly is true.

Descartes considered himself a loyal Catholic. Yet in a few paragraphs he has created a new kind of self, autonomous and self-defining, one who finds his criterion of truth within himself and who himself generates his own knowledge for himself out of his own resources. What has happened is that he has come to himself and got his first items of knowledge and his criterion of truth purely by himself and quite apart from God, the world or other people. Yet this modern autonomous self that has appeared still wishes to be Christian, and Descartes appeals to God for the further development of his system. It is significant that right at the beginning the modern self wishes, if it can, to remain on terms with Christianity.

The citizen

The accelerating growth of scientific knowledge, reaching its first great peak in Newton, was accompanied by a political change of perhaps even greater long-term significance for religion.

It was foreshadowed by Reformed Protestantism, which taught the priesthood of all believers and affirmed that the ultimate source of authority in the most important matters of all was 'the inward testimony of the Holy Spirit' in the conscience of the individual believer reading the Bible for himself. Radical Protestants such as the Quakers spelt out the implications. They rejected all outward distinctions of rank and title and refused to see religion as imposing a vast objective demand-system on each believer. Instead they internalised God, regarding him as an Inner Light within each member's own conscience. Every member of the Society of Friends had therefore an equal religious dignity and an equal right to make his or her own contribution to common worship. Church order did not depend on structures of authority inherited from tradition, but flowed up from the grassroots and was based on the belief that there was something of God in every man. A human being's worth and the direction of his life were not *assigned* to him in virtue of his place in the social structure and through the mediation of tradition, but were simply proper to him as a human person created by God. In 1648 the Digger Gerrard Winstanley declared that the indwelling within each person of 'the incomprehensible spirit, Reason' just *is* the Kingdom of God within man. He looks for a society in which

> There shall be none lords over others, but everyone shall be a lord of himself, subject to the law of righteousness, reason and equity, which shall dwell and rule within him, which is the Lord.

In the same years, only a century after the Reformation, the case for universal adult suffrage was being put forward by Colonel Rainborough and his friends in the Putney Debates:

The poorest he that is in England hath a life to live as the greatest he. And therefore, truly, Sir, I think it's clear that every man that is to live under a government ought first by his own consent to put himself under that Government.

The story is a familiar one: by internalising religious authority, the Reformation prepared the way for a momentous political transformation which was eventually brought about by the development of a market economy and by the Industrial Revolution. A new kind of man emerged, the free citizen of a democratic republic. People were no longer merely the subjects of a king who exercised absolute authority over them. Instead, sovereignty was vested in the people. Government became representative of the people, and accountable to them. They were subject to no law except that which through their elected assembly they had in effect imposed upon themselves. The work of politics was no longer merely to enforce obedience to sacred authority, but to establish consent by public debate. The politician was no longer a ruler, but a manager. The law was no longer seen as having dropped from heaven, but as being man-made and as expressing the current social consensus. When public opinion on some issue shifts, then in due course the law must shift to follow it. The people have become sovereign, self-governing and autonomous.

The change was enormous, and religiously ambiguous. On the one hand it was originally religiously motivated, and the religious case for making it continued to be put forward as long as the Protestant spirit remained vigorous. The arguments deployed by Tom Paine of Thetford (1737–1809), himself of Quaker stock, were lineal descendants of arguments advanced by radical Protestants almost 150 years earlier:

It is not the least of the evils of the present existing Governments in all parts of Europe that man, considered as a man, is thrown back to a vast distance from his Maker, and the artificial chasm filled up by a succession of barriers, or sort of turnpike gates, through which he has to pass. . . .

But on the contrary, says Paine, appealing to the story of creation:

all men are all of *one degree*, and consequently all men are born equal, and with equal natural rights . . . (For every child born into this world) the world is as new to him as it was to the first man that existed, and his natural right in it is of the same kind.

The fact that radical Christianity contributed so much to the rise of modern liberal democracy suggests that it might be possible in the new order for religion as well as morality to become autonomous and centred within man. 'My mind is my church', says Tom Paine, unabashedly carrying the principle of religious freedom to its limit. Yet – and here is the ambiguity – the new kind of society in many ways embodied the spirit of Lucifer and required his values. For if it is to work, it demands personal autonomy, critical questioning, innovation and enterprise. They can no longer be rejected as sinful.

A sign of the revolution in values came in 1759, when G.W. Lessing first questioned the damnation of Faust. The original Dr Johann Faust is alleged to have been a contemporary of Luther, with even a suggestion that he represents Luther's shadow-side; though the remote origins of the legend go back to Simon Magus in New Testament times. Faust developed into a typical wicked scientist who had sold his soul to the Devil in exchange for knowledge, power and pleasure in this life, and the story had always ended with a spectacular damnation-scene. Lessing began the rehabilitation of Faust by indicating that God might after all actually approve of his indomitable striving after knowledge. It became possible to imagine Faust's ultimate salvation.

Another portent appeared when Tom Paine's *Rights of Man* (1791–92) was speedily followed in 1794 by Mary Wollstonecraft's *Rights of Woman*. Just as Lessing begins to reverse the values embodied in the Faust legend, so Mary Wollstonecraft begins to reverse the values taught by the old contrast between Eve and Mary.

The response of the churches to the moral revolution in the change-over from absolute monarchy to liberal democracy has been very complex. They have made a positive adjustment insofar as they have relinquished their old function of exercising social control, have ceased burning heretics, have become culturally partially disestablished, and have taken to acting as a kind of pressure group campaigning for peace, for individual rights and so forth. On the other hand, in religious symbolism and in the corresponding structures of authority in the Church older patriarchal and monarchial ways of thinking persist strongly, giving rise to familiar tensions. There was a celebrated example on 18 December 1979 in Rome when, even as a Papal Message attacking the practice in the political realm of 'silencing those who do not share the same views' was being released, it became known that the Congregation for the Doctrine of Faith had withdrawn Professor Hans Küng's *missio canonica*, his licence to function as a Catholic theologian.

The problems are still unsolved, and presumably cannot be fully solved without doctrinal and structural changes that go further than most Christians are yet prepared to accept. In any case, they have been transcended by a still more profound challenge. The critical philosophy of Immanuel Kant opened the way to an anthropocentrism – a man-centred outlook – of a new kind.

Kant

As we have already seen, in the early eighteenth century there was a widespread confidence in the power of the human mind to build up a progressively increasing body of objective knowledge of the world. The philosophy of Descartes, the outstanding success of Newtonian physics and other advances in many fields of knowledge combined with new movements in economics and politics to create in many quarters a mood of great optimism.

Yet there were also doubts. There was sharp controversy about how far traditional theology would need to be revised (or even, as some hinted, abandoned altogether) in the new intellectual climate, which after all did not exactly encourage a reverent attitude to ancient super-natural mysteries that must be believed on authority. The first generation of liberal and radical theologians were proposing to demythologise Christianity into Protestant rationalism, into Deism or even into a Spinozist identification of God with Nature. At a more fundamental level yet, if man was set firmly in nature with no source of factual knowledge except his sense-experience, would it really be possible to justify our knowledge of universal laws of nature and of the basic principles of morality?

For those who had ears to hear, the great Scottish philosopher David Hume (1700–1776) had made these questions inescapable by proving that a consistent empiricism must lead to scepticism. The principle of the pinhole camera had been known for some time, and it suggested the theory that our retinas, along with our eardrums and other sensory surfaces, act as little screens on which images of external objects are projected. These pictures are then conveyed into the brain and there inspected by the mind or soul. But if that is the situation, then since we never get out of our own heads, we can never check whether or not the images we are receiving are pictures of an external reality.

The difficulty can be put in modern terms by supposing that we are obliged to spend our whole lives inside a darkened preview theatre receiving various inputs. A screen represents the visual input, a speaker the auditory, and so on. So we have nothing to go on but a series of flashes, buzzes, smells, tastes, squeezes. After a while we may notice some regular sequences in the flashes on the screen, or in the buzzes from the speaker. We may even learn to associate certain flash-patterns with certain buzz-patterns. But, as Hume puts it, 'All perceptions are distinct, (and) nothing is present to me but particular perceptions.' He is at a loss to explain how we can be justified in joining up our perceptions, as we obviously do, in order to form our ideas of things that we suppose to be out there in the world beyond the preview theatre, interacting with each other and causing our perceptions of them. He cannot even see how, from the stream of experiences alone, we can be justified in arguing that there must be a self that has these experiences. In the past philosophers had usually got themselves out of this difficulty by appealing to supposed self-evident and universal truths such as, 'every quality must belong to a substance', 'every change must have a cause', and 'every perception must belong to a perceiving mind.' But, Hume asks, how do we know that these statements are true? For they can certainly never be fully vindicated just from the stream of experiences. They seem to be both essential to our knowledge and unprovable.

Few in Hume's day even understood the questions he was raising, much less were competent to attempt answers to them. But Immanuel Kant (1724–1804) both understood and was competent. He was a keen exponent of Newton's vision of the world as a system of bodies moving about in space and time in accordance with universal laws. But he saw that in order to express Newton's philosophy of nature we have to begin with a number of statements about the nature of space and time, substances and their qualities, motion, causality and so on. These state-ments set up the framework of pigeonholes into which the stuff of experience is fitted. They have to be true prior to experience, for as Hume rightly pointed out they are not actually given *in* experience. Kant called these statements 'synthetic *a priori* judgments', and asked himself the question Hume had set him – How do I know these statements are true, and how can I explain and justify the move from raw, unstructured sense-experience to Newton's magnificent vision of the world?

Given his problem, Kant's answer had to be that it is our own minds which order our experience, for there was nowhere else for the order to come from. The ordering principles, the 'synthetic *a priori* judgments', must somehow be built into the human understanding. The human mind is pre-programmed to construe experience as being experience of an objective physical world.

However, this was not a sufficient answer to Hume. For Hume had also recognised that Nature has somehow pre-programmed us to construe our experience as being experience of a physical world. Certainly we are so constituted that we *believe* we are selves, set in a world of space and time and physical bodies and causal laws; but how do we prove that these beliefs about the world are actually *true*?

Kant's reply was to demonstrate that no other way to knowledge is possible. If a finite subject like you or me is to gain objective knowledge of a physical world through experience, then we must order our experience in terms of space and time, we must order it in terms of things and their properties, and we must impose universal laws upon it. In no other way could subjective experience be turned into objective knowledge: the only way to objectivity is by *conferring* it upon experience.

In his *Critique of Pure Reason* (1781) Kant provided an elaborate analysis of how the mind not only does, but *must*, convert the chaos of raw sense-experience into an ordered cosmos. The result was a form of idealism: where most previous philosophies had supposed that the mind copies or reflects an order that is out there in the world, Kant reversed the relationship between thought and things. The ordered world we see is the creation of our minds, and has to be so, for there is no other way that we could know it. The world mirrors the mind, and not the other way round.

Kant pointed out a whole series of stunning corollaries of his discovery. First, our mental machinery only produces knowledge when sense-experience is fed into it, which means that we can have no knowledge of things as they are in themselves apart from experience: we cannot have any knowledge of what lies beyond the boundaries of possible experience. We can for example use causal thinking to connect elements of experience together, but we cannot use it to connect the world or some part of it to God, for God is not part of the world of experience. The rules for thinking objects do not apply to him. Kant was therefore a strict agnostic about God. In his jargon, we can have no theoretical or speculative knowledge of God.

Secondly, on Kant's account, the autonomous human mind not merely discovers truth, but *constitutes* it. The man-centred approach to philosophy that had come in with Descartes is here taken a whole stage further. Anthropocentrism is not just a piece of human moral arrogance, nor is it just one possible starting-point among others. It has become a philosophical necessity. The creative work of turning chaos into cosmos, ascribed in the past to God, is now seen as something that is necessarily done by human activity.

The radical humanism implied here becomes still clearer when Kant turns to ethics. All of human thought and action is legislative: it imposes rules. Theoretical thinking imposes rule and order upon experience so as to make it into an intelligible world, the world of fact, the world that is. In practical, ethical thinking we autonomously impose rules on our own action in order to bring into being the world that our reason tells us ought to be. Kant's view of ethics, though rational and objective, was also thoroughly autonomous; it is our own reason which recognises the intrinsic authority of moral principles and our duty to adopt them as maxims that have a right to guide our action. Our whole moral dignity lies in the fact that we can and ought to be self-legislating.

This description may suggest that Kant's philosophy leaves no room at all for religion. That is not quite true. Kant saw human life as a pilgrimage, and was a kind of ultra-Protestant whose religion was wholly ideal and imperative. In a godless world the hero of faith soldiers on, following a guiding light, hoping for a state of things in which he himself is not merely heroically virtuous, but holy; in which the world of fact and the world of ideal value are harmonised, and in which things are as they should be and those who deserve it are at last truly happy. So God still figures in Kant's philosophy: though not known as the Ground of things as they are, he remains the transcendent ideal goal to which the man of faith aspires.

Kant's philosophy of religion, however, was not taken up by his immediate followers. What caught their imagination was the possibility of developing his thought further in the directions, first of idealism, and then of radical secular humanism.

The young Marx

Karl and Jenny Marx arrived in Paris from Switzerland in late October 1843. They settled at first at 23, rue Vaneau, among a small group of German political *emigrés* led by Arnold Ruge. Marx was to be co-editor with Ruge of a radical review, the *Deutsch-Französische Jahrbücher*, whose office was established in the large ground-floor room of no. 22 in the same street.

Karl Marx had been born in 1818 at Trier on the Mosel, the oldest town in Germany, and was the scion of a long line of rabbis. His father Heinrich had received Protestant baptism for the sake of his legal career just before Karl's birth, and Karl himself was similarly baptised before beginning school. Jenny was the daughter of the Baron von Westphalen, a professional colleague of Marx senior, and the two families had been on intimate terms for many years. The marriage of Karl and Jenny had been long opposed by some family members on both sides, partly because of their difference in rank and partly because Jenny was four years older, and had finally taken place only five months previously, in June. In spite of all the hardships of their later life together, the marriage was exceptionally successful, for Marx was somewhat unusual among great thinkers in being a robustly heterosexual and monogamous man whose wife would refer to him with relish as 'my big baby'. When they arrived in Paris she was already pregnant.

In Marx's student days the philosophy of Hegel was the dominant force in German intellectual life. G.W.F. Hegel (1770–1831) was a rationalist and an idealist. He had enlarged upon Kant's idea that the mind confers objectivity upon experience to such a point that he depicted the whole of reality as the product of the self-unfolding of Reason, as it moves towards absolute knowledge: perfect freedom, self-possession and self-expression. This self-unfolding of Reason takes place in accordance with a new dynamic logic of process, not the traditional formal and deductive logic, but a logic of transformation in which Spirit continually goes out and returns to itself, differentiates itself and then reunites itself, generates contradictions and then reconciles them at a higher level. Yet, Hegel claims, the whole process evolves by pure conceptual necessity towards a state of absolute knowledge in which everything is preserved and everything is perfectly reconciled.

So all-embracing is Hegel's philosophy that it unites in a single vision God, nature, history and the self. In the book that gives the first synopsis of his whole system, *The Phenomenology of Spirit*, Hegel analyses the development of consciousness from bare perception through understanding and reason towards the absolute knowledge of Spirit. Each stage in the process represents a temporary alienation of Spirit, dominant for a while but destined through its own inner logic to be overcome and taken up into a higher synthesis. As we read, we see that Hegel's idealism gives him a point of view from which he can describe all at once, and in a single vision, the spiritual journey of the individual human being, the whole world-historical process and the developing self-expression of the Divine Mind. The system is all three things at once; and it naturally assigns to politics, art, religion and philosophy each its proper place.

Hegel was a practising Lutheran Christian who claimed that his philosophy expressed the inner content of Christianity. The ultimate goal of Christian hope, that God shall be all in all and everything to everyone, appeared in his philosophy as the return of Absolute Spirit to itself. Hegel saw the whole world-process as being at once the creation and the self-revelation of Spirit. The incarnation of God in Christ was represented in the system by the ultimate identity of the human spirit with Spirit itself. The death and resurrection of Christ symbolised the principle of loss and gain, contradiction and reconciliation that permeated all Hegel's logic. Thus, he claimed, truths which the religious imagination apprehends in merely symbolic form were preserved and represented in purely conceptual terms in his system.

So formidable was Hegel's reputation that he was able to avoid the censorship troubles that had afflicted even Kant. Yet his departure from orthodoxy was radical. He had overthrown the traditional God-world distinction. His philosophy was purely immanent; that is, all the ultimate questions were resolved within the system, without appeal to any incomprehensible Transcendent outside it. No absolute mystery remained.

Hegel's system was so all-encompassing that it seemed to leave little to be said. It appeared to incorporate everything and all points of view, and during his lifetime few saw that because of its immanentism it was readily capable of being transformed into a completely secular atheistic humanism. Yet the hints were there. Religious ideas could be seen as projections of the human imagination. Anything whatever that stood over against man could be seen as a mere temporary alienation of Spirit – as something which evolving Spirit had projected out, something which for the moment might seem to stand over against man but which in time was necessarily destined to be reabsorbed into man as his consciousness advanced another stage. Thus the Old Testament picture of a God over against man is succeeded in the New Testament by a God who returns himself to man by actually becoming man. Finally, the keystone of Hegel's entire system, his idealism, his doctrine that Reason generates reality and thought is prior to being, might perhaps itself be overcome by applying his own logic to it. Hegel moves from the ideal to the real; but his own method surely requires us to go a step further and overcome even idealism itself. When we have taken this further step our apprehension of the real becomes completely concrete and immediate. Theory and practice become one and the same. We can advance the process not merely by philosophical reflection, but by revolutionary practice.

Marx gave an early indication of such a desire to complete the move from the ideal to the real. After an unsatisfactory year at the University of Bonn, he started again at Berlin in 1836 and there began to feel the full impact of the Hegelian philosophy. An extravagantly long and rhetorical letter to his father, dated 10 November 1837, expresses the whirling state of his mind at that time. In the course of it he says, 'I . . . came to seek the idea in the real itself. If the gods had previously dwelt above the earth, they had now become its centre.' Marx's romantic tirades made his father uneasy: 'I wonder whether the peculiar demon, to which your heart is manifestly a prey, is the Spirit of God or that of Faust.' As it was to turn out, the spirit in Marx was rather that of Prometheus.

After becoming a Hegelian, and then graduating, Marx joined the Berlin Doctors' Club, a discussion society to which many of the leading Young Hegelians belonged. With the publication of Strauss's *Life of Jesus* in 1835, followed by the even more radical work of Bruno Bauer, this group had moved from seeing religious ideas as valid imaginative projections to seeing them as outmoded and harmful illusions. The reduction of theology to anthropology and of Christianity to atheistic humanism was completed by L.A. Feuerbach in 1841 with his book *The Essence of*

Christianity. Meanwhile religious radicalism was leading to political radicalism, and the group were falling into official disfavour. Bauer, who still held a university post, was transferred from Berlin to Bonn. He had encouraged Marx to obtain a doctorate, in the hope that it might lead to a university post. Marx duly obtained his doctorate, moved to Bonn to work with Bauer, and began to write a qualifying dissertation; but then in March 1842 Bauer was deprived of his job and it became clear that Marx's hopes were at an end. From now on the Young Hegelians had no prospect of conventional careers, and must make a living as best they could by writing and freelance journalism. They founded or took over several political reviews, mostly shortlived, and Marx himself became the editor of one of them, the *Rheinische Zeitung*, in October 1842. The paper at first had some success, but it was suppressed by the authorities in the following March, and Marx found himself unemployed – and still unmarried.

The Young Hegelians at this time were mostly radical liberals and democrats rather than socialists. Industrially, and therefore politically, Germany was relatively backward and scarcely one man in twenty-five was an industrial worker. By contrast, Paris was more industrialised and already had a revolutionary tradition. French socialist thinking began to influence the Germans, and they became enamoured of the idea of an alliance between German theoretical sophistication and French practical experience – between, as Marx put it, thinking humanity which is oppressed and suffering humanity which thinks. Hence the plan to settle in Paris. Ruge had some money, and he and Marx would be co-editors of the review. All that remained now was to persuade the leading Young Hegelians and the leading French socialists to contribute.

This proved more difficult than had been expected. On the German side some leading figures such as Feuerbach were reluctant to commit themselves politically, feeling that the time was not yet ripe. As for the French, they were blessedly ignorant of the finer points of Hegelianism and reluctant to be evangelised by youths who had barely yet heard of socialism, who lacked political experience and whose most salient feature was a strange new form of militantly atheistic humanism which would merely bewilder and antagonise the public.

In short, the kind of thinking that was emerging among the Young Hegelians was not yet politically credible as a revolutionary doctrine.

When the first and last issue of the *Jahrbuch* appeared, therefore, it had only seven contributors, all writing in German. Apart from Marx and Ruge, the best-known authors were Heine, Engels and Moses Hess.

Marx's two articles are good examples of his combative and excessive journalistic style. The first had been written before he reached Paris, and is a criticism of Bruno Bauer's writings on the Jewish question. It shows that he had picked up from a recent essay by Hess 'On the Essence of Money' (1844), the idea of an analogy between God and money: both began as human symbols, had grown into great domineering abstractions that sucked the value out of life, and now needed to be demythologised and resolved back into their human basis. The article also shows Marx moving away from liberal individualism. He points out that in America complete political emancipation had supposedly been achieved, but the religious problem remained unsolved. 'As Christ is the intermediary on to whom man unburdens all his divinity, all his religious bonds, so the State is the mediator on to which he transfers all his godlessness and all his human liberty.' The State is free and secular, but in everyday civil life the spirit of Protestant religious individualism has become stronger than ever: 'religion has become the spirit of civil society, the sphere of egoism, the *bellum omnium contra omnes*' (the war of everyone against everyone else). The free-enterprise competitive spirit of Protestantism reigns unchecked. The lofty ideal of a citizen-republic masks the fact that in civil life man 'is active as a private individual, treats other men as means and becomes the plaything of alien powers'.

Marx's second article was a piece of work in progress, uninvitingly called *Towards a Critique of Hegel's Philosophy of Right: Introduction*. It marks a big advance in his thinking. Feuerbach had recently attacked Hegel's speculative idealism, saying that philosophy of that sort was no more than the ghost of theology and stood in just the same need of demyth-ologisation. Hegel's method of generating the real out of the ideal was merely mystifying: 'Thought arises from being, being does not arise from thought', or more simply, political thought should start with the facts. Marx himself was already reading less and less philosophy, and more and more of history and economics.

The other major new influence is that of the working-class leaders whom Marx had been meeting in Paris, including not only native French-men but also German immigrants. The main theme of the article shows Marx moving towards revolutionary socialism, though by no means reaching it yet. Germany, he argues, is so backward that it needs a social and not merely a political transformation. A particular class, such as the bourgeoisie, could not do more than reform society from its own point of view and in its own interests. Only those who have nothing and are outside the class system altogether, the proletariat, can accomplish the total emancipation of society. Radical philosophy can supply them with the necessary theoretical backing and tools.

The article is particularly famous for the passage about religion with which it opens. The main themes were some years old, and come from the work of Strauss, Bauer and Feuerbach. For too long man has looked up to the heavenly world to learn the truth about himself. Now he knows that what he sees there is nothing but a distorted reflection, and he must turn to this world, to the State and society. Criticism of religion must give place to criticism of politics.

The message was not original, but it was expressed with great force in a tumbling cascade of striking images:

> As far as Germany is concerned the criticism of religion is essentially complete, and the criticism of religion is the presupposition of all criticism. . . .
>
> The foundation of irreligious criticism is this: man makes religion, religion does not make man. Religion is indeed the self-consciousness of man who either has not yet attained to himself or has already lost himself again. But man is no abstract being squatting outside the world. Man is the world of man, the state, society. . . .
>
> Religious suffering is at the same time an expression of real suffering and a protest against real suffering. Religion is the sigh of the oppressed creature, the feeling of a heartless world, the soul of soulless conditions. It is the opium of the people. . . .
>
> The abolition of religion as the illusory happiness of the people is at the same time the demand for their real happiness. The demand to give up the illusions about their condition is a demand to give up a condition that requires illusions. Criticism has plucked the imaginary flowers from the chains so that man may throw off the chains and pluck real flowers. Religion is only the illusory sun around which man revolves so long as he does not revolve around himself. . . .
>
> The criticism of religion ends with the doctrine that man is the highest being for man – with the imperative to overthrow all circumstances in which man is humiliated, enslaved, abandoned and despised.

The rhetoric is brilliant, but even some of Marx's colleagues disapproved of such fireworks. To understand the feeling behind it one needs to recall some of those nineteenth-century prints which show working men toiling with a vast many-tiered burden on their backs that they are obliged to support. It is composed, successively, of the police and the military, the bourgeoisie, the judges, the clergy, and topping all, the Crown. A whole social order which in previous ages had been more or less grudgingly accepted was now felt, with the advent of industrialism, to be a monstrous burden.

Although most of the commentators deny it, some of the language used about the proletariat in the closing paragraphs of the article has a decidedly messianic ring. The most striking sentence reads:

When the proletariat proclaims the dissolution of the hitherto existing world order, it merely declares the secret of its own existence, since it is in fact the dissolution of this order.

This surely reflects knowledge of Gospel criticism, and in particular the debate about Jesus' eschatological message, the secret of his own identity, and his part in the coming kingdom of God. As for the question of why Marx decided that it should be the relatively tiny proletariat rather than some other social group which would become the nucleus of the new humanity, it appears that Marx's study of French political and economic history had led him to think that as it had been the turn of the bourgeoisie in 1789, so it would be the turn of the proletariat next time.

None of all this mattered immediately, for the *Jahrbuch* was a failure. The French public would not buy it, and the German government promptly banned it, issuing warrants for the arrest of Ruge, Marx and Heine. To add to their troubles, the group even began to quarrel among themselves.

Nevertheless Marx had a tremendous year, reading, writing and disputing with furious energy. His first child was born in May and named Jenny after her mother. In September Engels, whose contribution to the *Jahrbuch* had been sent from Germany, arrived in Paris. When they met the two men at once became fast friends, and their long collaboration began.

Marx's subsequent development is outside our scope. What is at present important to us is the fact that by the second half of 1844 he had reached a point of view which utterly precluded any serious interest in religion. The following passage shows why:

Since for socialist man what is called world history is nothing but the creation of man by human labour and the development of nature for man, he has the observable and irrefutable proof of his self-creation and the process of his origin.

From this point of view even atheism has become a term without meaning, for it is no longer necessary to deny something in order to affirm man. Socialism simply starts with man and nature. Through his historical, social activity man makes himself, and nature for himself.

This radical humanism, in which traditional religious questions are quite forgotten, came ultimately from two sources. There was Kant's demonstration that man not only does but must autonomously order the realms of knowledge and morality, and there was Hegel's immanentism. For Kant himself, that tough old ultra-Protestant, the traditional ultimate questions had still been very much alive. In his jargon, 'the highest good is not immanently realisable'. The soul must ultimately look beyond this world. But Hegel's philosophy purported to resolve all the ultimate questions immanently, while still professing to be Christian; and after his death his younger and most talented followers quickly transformed it into the most thoroughgoing secular humanism yet known.

To challenge this development it would be necessary to go back to Hegel and question his claim to have solved the ultimate questions of life within his system.

Kierkegaard

At the end of the eighteenth century some prophetic thinkers began to express unease at the way modern society was developing. The mechanisation of the physical world had been followed by a proliferation of new sciences and trades, and the growth of a market economy. The result was a certain fragmentation of life. People were losing the ability to integrate their own private life-aims and specialisms into a larger public whole. Friedrich Schiller, idealising the Greeks as was the German custom, complained that the old ideal of

> the Greek states, in which every individual enjoyed an independent existence but could when need arose, grow into the whole organism, now made way for an ingenious clockwork in which, out of the piecing together of innumerable but lifeless parts, a mechanical kind of collective life ensues.

In such a world the individual is diminished:

> chained to a single little fragment of the whole, a man himself develops into nothing but a fragment; everlastingly in his ear the monotonous sound of the wheel he turns, he never develops the harmony of his being, and instead of putting the stamp of humanity upon his own nature, he becomes nothing more than the imprint of his occupation or of his specialised knowledge.

When the great institutions such as the Church and the State are no longer able to unify the life-aims of individual citizens, they come to be thought of as irrelevant and oppressive. Society becomes dangerously sick and restless.

This influential diagnosis suggests that what is wrong with the modern human condition is that the subjective aim of the individual is not fulfilled by being taken up into the larger objective institutions and goals of society. The result is alienation in the strict sense of that overused word: a person has become like a foreigner in his own country. Hegel proposed to cure it by teaching a grandiose and optimistic philosophical scheme of redemption, and Marx by socialist revolution. Both sought to overcome the contradictions and oppositions of our present state, and re-unite the self with society and nature.

However, by the end of 1844 Marx's vision had become so completely naturalistic that all the questions of life, without remainder, had become questions of politics. The old Greek doctrine that man is a political animal, a creature for whom the *polis* or city is life's chief end, had reached its furthest development, and the result was a certain shallowness. Marx lacked any deep personal interest in religion. For him, man has created himself, for man makes history and history makes man. Man has even created the world, in the sense that the only world that concerns us is the world so far as it had been humanised – made intelligible and appropriated by human creative activity. Always the 'man' in question is mankind at large, humanity in general, as if the uniqueness of each individual were not a question of prime importance. Marx always talks as if the ideas of man and self-consciousness and liberation were quite straightforward. He has no deep dread of existence. Even death seems not greatly to concern him: the individual is mortal, but the species goes on and that is all there is to it.

There was room for a protest to be made that something was being lost. It came from Denmark, a country which had had a painful intro-duction to the nineteenth century. Still feudal and backward, Denmark suffered badly in the Napoleonic wars. It was struck by violent inflation, and the king had to close the State Bank in 1813. Thereafter, modernising influences began to enter the country: English economics, German Ro-manticism and philosophy, French political thinking, natural science, and in due course the beginnings of industrialism – the electric telegraph, the railway. The development towards a modern liberal democratic state was completed when the king signed a new Constitution in 1849.

The Church had naturally bulked large in the old Denmark, both in the University at Copenhagen and in intellectual life generally. The clergy were early exposed to the challenge of modernisation, as Hegelianism, liberal theology and biblical criticism became known in the University. In religious thought, there were disputes between conservative Lutherans and liberals. But on the whole the Church leadership supported the social transformation of the country: the new order could and would be still a Christian order.

In the 1760s, in the old Denmark, Saeding on the Jutland Heath was reckoned one of the poorest parishes in the poorest district of all. Since it could not afford a pastor of its own, the parsonage house was let to a peasant family. Surnames were still not fixed, and the family were named after their address – Kierkegaard, 'Churchyard'. An eleven-year-old son of the family, Michael, worked as a shepherd. His son later recalled

> the dreadful case of a man who when he was a little boy suffered much
> hardship, was hungry, numb with cold. He stood on a hillock and cursed
> God – and the man was not able to forget this when he was eighty-two
> years old.

A year later an uncle rescued the young Michael Kierkegaard from this
life by taking him into the hosiery business in Copenhagen. Years passed,
and Michael Kierkegaard became rich enough to retire while still in his
forties. His first wife died childless, and very soon afterwards he got his
housekeeper with child and married her. There were seven children of
the marriage of whom the last, Søren (1813–1855), was born when his
mother was forty-five and his father fifty-six. All were gifted, but they
grew up not knowing why their mother was a cipher in the household or
why their father, though outwardly both rich and devout, had an air of
guilt and dread about him.

At last the retribution that he had long awaited fell upon the old
man. The wife and five of the children died. Two sons remained. The
elder, Peter, somehow escaped, eventually to live a more-or-less normal
life as a bishop, though always troubled by feelings of unworthiness that
led him in the end to resign his see prematurely. Søren alone was left,
and to him the old man gave all his attention:

> As a child I was sternly and seriously brought up in Christianity.
> Humanly speaking, it was a crazy upbringing. The depth of my melan-
> choly was only equalled by the depth of my skill in concealing it. My only
> joy was that nobody could discover how unhappy I felt. I have never had
> any immediacy, and in the ordinary human sense of the word I have
> never lived. I did not gradually learn reflection: I *am* reflection from first
> to last. I was forced back on myself and my relation to God.

Always physically small in any case, Søren was additionally handicapped
by a fall from a tree in childhood which left him with a slight curvature of
the spine. To protect himself he developed a singularly sharp tongue and
a dandified eccentric manner. Having been educated by his father for
precocity, he was highly aware of his gifts, and realised quite early in life
that he would never meet an equal. By the same token, he would never
be a normal person. He sensed that he was condemned to live outside the
mainstream of life, an observer and an exile doing penance for a crime
whose nature he did not even understand.

> Once upon a time there lived a father and a son. Both were very gifted,
> both witty. Usually they talked together and amused one another like
> any two intelligent people. But once, the father looked upon his son, saw

that he was deeply troubled, and said, 'Poor child, you go about in silent despair.' But he never questioned more closely: he couldn't, for he was himself in silent despair . . . The father believed that he was the cause of the son's melancholy, and the son believed that he was the cause of his father's melancholy, and so they never discussed it.

Given this strange background, it is scarcely surprising that Kierkegaard's young manhood was somewhat turbulent. He was highly introspective, with an obsessive need to understand himself and his relationship to his father which made him a psychologist and a minute analyst of the spiritual life. He was probably the first writer to think of himself as a thief and a spy: a thief because he became expert at burgling the secrets of other people's lives, beginning with his own father's, and a spy because unknown to others he was 'in higher service' and had a special mission and identity. Later he was to think of himself as a smuggler with the paradoxical aim of 'smuggling Christianity into Christendom', teaching the truth to people who thought they knew it already. No doubt these criminal images reflect his unusually strong dual sense of being both a sinner and an exception.

Kierkegaard spent no less than ten years at the University of Copenhagen, oscillating between brilliance and dissipation. He penetrated his father's secrets, and went through a period of romantic revolt and despair. Then there was a reconciliation which was sealed by the old man's death.

In spite of the turmoil, Kierkegaard got the education he needed. He was proficient in ten languages, and had a special love for Homer, Shakespeare, Mozart and Goethe. The philosophers who most influenced him were, in order, Hegel, Plato and Kant. He had an actor-dramatist's facility at impersonation, and would compare himself with Faust, Don Juan, Peter Abelard and Hamlet – all of them characters whose relations with women were in various ways disastrous.

In all, on the arts side his education and equipment were superlative. His one lack was a good grounding in natural science. In many ways his general cultural background was very similar to Marx's: that he developed in the opposite direction is largely due to the immense influence upon him of his father and of a strongly traditional Lutheran piety.

His father's death left Kierkegaard with independent means, and so the chance to avoid ordination and become a freelance writer and thinker. In his contempt for academics, his solitary life and caustic wit, his love for the theatre and music and his ascetical temperament, he later recognised an affinity with Schopenhauer. But he was even more unusual; for no thinker of Kierkegaard's eminence had been so strongly Christian

for a long time past, or would be again. His oddity in this respect has led
to some resistance to his ideas: Nietzsche avoided reading him, and Sartre
(though learning a great deal from him) saw him as giving the lie to
Hegel by proving that it is after all possible for a past form of consciousness
to be reborn out of its time. In fact, however, Sartre's opinion is mistaken:
Kierkegaard does not represent simply a restoration of traditional Christian
consciousness, but a more radical transformation of it than is yet fully
realised.

One further episode completed Kierkegaard's formation as a writer.
In May 1837 he met the fourteen-year-old Regine Ølsen and fell in love
with her.

> Today I got out to the Rordam's house – Merciful God, why should that
> inclination awaken just now? – Oh, how I feel that I am alone – Oh,
> cursed be that arrogant satisfaction in standing alone!

He said nothing, but chose instead simply to wait quietly for her to grow
up. Next year, at the age of twenty-three, he reports an intense experience
of religious joy:

> *May 19. Half past ten in the morning.* There is an indescribable joy which
> kindles us as inexplicably as the Apostle's outburst comes gratuitously:
> 'Rejoice, I say into you, and again I say unto you, rejoice.' – Not a joy
> over this or that, but the soul's mighty song 'with tongue and mouth,
> from the bottom of the heart': 'I rejoice through my joy, in, at, over, by
> and with my joy' – a heavenly refrain, as it were, suddenly breaks off our
> other song; a joy which cools and refreshes us like a breath of wind, a
> wave of air, from the trade wind which blows from the plains of Mamre
> to the everlasting habitations.

During the following two years Kierkegaard seemed to be heading for
normality, 'the universal' as he called it. He returned to the Church from
which he had been estranged for a while, worked at his studies, and
passed his final examinations for the ministry. He became engaged to
marry Regine and dreamt of taking Orders and settling down with her to
the life of a country pastor. Trying out the idea, so to speak, he revisited
Saeding, staying at his aunt's poor cottage. He went to the parish church
and was moved by the appropriateness of the appointed Gospel: 'From
whence can a man satisfy these men with bread here in the wilderness?'

In the end he could not go through with it. His sense that he was
irrevocably an 'exception', called to be a lonely individual, prevailed
over his hopes of joining the majority. He was, 'an eternity too old' for
Regine, and their natures were too disparate. She was all 'immediacy',
he all 'reflection'. He broke off the engagement, behaving badly in the
process, and fled precipitately to Berlin to escape the subsequent scandal.

In Berlin he attended Schelling's lectures, in an audience that included Engels and Bakunin. Schelling had just been appointed to counteract the influence of Hegel's teaching, but, like the other two, Kierkegaard was unimpressed by his performance. More importantly, by his action he had committed himself to his vocation.

In the next six years Kierkegaard produced the very large body of books which together comprise his 'pseudonymous authorship'. He wrote furiously, standing at his high desk, and during the night surrounded by candles. At first the emotional driving-force behind the production was in large part the need to explain himself to Regine. She was the 'individual' to whom they were addressed and who would be able to penetrate the layers of pseudonymity and divine their true meaning. Thus *Fear and Trembling* (1845) is by 'John of Silence', and discusses Abraham's readiness to sacrifice Isaac. A higher religious imperative may oblige one to act inhumanly, and the pseudonym is that of one who may not openly disclose why he himself has had to act in a similar way. One who could understand would see in the book a reflection of what his father had done to Kierkegaard, and what he in his turn had done to Regine. At the same time the book teaches a general law of the spiritual life, that it is through maintaining and enduring the tragic contradictions of life, and not by resolving them, that the human spirit is tuned to its highest pitch. Another book of the same year, *Repetition* by 'Constantine Constantius', teaches a similar message. It tells of a young man who by falling in love became a poet, but then had to renounce his love to remain a poet. How can you explain such a thing to a girl? – yet the pseudonym suggests a hidden fidelity at a higher level.

These two early books already suggest the main lines of Kierkegaard's divergence from Hegel. Hegel fully recognised that the spiritual life is defined by the various oppositions or polarities between which it is suspended: the ideal and the actual, the necessary and the possible, the temporal and the eternal, the subjective and the objective and so on. But as Hegel saw it the task of philosophy was to 'mediate' between these opposites by showing how each implies the other, and how both can be preserved and yet reconciled in a synthesis at a higher level. Thus Hegel's philosophy is intended to lead his reader towards a condition of perfect spiritual fulfilment in which all the contradictions are overcome, and claims to be a translation into philosophical language of the Christian doctrine of redemption.

Kierkegaard's thought is an attack on Hegel's idea of mediation. In his view Christianity is a message about and for the concrete existing human individual, whereas the effect of Hegel's teaching is to dissolve away concrete individuality by merging it into the Absolute. 'Speculative philosophy', he writes, 'deduces paganism logically from Christianity.' What is more, Hegelian mediation is exactly the wrong doctrine for the present age, when democracy, industrialism and the Press are all conspiring to persuade the individual to 'draw in his antennae and become part of the public'. These new forces are introducing an objective, statistical way of thinking that persuades a person to think of himself as if from the outside, as a mere component of such abstractions as 'the economy', 'the worker', 'the housewife', 'the voter', 'the ratepayer'. In his book *Morgenröte* (Daybreak, 1881) Nietzsche urges factory workers to abandon their jobs and their countries and become poor, wandering, exiled 'free spirits' like himself; and Kierkegaard's opinion was not very different. It is more important than anything else that one should become an individual, which means that one must resist 'mediation'. As he says, 'In defiance of the whole nineteenth century, I will not marry.' To become spirit one must cleave to paradox, and unlike Nietzsche Kierkegaard regards Christianity as showing the only path to true selfhood because it is above all a tragic and paradoxical faith. 'It is terrible to be born outside the universal, to walk without meeting a single traveller', but that is what the disciple of Christ must do:

> The spiritual man differs from us men in being able to endure isolation, his rank as a spiritual man is proportionate to his strength for enduring isolation, whereas we men are constantly in need of 'the others', the crowd; we die, or despair, if we are not reassured by being in the crowd, or of the same opinion as the crowd, etc. But the Christianity of the New Testament is precisely reckoned upon and related to this isolation of the spiritual man. Christianity in the New Testament consists in loving God, in hatred to man . . . the strongest expression for the most agonising isolation.

Kierkegaard's insistent dualism is reminiscent of Luther, the Luther who said that the believer is 'at once righteous and a sinner', and that one should 'sin hard and believe harder still'. Faith steadfastly holds opposites together in tension, which is why in Lutheranism the hero of faith replaces the more traditional ideal of the saint.

Still more reminiscent of Luther, and also more innovative, was Kierkegaard's attitude to the truth of Christian doctrine. Luther had made a distinction between historical faith and divine faith. The mere historical statement that 'Christ died' is devoid of religious significance. It only acquires religious value by the addition of the suffix 'for my sake'. Thus religious truth consists not in the objective fact but in the subjective appropriation of it when I act upon it. Kierkegaard takes this theme still further, for his general position precludes objectivity in faith. Hence his unwearying polemic against the established Church, in which the bourgeois Christian recites the Creed as objectified dogma and then waddles comfortably home to his dinner – and nothing in him has changed at all, except that his conviction that he is a fine fellow has become a little stronger than ever. But on the contrary, says Kierkegaard, the ideal and and the actual must remain in opposition and Christianity must not be allowed to decay into objective truth, for its truth consists solely in its continual subjective appropriation and enactment in the believer's practice; and even that truth can never be possessed but only lived-towards.

Kierkegaard demythologised Christianity into spirituality, and did so quite naturally, without any special effort, because living as he did after the Enlightenment, after Kant's demolition of dogmatic metaphysics, and in the shadow of idealist philosophy, all the problems with which he was concerned presented themselves to him as problems in spirituality. It came quite naturally to him to think that everything is decided within the sphere of human subjectivity. All the different ways of life that he discusses, aesthetic, ethical, religious and Christian, appear simply as various possible forms of consciousness, shapes that the human spiritual life may assume and worlds that it may construct around itself. None was assessed in terms of its correspondence with objective facts and structures out there; all were assessed from within, and in terms of their inner logic and movement.

Kierkegaard's attitude to his dead father is a good example of the non-realism of his thought. In all that he wrote, directly or indirectly, about his dead father, there is no suggestion that he thinks of Michael Kierkegaard as somehow 'literally' continuing to live in another world. On the contrary, MK is simply fixed in the finality and changelessness of death, and it is in that aspect that he bulks so large in SK's consciousness. SK's own spiritual life is of course ordered by the hope of an eternal blessedness, but that hope is simply a vital reference-point in the guidance of SK's *present* spiritual life. The plain man's notion that there is 'literally' a life after death, presently for MK and in the prospect for SK, never arises and cannot arise from SK's point of view.

The same considerations apply to Kierkegaard's doctrine of God. Some commentators complain that he believed in two or more gods, because God appears in various aspects in his writings. Sometimes God appears as an impersonal Greek absolute, 'the Eternal'. Sometimes God is an inexorable Father, bound by his own immutability and yet anguished by it, as when Kierkegaard imagines how terrible it must have been for God to hear Christ's cry of dereliction on the Cross and yet to be able to do nothing about it. Again, God is sometimes a loving Father, constantly attentive to his children's needs. Why does Kierkegaard operate with these different images of God? Because they are all part of the tradition, and they all have a part to play in the formation of a Christian. We do not have any objective knowledge of God, and Kierkegaard was emphatic that God's existence cannot be proved; so that to suppose that our various images of God can be checked for their accuracy against an independently-known Original in order to harmonise them and remove their mutual inconsistencies is to fall into the absurd and impious fancies of objectifying dogmatic theology. For us, God is the various roles God plays in the formation of a Christian, and no more can or should be said.

In opposition to Hegel's immanentism, Kierkegaard insists vehemently upon God's transcendence, but it is sheer laziness to suppose that he is here restoring the very objectivity that elsewhere he invariably attacks. God's transcendence is to be understood in terms of Kierkegaard's view of the spiritual life: it functions to prevent any merely speculative reconciliation of the opposites, such as Hegel aimed at. God's transcendence cannot be so assimilated within the system that the spirit may allow itself to slumber in peace, but must be maintained to keep the spirit tense and tuned-up. Kierkegaard will not allow us to rest in the indolence of the bourgeois Christian with his objective God, nor in Hegel's speculative overcoming of God's transcendence. He does not permit either way of assimilating God. Instead, the paradoxes of the spiritual life are maintained unresolved with the aim of forcing the spirit to decision, to action. This return to the concrete Kierkegaard calls 'repetition'. It obliges us to become real individuals who act in faith, in time, in 'the Moment'.

Kierkegaard sees the tragic contradictions of life focused most sharply in Christ. As Pascal had already said, when God comes closest to us his mysteriousness, his incognito, his infinite distance from us become more apparent than ever. The believer's religious suffering reaches its climax in his participation in the passion of Christ. Through this experience he becomes at last an authentic self, in the world but not of it, fully responsible for his own future, obliged to act and to do the works of love in imitation of Christ. Having now become a Christian, he returns to the world so fully that Kierkegaard was eventually able to look back and say to himself, 'If I had had faith, I would have married Regine.' But he always found this final movement difficult to make and to hold: because his task was to show his generation what is involved in becoming a Christian, he stops at the gate more often than he passes through it.

Yet, again, the entire discussion takes place within the sphere of spirituality – because for Kierkegaard, with his idealist background, that is all there *is*. For Hegel, the world is the embodiment or self-expression of Spirit; for Kierkegaard the various worlds men may construct and inhabit are products of their own inner lives. What we see is a reflection of what we have chosen to be. Because all human beings, and especially Anglo-Saxon ones, are born into this world little realists who think that the ideas in their heads mirror pre-existing objective structures out there in the world, the ordinary person is an incorrigible theological realist. As I have reason to know, if Kierkegaard's position is explained to him too clearly he is sure to react with a charge of 'atheism'. But Kierkegaard launches a vehement attack on that kind of naive objectification, and does so upon religious grounds; and certainly from his own point of view he is no kind of reductionist, nor did anyone charge him with being a reductionist. On the contrary, he is more often charged with putting up too high the price of becoming a Christian.

Kierkegaard remains the most important modern Christian writer, because he fully accepted the radical anthropocentrism which first appeared in European culture with Kant and his idealist successors and yet showed that it was possible, within these seemingly narrow limits, to express an uncompromisingly Christian faith. He does not represent, as Sartre suggested, a reversion to an earlier stage of consciousness; rather, he illustrates Christianity's power of entirely transforming itself and yet remaining the same.

How do Kierkegaard's views stand today? The charge that he is excessively individualistic is usually based on lack of knowledge of his later writings, and in any case Christianity has always had within it a tradition of individual perfectionism as well as the social and ecclesiastical strain. On the other hand he does not provide much support for his claim that authentic selfhood can be realised only through Christ and not through, perhaps, some other religious tradition, or indeed through a secularised version of his own existentialist teaching. He did not anticipate the severe criticisms that would after Darwin be levelled against his very Western, very dualistic type of religious psychology. From reading D.F. Strauss's *Life of Jesus* he did, however, get a hint that biblical criticism might fail to support his very extreme idea of the Incarnation, and this may partly account for the switch towards Christian ethics and the imitation of Jesus in his last years.

Not that he had many years, for he died burnt out at forty-two, after having refused the ministrations of the Church on his death-bed. He had once expressed the hope that the words 'that individual' might be inscribed on his tombstone, but there was some disorder at the funeral and his brother, Bishop Peter Kierkegaard, afterwards delayed erecting any monument over the grave. Perhaps it was a fitting gesture for so deeply disturbed and disturbing a figure. Almost the last words in his journal are these:

> A human being must live in such a state of anguish that if he were a pagan he would not hesitate to commit suicide. In that state, then, he must – live! Only in that state can he love God.

Kierkegaard himself lived in that state, but perhaps he was reluctant to recognise just how few are capable of it. Hermine Wittgenstein once reproached her brother about his wayward life. He looked at her and said that she was like a person indoors who sees through the window a man staggering outside, and thinks his behaviour odd because she does not realise that he is out in a storm and has difficulty keeping his feet. This, she says, silenced her.

Yet to end on such a note could be to suggest that Kierkegaard was a side-show freak: we wonder at him, and then return to our humdrum lives. Not so. Kierkegaard, more than any other writer of recent centuries, has the power to make us believe that we might actually succeed in becoming something of worth. Put it this way: suppose we see really clearly the utter futility of everyday life as it is lived. Ordinary folk may suppose that it is possible to give the value to life by begetting children, or by creating some imperishable work that will become a permanent constituent of the human scene, or by performing some great deed. But where's the point of leaving children to live lives as futile as our own, or of leaving a work or a deed as a constituent of a scene that is itself futile? Time will come, we are assured, when the last human being is dead and gone, and the universe will in the end consist of nothing but radiation. When we have fully grasped that time reduces everything to dust, including all the various monuments that people try to erect to prevent it from doing so; when we have grasped that nothing outside us can save us from our own futility; when we are reduced to Kierkegaard's 'state of anguish' – then, he says, we might grasp what it means to love God and to become an individual.

Chapter 6
RELIGION-SHOCK

The crucible

Where today can we find the world's greatest religious diversity within a single society? In California? I doubt it, because prolific though California is in new religious movements, many of them are very similar to each other. They share an interest in psychotherapy. They are of what used to be called the 'mind-cure' type that seeks to relieve guilt and anxiety and to promote personal integration and a heightened self-awareness, and as such they are rather alike. By contrast, we might discover a more profound diversity and a more genuinely cosmopolitan mixture of faiths if we looked today not at California, but at certain British cities – London, Birmingham, Wolverhampton, Leicester, Leeds, Bradford, Glasgow and a few others.

Birmingham, for instance, has among its million inhabitants over 30,000 Muslims, over 15,000 Sikhs, over 10,000 Hindus, about 6000 Jews, and a smaller number of Buddhists. In addition there are naturally all the main branches of Christianity and the usual marvellous variety of small sects of every description – Rastafarians and Christian Scientists, Theosophists and Mormons, Transcendental Meditators and Unitarians.

For practical purposes most religious activity in Birmingham that can claim any public significance occurs in one or another of seven groups – three kinds of Christianity and the four principal other religions. It is these seven groups that are commonly represented on the various multi-faith bodies that have grown up. The committees find that they need a Catholic, an Anglican, a Free Churchman, a Muslim, a Hindu, a Jew and a Sikh.

The mixture is extraordinary and yet in practice, and with patience, it works. One problem the newer faiths have faced is that of establishing places of worship. Among local people and in the Town Halls there is often uncertainty about just what is involved in the worship of a religion that is new to their area. Here Christians have been able to play an active part in helping to allay fears and to extract planning permissions, and in several cases they have even supplied a suitable building, for of Birmingham's eight Sikh gurdwaras or temples four are converted chapels – one Congregationalist, two Methodist and one Elim Pentecostal. Thus Christians have proved willing to help in very concrete ways to get the worship of a new and incoming religion established in the area. The bitter rivalry between different faiths that was normal in the past is gradually being replaced by a new spirit of mutual tolerance, respect and even collaboration. Historically speaking, it is a remarkable reversal of policy and our ancestors would doubtless have been horrified – but then, they never foresaw the day when Birmingham would have, as it now does, two Muslim mosques and twenty prayer-houses.

In some inner-city schools in Birmingham it is possible for Christians to be in a minority among the children. This lands added weight to the argument often put forward by the leaders of the new communities, that exclusively Christian religious teaching in the schools is unjust and propagandist. The solution that has been reached after years of discussion allows for each pupil to major in one faith (normally of his or her own choice) while taking minor courses in two other faiths, provided that Christianity as the historic religion of the country is taken by everyone as either a major or a minor. This allows everyone to put his own faith first, while making the point that British society and culture have been historically and in some respects still are profoundly Christian; and it also obliges everyone to face the fact that Britain is now a multi-faith society which cannot afford to encourage people to live in sealed-off private religious worlds.

Incidentally, it is also possible to minor, but not to major, in a non-religious philosophy of life such as Humanism or Communism.

A shift of this sort, from an exclusively Christian to a multi-faith syllabus, is taking place in many parts of Britain. It creates a demand for suitable teaching materials, and so an increase in the quantity of material published in the field of comparative religion; and since it requires suitably qualified teachers, it also brings about a corresponding syllabus-change in the university and college departments where future teachers study.

We must not exaggerate the extent of these changes so far. As yet only a small minority of people have any first-hand experience of the worship of a religion other than their own ancestral faith. Only a few even read the religious literature of any faith but their own. Nevertheless, there is no doubt that a gradual shift towards a more multi-faith outlook is taking place. It is happening even among the more strict and exclusive believers. Today some initiatives towards other faiths come even from Muslims, Orthodox Jews and conservative Evangelical Christians. The Second Vatican Council issued a notably respectful Declaration on the Relationship of the Church to non-Christian Religions (28 October 1965). It rejected as 'foreign to the mind of Christ' any discrimination against people because of their religion.

The implications of that Catholic statement are considerable. There was certainly no intention to withdraw any of the Catholic claims to final truth and authority in matters that concern human salvation; but nevertheless it is accepted that the State as such cannot take cognisance of such claims in the determination of public policy. It seems that (except in a few special cases) the State must regard all religions as being equal as all men are equal, and should not see any of them as being intellectually or morally superior to the others in a way that justly entitles it to special status and privileges. In effect, the Church is recognising that the growing pluralism and concern for human rights in all modern societies will eventually mean an end to the constitutional establishment of any one religion. Modern society says, *Equal rights for many truths*! Anti-discrimination and acceptance of pluralism go together.

All this is new. I do not mean that pluralism itself is novel, because there have been many pluralistic societies in the past. In their different ways India, the Roman Empire, and especially Iran were at certain times in the past highly pluralistic. Iran has known at least a dozen religions, including five indigenous ones (Aryan, Zoroastrian, Zurvanite, Mithraic, and in modern times the Bahai), plus the three Abrahamic faiths (Jewish, Christian and Muslim), plus the religions of India which have at times spread to Iran, plus other incoming faiths of Middle-Eastern origin such as Mandaism and Manicheeism. One could scarcely expect that record to be beaten anywhere. But in the past a religion was understood to be a total, society-defining way of life, and it was commonly thought impossible to mix religions socially. The usual custom was segregation: people of different faiths occupied different quarters of the city as they do in the Old City at Jerusalem to this day, and in the country they often lived in separate villages. Broadly speaking, Jews in Poland and Christians under Islam accepted segregation. Many religious doctrines and rituals stress the distinction between believers and infidels, and strongly encourage believers to stay in a closed world of like-minded people. It was a duty to be clannish.

In Isaac Bashevis Singer's well-known stories about Jewish life in

Poland in the old days before the Nazis this self-sufficiency and enclosed-ness of a religiously-defined society emerges very clearly. Singer's Polish Jewry is a rich and complex social world, a creation of genius, but very few of his hundreds of characters seem aware of the existence of Gentiles as individual human beings with souls of their own. Gentiles are shadowy background figures to whom, frankly, one pays little attention. They are not quite members of society. They are in fact ritually unclean. There is nothing especially Jewish about this: it is a common phenomenon. But a consequence of it is the paradox that although people have in a sense always known of the existence of religions other than their own, they have begun to pay close attention to those other faiths only within the last one hundred years, or even less. Christians rubbed up against Muslims for over a millennium without ever really learning to understand Muslim beliefs and customs. It is only in the last generation, for example, that the offensive old misnomer 'Mohammedanism' has at last been dropped.

There is an obvious link between a religion's claim to complete and exclusive truth and its tendency to segregate by sealing up its adherents in a closed world. The two features of religion work to confirm each other. Vivid religious faith often tends to shut one up in a sub-culture of like-minded people. Within that world the truth of the faith seems obvious and unquestionable, something so much taken for granted that it is rarely mentioned. A tacit consent of this kind creates a strong and distinctive atmosphere that works to exclude sceptical outsiders and their uncomfortable questions. And the more we are able to assume that our truth is *the* truth and our world *the* world, the less we shall be aware of any world outside our own world.

However, the modern world has decided against segregation. It is now thought to be a political and moral impossibility, whether it be voluntarily chosen or forcibly imposed. And not without reason: look where Polish Jewry ended. Today we wish people of different faiths not to be separated into different social worlds, but to be able to mingle easily as co-equal fellow-citizens in one and the same social world. We want both full equality and the freedom fully to affirm our religious and cultural differences. This rather paradoxical double demand is having the effect of forcing the religions upon each other's attention and obliging them to take notice of each other as never before.

There lies the novelty; not in pluralism as such, but in the way modern society compels us to realise that in matters of religion, philosophy of life, morality and customs there is not just one truth, but many truths. Ours is not the only way; there are many ways. Once again, if on moral grounds we are agreed in condemning all forms of racial, cultural and religious discrimination, then we have accepted the principle that at least where religion is concerned there are many truths, and not just one truth. And these many truths, we seem to suppose, no longer need each to create its own separate social world: they can fit together as diverse constituents of a single social world.

And if it is true that thought eventually bows out to social facts, then *that* means that the religions must in the end come to be seen as being all of them different aspects of a single totality.

Toleration

In the year 385 the Spanish layman Priscillian and a number of his followers were executed for heresy at Trier. They were the first people to be martyred for their beliefs by the Church, and the first of many, because for the next thirteen centuries Christianity was, frankly, totalitarian. A few years later Augustine, Bishop of Hippo, was not only urging the physical punishment of heretics but also working out the theory to justify it.

Given his premises, it was not difficult for Augustine to devise a justification for religious intolerance. There is one God, one perfect and absolute Mind. This God has given a revelation of saving truth to the Church, and being perfect and all-powerful he will surely see to it that the Church does not slip into error but remains indefectibly in possession of the fullness of truth. So there is one God, and one faith in the custody of one Church; and given that there is but one absolute Truth that is vital to everyone's salvation and is known to the authorities, totalitarian ideological government seems inevitable. Error is too dangerous to be tolerated. Other religions and Christian heresies are simply wickedness and lies and ought to be stamped out.

It is part of the argument that the revealed Truth is not merely diffused generally through the Church but is specially vested in the authorities, who know just what it is, have a duty to safeguard it, and must use their power to drive out error.

So it came to be argued that by baptism one puts oneself irrevocably under the Church's jurisdiction for life. Since the Catholic faith is the one true religion and the basis of Christian society, anyone who departs from this true faith threatens the foundations of society and deserves the punishment of a rebel and a traitor, so that for over a millennium death was the ultimate penalty for obdurate heresy. Non-Christians like the Jews, being outside the rules, were in some respects better off than Christian heretics, but even they needed to keep their heads down. There did not seem to be any good arguments, or indeed any other defences, against religious persecution in a society where it was so much the norm.

The Protestant reformers were no different. Luther, Beza, Calvin and Zwingli approved the cruel persecution of Protestants more radical than themselves, and death continued to be thought the fitting penalty. The Reformation was not at all about private judgment or religious freedom. At the Peace of Augsburg in 1555 the principle was formulated *cuius regio eius religio* (the religion of whoever rules), meaning that it must be accepted that the German and some neighbouring lands were henceforth effectively partitioned along religious lines, some states being Lutheran and others Catholic. But this agreement was an attempt – unsuccessful as it turned out – to secure peaceful coexistence between two total systems. It was not toleration.

In the seventeenth century there did at last begin some practical experiments in genuine religious toleration, especially in America. Roger Williams of Pembroke College, Cambridge, sailed to America and founded in 1636 a settlement at Providence which was intended to be truly tolerant. When it got its charter, it incorporated the principle of freedom of religion in its constitution. It came to be called Rhode Island. Also in the 1630s, Maryland was a refuge for both Catholics and Protestants.

In Europe, England was first. Voltaire paid his characteristic tribute:

> If there were only one religion in England, there would be danger of tyranny; if there were two, they would cut each others throats; but there are thirty, and they live happily together in peace.

This religious liberty was not very extensive. It derived from the Toleration Act of 1689, which granted conditional freedom of worship to Protestant dissenters. It did not remove their civil disabilities, which remained until the nineteenth century, but at least it was a beginning. On their accession William and Mary had been confronted by two great facts: one was the need to unite the nation against the deposed Roman Catholic monarch James II, and the other was the fact that after all the wars, controversies and religious upheavals that the country had suffered since the days of Henry VIII no one party had clearly prevailed. There were still episcopalians who believed in a traditional sort of Church governed by bishops, and there were still various sorts of Presbyterian and other dissenters. There was no choice but to try to build a coalition of orthodox Protestants, some of them Church and some Chapel. But toleration went no further than it had to. It was not proposed to extend religious liberty to atheists, to Catholics or to overt anti-trinitarians, and in his writings John Locke, the chief apologist for the new regime, did not defend freedom for Catholics and atheists but only for the various kinds of Protestant.

The toleration that William and Mary introduced and that Voltaire admired was therefore strictly limited, but it was nonetheless a portent for the future. The Age of Reason was beginning, and England's modest concession was a precedent that could be quoted when arguing for freedom of thought and expression in other countries.

To Voltaire, different 'religions' meant mostly different versions of Christianity. But the argument could easily be extended. G.E. Lessing, one of the great figures of the German Enlightenment, developed it further in his play *Nathan the Wise* (1779).

In the play the character of Nathan, the tolerant and liberal-minded Jew, is modelled on Lessing's friend Moses Mendelssohn, the founder of the Reform movement in Judaism. Another character, Saladin, is a Muslim, and Christianity is represented by a Knight Templar. At the play's climax Saladin asks Nathan which of their three religions is the true one. Nathan in reply tells his story of the three rings, as follows:

Once there was an old man who had a marvellous ring which could make its wearer beloved by God and by men. He left it to his son and so it passed down in the family for several generations. Eventually it came to a man who had three sons. Not wishing to show favouritism, he had two replicas made and gave each son a ring; but then he died without telling them which of the three rings was the genuine one. The sons began to quarrel sharply, each claiming to possess the true ring. A judge was called in to arbitrate, and he ruled that there was no way of telling which ring was genuine, or indeed whether any of the rings was genuine. For all that anyone could tell, the original had been lost, and the father had caused *three* replicas to be made. All that any of the brothers could do was to try to show by his conduct that his own ring was the true one. In effect, the only criterion of religious truth is morality.

The parable of the rings does not altogether rule out the possibility that one of the three religions may indeed be absolute and revealed truth. In the next century John Stuart Mill, in the most famous essay on liberty in the English language, took the question a stage further. One of his chief arguments for toleration was that we can never be so sure we are right as to be fully justified or even prudent in repressing other opinions. For, says Mill, all human grasp of truth is provisional and imperfect. We are always influenced by the age we live in, the company we keep, the ways of thinking available to us and so on. Nobody is infallible. We can all learn something from other people, other ages, other cultures.

Mill thus frankly welcomes pluralism. He is in favour of toleration not because we cannot tell which religion is finally and irreformably true, but because we can be sure that no religion is so. In an uncertain world the best hope of arriving at the truth is by unfettered debate. If all human thinking and language are historically conditioned and in continual change, then all human understanding is imperfect and conditional, and there cannot be any absolute and incorrigible formulation of the truth. Everything dates, everything will eventually need to be reconsidered. It follows that there cannot be a religion that consists in a tightly interconnected system of immutable revealed truths, defined in doctrinal statements whose meanings are not eroded or altered in any way by the passage of time. That view of religion is simply a mistake. Once you have understood the nature of history you will have to acknowledge that a religion cannot be an immutable ideology, for history shows that a faith such as Catholicism is a continuous living stream of community life and devotion, thought and debate, which has been evolving and changing from its very beginning and has always embraced a variety of standpoints. What is more, history also shows that the religions have in the past overlapped with each other, borrowed from each other, and are in general much more many-sided and eclectic than is usually realised.

Thus the modern argument for religious toleration is based on the recognition that religion is human, historical, multifarious and ever-changing. Religious totalitarianism and religious exclusivism rest on misconceptions. There cannot be the kind of absolute and uncontaminated revealed truth that people used to believe in. The arguments that were used to justify the totalitarianism, the exclusivity and the intolerance have nowadays ceased to matter. Doctrine used to say things like 'Nobody can be saved except by the means provided in my tradition', but today we find we are easily able to recognise genuine sanctity in someone who is not of our tradition at all. If such a person is obviously a saint then it seems absurd to call him an infidel merely because he does not subscribe to our doctrines. Again, today we are used to the idea that we can recognise good religious writing and good religious art quite outside our own tradition. We are evidently learning to make a distinction between good and bad religion that is independent of the traditional criteria of orthodoxy and heresy.

It thus seems that the gradual movement towards greater religious toleration in the past few centuries is now being accompanied by a considerable change in the way people perceive religion. People are coming to see religion as deeply embedded in human nature, in culture and in history. It expresses a community's sense of its corporate origins, values and destiny. Through myth and ritual, doctrine and ethics, it provides the individual with an itinerary for his path through life. In the past most individuals had only one option, but as faiths and cultures intermingle in modern societies people are beginning to examine other traditions, to weigh what they see there, and to borrow freely. Religion is becoming less of a socially compulsory, sacred and monolithic deposit and more voluntary, something that many people now prefer to put together for themselves from the resources available to them.

The meeting

Asian ideas have reached the Mediterranean world intermittently since early times. They are thought, for example, to have influenced the Pythagoreans and, through them, Plato. Alexander's conquests in Asia led to some interaction between Graeco-Roman and Buddhist culture, and the Buddhist scriptures include a celebrated dialogue between a group of monks and the Greek King Menander, or Milinda. One of the Christian Fathers, Clement of Alexandria, mentions the Buddha in about AD 200.

The first European Christian writer to argue that Christians could actually learn something from another faith came very much later. In 1583 the energetic Jesuit Matteo Ricci entered China. Unlike Marco Polo and other earlier travellers, he did not simply see marvels and monsters, but learnt Chinese and studied Confucian texts. He decided that the Chinese had sufficient of a 'natural religion' – a set of basic ideas about God, ethics and the immortality of the soul – for it to be possible to build an indigenous Chinese Christianity upon it.

Over the years the Jesuit mission slowly began to prosper, moving to the capital and even acquiring some influence in court circles. The Jesuit astronomers were particularly respected by the Chinese. By the 1690s there were hopes of converting the Emperor K'ang-Hsi and so eventually perhaps the whole country.

Meanwhile, back in Europe the Jesuits' progress was followed with interest. Chinese goods were arriving and becoming fashionable, and Confucius could now be read in translation. Unfortunately the Jesuits, as always, had their critics, and questions began to be raised about the theological basis of their mission. Finally, in 1704, the Pope condemned Confucianism as atheistic, forbidding Chinese Christians to use the Confucian rites and names for God. The Chinese were naturally affronted, and the Emperor in due course retaliated by prohibiting Christianity. A chance to evangelise China was lost.

In Europe, where there was great admiration for Chinese ethics and the Chinese social system, the papal decision caused much controversy. The philosopher G.W. Leibniz (1646–1716), who was himself a Catholic, argued at length that the Church's condemnation of Confucianism had been based on a misreading of the texts. He went so far as to urge a policy not only of cultural but of religious exchange. China would teach Europe her natural religion, ethics and political organisation, and Europe would in return give to China the Gospel and modern science. Leibniz even talked to Peter the Great about the possibility that Russia might act as the intermediary between China and the West.

Leibniz was thus the first European of standing to recognise that we live in a multi-faith world whose different traditions can and should enrich each other. It was an idea with a future: the Chinese experiment may have failed, but a more lastingly effective two-way link between the East and West was to be forged through the British rule in India.

There is one rather puzzling early example of knowledge of Indian religion. John Toland (1670–1722), an eccentric freelance Anglo-Irish writer and pamphleteer, was a man known to Leibniz. A theological radical, he was the inventor of the word 'pantheism', and in quoting precedents for this idea he mentions 'the Brahminical theology'. Where Toland had learnt this, I do not know. It is usually said that the first translations of Indian sacred texts into European languages came much later: Charles Wilkes's version of the *Gita* (1785), Sir William Jones's *Shakuntala* (1789) and *The Laws of Manu* (1794), and above all the French adventurer Anquetil de Perron's translation of some fifty of the *Upaniṣads* (1802). Perron's version was from Persian to Latin, so that a European reader was receiving the Upaniṣads at third hand; but they still made an impact.

Of those influenced by Indian religious thought the most remarkable is Arthur Schopenhauer (1788–1861). Although he always retained a deep respect for Jesus, Schopenhauer broke with both Christianity in general and belief in God in particular more openly than any of his predecessors in the line of German philosophers. It now appears that an important turning-point in his development was a short period he spent as a schoolboy in, of all places, Wimbledon in south-west London.

Schopenhauer was the son of Heinrich Floris Schopenhauer, a rich merchant of Danzig (Gdansk), an old free city then, as now, distinguished by a passionate love of liberty. When the Prussians annexed the city the family left it, and the young Schopenhauer was educated mainly by travel. It was in order to perfect his English that his parents placed him for some months at the Nelson House School, then established in what is now Eagle House in Wimbledon High Street. The headmaster was the Reverend James Lancaster, an old-fashioned Georgian High Churchman and Tory. Lancaster was also Vicar of Merton, a parish which had an old connexion with the Nelson family, and in that same year of 1803 the children recited to Nelson and Lady Hamilton when they visited the school.

Schopenhauer was not happy at Wimbledon. At fifteen he was older than the others and out of place; but he particularly disliked being compelled to experience, three times a Sunday, the worldly religion of Jane Austen's England. He could admire the asceticism of figures like Jesus and the Buddha who had seen all of human life in this world as pervaded by folly and suffering, but this was something quite different. His letters to his parents are full of complaints about the cant and hypocrisy of English religion. His later verdict was this:

> [Protestantism has given up the inmost kernel of Christianity by eliminating asceticism]. In the end this results in a doctrine of a loving father who made the world in order that things might go very pleasantly in it (and in this, of course, he was bound to fail), and who, if only we conform to his will in certain respects, will afterwards provide an even pleasanter world (in which case it is only to be regretted that it has so fatal an entrance).
>
> This may be a good religion for comfortable, married and civilised Protestant parsons, but it is not Christianity.

Two years after Wimbledon, Schopenhauer's father died and his mother settled in Weimar, where she enjoyed success as a society hostess and a popular novelist. There he met Goethe, who gave him some encouragement, and there he was presented by a visiting orientalist with a copy of Perron's *Upaniṣads*. He loved it:

> This book provides the most rewarding and the most elevating reading . . . the world has to offer. It has been the consolation of my life and will be my consolation when I come to die.

Most historians of philosophy argue that Schopenhauer's thought would have developed as it did even without the Indian influence. His own testimony, though, is very strong. For example:

> We . . . send the Brahmans English clergymen and evangelical linen weavers to . . . show them that they are created out of nothing, and ought thankfully to rejoice in the fact. But it is just the same as if we fired a bullet against a cliff. In India our religions will never take root. The ancient wisdom of the human race will not be displaced by what happened in Galilee. On the contrary, Indian philosophy streams back to Europe, and will produce a fundamental change in our knowledge and thought.

Schopenhauer made one attempt at a career. He obtained a lectureship at Berlin, and then with typical arrogance announced his lectures for the same hour as those of Hegel, whom he despised. He failed to gain an audience and resigned in disgust, with a grievance against academic philosophers which he was to nurse for the rest of his life. His relationship with his mother was equally unhappy, for he quarrelled hopelessly with her and left to live alone. Though he did not wholly abstain from the company of women he became a notorious misogynist, the bachelor recluse of Frankfurt with his rigid two-hour daily walk by the river and the statues of Kant and the Buddha upon his desk.

All are agreed that Schopenhauer was cantankerous and ungracious to a degree rare even among vain and neglected men of letters. It is otherwise with his prose, which is like the lament of gulls heard above the roar of breakers: as its long sombre periods unroll we hear his cry of grief at the human condition. His thought was formed early in life, and although he later doubled the size of his masterpiece, *The World as Will and as Representation* (1818), he did not change its message.

In his view of our knowledge of the world about us, the phenomenal world, Schopenhauer was close to Kant's idealism. 'The world is my representation', that is, a product of the ordering activity of our own minds:

> The assumption that things exist as such, even outside and independently of consciousness, is absurd. . . . Between us and things there always stands the intellect, whose forms of knowledge, namely space, time and causality, mould our image of the world.

Science does no more than connect up appearances. It cannot penetrate to the real truth about the world — which, unlike Kant, Schopenhauer nevertheless believed could be known. The route to knowledge of the world's inner nature runs through the self. As an object of factual and scientific knowledge, the self is naturally as much part of the world of representation as anything else; but the introspective philosophical psychologist can penetrate deeper:

> All philosophers before me placed the true and inner nature of man in the knowing consciousness. But it is the *will* that is the primary and fundamental thing, which throughout asserts its pre-eminence over the intellect.

By the 'will' in man Schopenhauer means, not a rational will, but a blind, timeless and indomitable striving, the will-to-live. Its most characteristic expression is the sex-drive, in which it reveals its will to extend itself beyond our individual lives by snatching our behaviour out of our rational control – much as even a suicide struggles as he dies. The will is not in time, because time is merely a form of the human understanding; it extends beyond the human individual, who is merely its transient expression and prisoner; and it is manifested in all biological life. These considerations persuade Schopenhauer that the will is not merely our own inner nature, but that of all reality.

> The *will-to-live* is the only true description of the world's innermost nature. Everything presses and pushes towards existence, if possible towards organic existence, and then to the highest possible degree thereof.

The nature of the will is such as to ensure that our desires can never be fully satisfied, and happiness is in principle unattainable in this life.

> There is only one inborn error, and that is the notion that we exist in order to be happy. . . .
> Life is deeply steeped in suffering and cannot escape from it. Our entrance into it takes place amid tears, at bottom its course is always tragic, and its end is even more so. . . .
> Dying is certainly the real aim of life. It sums up all that life teaches, namely that fate's purpose is the destruction of our happiness, the mortification of our will, the elimination of the delusions that chain us to the world.

So far Schopenhauer's message appears to be one of simple pessimism; but it is not unrelieved. We can escape from our melancholy and self-absorbed musings into a measure of disinterestedness through an ethic of compassion for the sufferings of others, and by the contemplation of works of art. And Schopenhauer has a doctrine of salvation, for he holds that it is possible to deny the will to live, freeing ourselves from it by turning it back upon itself:

> He who has attained to the denial of the will to live, however poor, joyless, and full of privation his condition may appear externally, is yet filled with inward joy and the true peace of heaven. . . .
> How blessed the life of a man must be whose will is silenced, not merely for a moment, as in the enjoyment of the beautiful, but for ever. . . .
> Such a man, who, after many bitter struggles with his own nature, has finally conquered entirely, continues to exist only as a pure knowing being, the undimmed mirror of the world. Nothing can trouble him more, nothing can move him, for he has cut all the thousand cords of will which bind us to this world, and, as desire, fear, envy, anger, drag us hither and thither in constant pain. . . .
> And what I have here described with feeble tongue and only in general terms is no philosophical fable invented by myself; no, it was the enviable life of so many saints and beautiful souls among Christians, and still more among Hindus and Buddhists, and also among the believers of other religions. However different were the dogmas impressed upon their reason, the same inward, direct intuitive knowledge, from which alone all virtue and holiness proceeds, expressed itself in precisely the same way in the conduct of life.

Here Schopenhauer adumbrates an idea that was greatly to influence Tolstoy and Wittgenstein: the essence of religion is not doctrine but holiness itself, something wonderful and very rare, possible only on the basis of a kind of knowledge that cannot be put into words. However much its intellectual superstructure may have become discredited, there remains at the heart of religion something supremely important but ineffable. It is 'the mystical'.

The mystical really is ineffable, and Schopenhauer leaves us with nothing but riddles. Consciousness, he says, can no more exist without the brain than digestion without the stomach. The extinction of the will, it seems, must be our complete extinction. And yet —

> No will: no representation: no world. We freely acknowledge that what remains after the complete abolition of the will is, for all who are still full of the will, assuredly nothing. But also, conversely, to the saints in whom the will has turned and denied itself, this very real world of ours is — nothing.

Well, yes, the saints are nothing to the world, and the world is nothing to the saints; but is there anything else that *is* something to the saints? We put the question to the empty air, because Schopenhauer does not even raise it, much less attempt to answer it. His book is intended to leave us with the realisation that we should not have asked that foolish last question.

As for the external apparatus of religion, 'truth is like water; a vessel is needed to carry it'. Men will always wish to see a flag flying overhead, and it does not much matter what particular emblems are painted upon it:

> The ephemeral generations of men are born and pass away in quick succession; individual men, burdened with fear, want and sorrow, dance into the arms of death. As they do so they never weary of asking what it is that ails them and what the whole tragi-comedy is supposed to mean. They call on Heaven for an answer, but Heaven stays silent. Instead of a voice from Heaven there come along priests with revelations. But he is still in his childhood who can think that superhuman beings have ever given our race information about the aim of its existence or that of the world. There are no other revelations than the thoughts of the wise, even if these . . . are often clothed in strange allegories and myths, and are then called religions. . . .
>
> The weak point of all religions remains that they can never dare to confess to being allegorical, so that they have to present their doctrines in all seriousness as true [in the strict sense]; which, because of the absurdities essential to allegory, leads to perpetual deception and a great disadvantage for religion.

Schopenhauer follows the Indian faiths – and Plato – in his readiness to distinguish between the religion of the populace and the higher teachings that are for the élite alone. His general message is evidently close to that of the Buddha: all life is pervaded by suffering, the cause of suffering is desire or craving, and the way to blessedness is by the extinction of craving. For both him and the Buddha, the ultimate goal of the religious life cannot be satisfactorily described in language. Yet there is a difference between them which reflects rather badly on Schopenhauer's religious seriousness. The Buddha gives us some idea of where he is going by prescribing the Path in detail. He commits himself to, and he requires of us, the practice of various ethical and spiritual disciplines which at least point us in the right direction. Schopenhauer, by contrast, signally fails to do anything of the kind, leaving us with nothing but a tantalising question-mark, as if he scarcely expected his own teaching to be seriously *practised* by himself or anyone else. It was for this reason, I believe, that Wittgenstein – having at one time been greatly influenced by him – ended by thinking that he compares unfavourably with Kierkegaard.

Schopenhauer's reputation grew very slowly, but after twenty years a second edition of *The World as Will and as Representation* was called for, and after a further ten years, a third. He ended his life with the satisfaction of knowing that his name would live, and by the end of the century almost every young artist and writer in Europe of really high talent was a follower either of him or of Nietzsche. But because he lacks weight as a religious teacher, and in any case interprets it too pessimistically, he did not in the end greatly advance the cause of Indian religion. The true reason for his great popularity, especially between 1850 and 1900, was rather that he provided a philosophy of life for unbelievers in an age when, for the first time, most of the educated had lost their faith. There must remain a suspicion that he and his followers were more keen to use Indian religion as a stick to beat Christianity than they were actually to practise it for themselves.

There were, however, some exceptions to this generalisation; people who embraced Indian faiths with ardour and found them liberating. One such was Annie Besant (née Wood, 1847–1933), whose story is both touching and instructive – although I must hasten to add that she was no thinker.

The missionaries

By the end of the nineteenth century Europe had many distinguished orientalists who had done much to publish the scriptures and trace the history of Asian religions, though knowledge of what those faiths were now like on the ground remained rather hazy. There are several stories of dedicated orientalists who on first actually visiting Asia were shocked by what they found.

Annie Wood was one of those Victorians for whom India was the goal of a personal spiritual quest. She was born in 1847. Her father died young, and the family were left poor. It was taken for granted that their whole effort should be spent on the son's education, so the mother opened a small boarding-house in Harrow for pupils at the school in order to finance her own boy's education there. As for Annie, her education was to consist of eight years of French and evangelical piety, together with a little German and Latin, at the home of Miss Marryat, the sister of the well-known novelist.

Because, like many women in her day, Annie Wood was grossly under-educated in relation to her talents, she became vulnerable to crankiness and belief in occult revelations. Nevertheless, she managed to live a pretty full life. At nineteen, full of romantic devotion to Christ and desire for service and sacrifice, she did what all the world told her was the obvious thing: she married a clergyman, the Reverend Frank Besant.

As she remarked afterwards, in those days it was thought right that girls should enter marriage knowing nothing at all about sex, about men or about the world. She was quite unprepared for what she found in her husband, and the marriage was a disaster.

At Sibsey Vicarage in Lincolnshire, in the early 1870s, she went through the loss of faith. Even before her marriage she was already having difficulty in harmonising the Gospel narratives. Now her faith was additionally tested by her unhappy marriage, by the strain of her baby daughter's long and near-fatal illness, and by the sufferings of the farm labourers in the parish.

> The agony of the struggle was in the first nineteen months. No one who has not felt it knows the fearful anguish inflicted by doubt on the earnestly religious soul. It seems to shipwreck everything. Is all blind chance, is all the clash of unconscious forces, or are we the sentient toys of an Almighty Power that sports with our agony?

In that retrospective account from her autobiography she clearly sees herself as having been like a heroine from a novel by Thomas Hardy.

Her first doubts concerned the infallibility of the Bible, the problem of evil, the justice of Christ's vicarious punishment for our sins, and the idea of Hell. By reading liberal theology she successfully eased herself out of the harsh old evangelical beliefs; but the respite was only temporary. She next moved on to question more specifically Christian beliefs, such as the credal insistence that Christ was God's *only* Son:

> In the course of my reading I had become familiar with the idea of *Avataras* in Eastern creeds, and I saw that the Incarnate God was put forward as a fact by all ancient religions. Thus after the morally repulsive doctrines had been cleared away, the way was now paved for challenging the especially Christian teaching.

The only Christianity that was available to her was a strongly dogmatic and revealed faith. As it slipped away bit by bit, she found herself left with nothing. She consulted Dr Pusey at Oxford, but got no help from him. Her doubts were sinful; she should pray to be delivered from them. But she was not delivered, and gradually her faith in Christ, and then in God, faded away.

At the same time she began to discover that she had powers of expression. She earned a little money by writing, but her husband pocketed it because a married woman could not own money. Once, she locked herself into the empty church, climbed the pulpit to deliver an address – and realised that she could speak.

A few months later, the crisis came. One Sunday morning she refrained from communicating and instead walked out of the church. There was an ultimatum: she must conform, or leave home. So by the end of 1873, at the age of twenty-six, Annie Besant was legally separated from her husband and living in genteel poverty in Colby Road, Upper Norwood, South London, with her two babies.

Her energies were released. She began attending Free Thought Halls and reading the atheist journal, *The National Reformer*. She joined the National Secular Society, met the celebrated atheist campaigner Charles Bradlaugh, and became his co-worker. She edited a paper, poured out tracts, and was assailed, often physically, at public meetings all over the country. With Bradlaugh she stood trial before the Lord Chief Justice in 1877 in the great test case over the right to publish information about birth control. They won on appeal but the case cost her the custody of her children, for she was deprived of them on the ground that her views made her unfit to care for them. With Bradlaugh she fought the long legal proceedings over his admission to Parliament, and in the same years she also managed to work for a science degree at London University.

By 1877 she was moving away from Bradlaugh's rather narrow and sectarian atheism. She became an active socialist, and the friend of people like William Morris, Sidney Webb, Bernard Shaw, the Avelings, the Blands, and the radical clergyman Stewart Headlam. She was active in the bloody demonstration of 13 November in the same year, when socialist marchers were met in Trafalgar Square by police with truncheons and guardsmen with fixed bayonets. In her circle there were dreams at this time of founding a universal Church of Man, that would draw together socialists, radical Christians and freethinkers.

Yet still Annie Besant's spirit had not come to rest. She seems to have felt a need to come to terms with the memory of her mother and her upbringing. After dabbling with spiritualism she read Madame H.P. Blavatsky's *The Secret Doctrine*. In 1889 she met Madame Blavatsky and, to the consternation of her friends, became a passionate Theosophist.

Gandhi reports his first encounter with them both, a year later. In 1890 he was a law student in London, living in lodgings and eating frugally in vegetarian restaurants:

> Towards the end of my second year in England I met two Theosophists who talked to me about the *Gita* and invited me to read the original with them. I felt ashamed, as I had read the divine poem neither in Sanscrit nor in Gujerati. Indeed, my knowledge of Sanscrit was meagre . . . but I began reading the *Gita* with them. The book struck me as one of priceless worth.
>
> They took me to Blavatsky Lodge and introduced me to Madame Blavatsky and Mrs Besant. The latter had just joined the Theosophical Society, and I was following with great interest the controversy about her conversion. . . . I also read Madame Blavatsky's *Key to Theosophy*, which stimulated me to read books on Hinduism, and disabused me of the notion fostered by the missionaries that Hinduism was rife with superstition.

Gandhi's comments are illuminating. Even a person of his standing needed to be taught to respect his own religion and to read its scriptures – by Theosophists in London! If Theosophy today seems a marginal movement, it was not so then. In the West, it popularised belief in reincarnation and the idea of the wisdom of the East. It was progressive politically, founding schools and campaigning for emancipation on all fronts. Above all, people like Annie Besant awakened India by taking to it their own enthusiasm for it.

Mrs Besant moved to India in 1893 after attending the great Parliament of Religions in Chicago, the first event of its kind. At that time Chicago was the most dynamic city in the world, already building skyscrapers and eager to absorb all humanity in its vast embrace. For the World's Columbian Exposition in 1893 two hundred Congresses were planned, of which forty-one were devoted to religion. The Parliament of Religions was intended to link them, and Annie Besant addressed it on behalf of Theosophy. But the biggest sensation was created by another figure moving in the opposite direction, from India to the West. He was Vivekananda (1863–1902), the first Hindu missionary to the West.

The surviving photographs do not do justice to Vivekananda, for they make him look like a plump and playful drawing-room guru, and he was more than that. He was a considerable religious figure. As a pupil of Ramakrishna he taught, not popular Hinduism, but the Vedanta. He stayed in the West for several years, setting up the Ramakrishna Mission and the Vedanta Societies of America and Europe. Two of his doctrines became part of the consciousness of the West. He spread the idea that all religions are one, treading different paths to the same goal. The goal is that described in Vedantic teaching, the union and indeed the identity of the soul with God. Secondly, he rejected the Christian idea of sin, and taught that by living a virtuous life you can realise God in yourself.

His idea of what it is to live a virtuous life came from the *Gita*, where Krishna teaches that the way to free yourself from *karma*, the chain of cause and effect and the wheel of rebirth, is not to withdraw from the world like an ascetic but to learn to act disinterestedly *in* the world. You must do what is right for its own sake – and then move on, forgetting about consequences and about praise or blame. You can learn to act in such a way as continually to be freeing yourself from yourself. Liberated in this way from being tied down by your own life, you could learn a godlike freedom and could become the God within.

In this way Vivekananda modernised the ancient higher teachings of India and made of them a universal faith. It became possible for an ordinary person living an active life in the world to realise the goal of the ascetic and the mystic through public activity:

> When we have nobody to grope towards, no devil to blame, no personal God to carry our burdens, when we are alone responsible, then we shall rise to our highest and best. I am responsible for my fate, I am the bringer of good to myself, I am the bringer of evil. I am the pure and blessed One. . . . I am not bound by either virtue or vice, by happiness or misery. Pilgrimages and books and ceremonies can never bind me. I have neither hunger nor thirst; the body is not mine, nor am I subject to the super-stitions and decay that come to the body. I am existence, knowledge and bliss absolute.

Vivekananda was usually successful among modern religious reformers. He was rooted in the ancient tradition that sought to realise the identity of the soul with the Absolute, and yet he managed to fuse it with the spirit of modern radical humanism. His converts were not simply chaise-longue mystics. Miss Margaret Noble, the principal of the Ruskin School in Wimbledon, first heard him in Lady Isabel Margesson's drawing room in London on a Sunday evening in 1895. She became Sister Nivedita, a notable pioneer of women's education in India, and perhaps the ablest of early European converts to Hinduism.

Religion-shock

The encounter of the world faiths is still only just beginning, even today. There are many historical and sociological reasons for the delay. Chief among them, no doubt, is the understandable belief that one's own tradition, after long centuries of development and diversification, contains within itself resources varied enough to meet the needs of all types of individual. This argument for staying within one's own camp is, however, vulnerable to something that we might call 'religion-shock', on the analogy of culture-shock. Religion-shock occurs when someone who is a strong and sincere believer in his own faith confronts, without evasion and without being able to explain it away, the reality of an entirely different form of faith, and faces the consequent challenge to his own deepest assumptions.

One example of it is the modern Christian's belated discovery that Judaism is after all not an obsolete religion that died away when Christianity superseded it, but a continuing and living faith, deeply biblical and yet very different in temper from Christian biblicism.

Traditional Christianity had a strong built-in resistance to recognising the religious reality of Judaism. It was believed that the Jews no longer constituted a significant religious community. By rejecting the Messiah they had forfeited their old special relationship with God. The title of 'Israel' was now transferred to the Church, with which God had instituted a new covenant. To put it bluntly, even the Hebrew Bible no longer properly belonged to the Jews, for its promises no longer referred to them. It was not their book any more. It was now the Christian Old Testament, and its ancient promises were all fulfilled in Christ and his Church.

In addition, much of Christian doctrine was habitually expounded by setting up a contrast, highly unfavourable to the Jews, between the bad old way things used to be in Judaism and the way they are now in the Christian dispensation after God has put things right. At every point Judaism was used as the classic case of how to get it wrong in religion. So – on the Christian view – the very existence of Christianity as a distinct faith was founded on God's rejection of the Jewish people, and the definition of Christianity was accomplished by contrasting it with a caricature of Judaism.

Worse still, Jesus himself was made to endorse this strategy. He had been a Jewish teacher criticising certain of the Jewish leaders, just like the prophets before him, but he came to be seen as if he were a non-Jewish figure, God Incarnate pronouncing his divine judgment upon Judaism as a whole.

Whether all this is or is not properly to be described as 'antisemitism' does not matter very much. The point is that, quite apart from the charge of 'deicide' and similar absurdities, Christians have always had a deep doctrinal prejudice against Judaism as a religion. The Jews tended to be seen as a particularly obdurate group of unbelievers who needed to be evangelised by tough specialist missionary agencies. Christians never attended Jewish worship and knew nothing of Jewish literature.

It was above all else the horrific Nazi persecution of the Jews that obliged Christians to examine their own old prejudices and so opened the way to recognition of Judaism as a living, biblical faith. Things had already begun to change some years earlier. An English priest named James Parkes began in the 1930s his life's work of trying to improve Christian–Jewish relations. In Germany, by a sad irony, serious Christian–Jewish conversations began in the very year of Hitler's rise to power. But it was in 1942, as the Allies first learnt about the Final Solution, that the Council of Christians and Jews was formed. In 1948 at its First Assembly the World Council of Churches considered the Christian 'approach' to the Jews in the first of the long series of Church statements that have sought to redefine positions and to make amend for the past.

Today, few Christians would wish to convert their Jewish friends. Understanding of the Jewish religion is better than it was in the past, and many Christians would now agree with Parkes that the Jews evidently continue as a living community of faith, with their own place in God's purpose and a theological right to exist as a community distinct from the Church.

But if this is so, then what happens to the old exclusive doctrines asserting that baptism into the Church is universally necessary to salvation and that nobody can know God except through Jesus, that is, by believing in his messiahship, his divinity and his atoning death? It looks as if these doctrines were intended to safeguard the Christian experience of salvation, and it seems that they have functioned as a justification of the Church's authority and its claims; but their traditional status is called in question by the admission that for all these years Israel has truly known the very same God, without approaching him via Jesus. It is no use saying – as certain theologians do say – that the Jews have been 'virtual' or 'implicit' or 'anonymous' Christians, because the Jews still reject Jesus' messiahship, and will not thank Christians for granting to them honorary-Christian status. They are bound to decline all offers of that kind.

So Christians will have to say, 'We find salvation this way, and we think it is a way open to anyone, and in that sense we still say Jesus is the Saviour of the world. Yet we must admit that there seem to be other ways to salvation that also work.'

Another example: Christians sometimes talk as if they have a monopoly of the idea that God is loving and gracious, and as if salvation by faith alone were a distinctively Christian idea. And so far as Hinduism is concerned, many Westerners have heard of the Advaita Vedanta (the non-dualist interpretation of the Upaniṣads that had been taught by Śankara) and it has given them the impression that Hinduism as a whole is a form of pantheistic mysticism.

For these two reasons Christians expect Hinduism to be strange and alien to them. It is a shock to discover that most Hindu piety has long been of the *bhakti* kind which is theistic and devotional. *Bhakti* seems to have begun among the Tamils of southern India, and thence gradually to have spread over the whole sub-continent. It rejects the way to salvation by discovering an eternal element within the self, and teaches instead a new way: sinful man must surrender himself completely in loving devotion to God. The message is that the more you give yourself to God, the more God will give himself to you. The ninth-century poet Manikka Vasagar addresses God as follows:

> Thou gav'st thyself, thou gainedst me;
>   Which did the better bargain drive?
> Bliss found I in infinity;
>   But what didst thou from me derive?
> O Śiva, Perundurai's God,
>   My mind thou tookest for thy shrine:
> My very body's thine abode;
>   What can I give thee, Lord of mine?

Traditionally, Christians supposed this kind of piety to be distinctively Christian and possible only through Christ. But *Bhakti* can encompass not only the tender 'metaphysical' wit of the first couplet just quoted but also something else equally reminiscent of seventeenth-century Christian piety, namely ecstatic and erotic self-surrender. Yet the psychology can scarcely have been the same, for the Saivite saints wore the lingam (the penis, Śiva's symbol) around their necks, a practice not exactly common among Christians. It seems that Saivite love-mysticism and Christian devotion could reach much the same religious experience from very different doctrinal and psychological starting points.

Jewish faith and Hindu faith both startle the Christian, but for opposite reasons: the Jew because he knows the same God in a different way, and the Hindu because he knows a very different God in the same way. The Jew is shocking because he does not use the Christian categories when he approaches the God of the Bible. The Hindu is shocking because he seems to have something very like the Christian categories, but not from Christ, and to use them in approaching a God very unlike the God of the Bible. Yet there is a third faith, the Buddhist, which is perhaps more startling than either, for it raises the question of whether God or an immortal soul are needed in religion at all. In all faiths people seek deliverance from suffering, wickedness, futility, transience and spiritual confusion. Commonly we are recommended to break out of the old narrow and grasping Ego and move out into spiritual wakefulness, tranquillity, disinterestedness and universal compassion. The centre of religion is surely this demand for the inner transformation of the believer himself. And if religion is indeed a way of inner transformation that seeks to overcome evil, ignorance and futility then Buddhism is not just a genuine religion but one of the purest of all religions, for it presses the demand for inner clarity and non-attachment so far that much of the metaphysics of religion falls away. One should not be attached either to one's own personal immortality or to any god.

To most non-buddhists this is very disturbing, for we have it fixed so firmly in our minds that only metaphysical facts and nothing but metaphysical facts can justify religious activity. If it is a fact that there is a God and a life after death then religious practices are rational, but if there is no God and no life after death then there cannot be any sense in pursuing religion – or so most people in the West think. But Buddhism suggests that if we take such a view then we show that we have entirely missed the point of religion. For religion is essentially about becoming unselfish or disinterested. We must give up all forms of futile, quasi-erotic craving or yearning. Attachment is dependency is spiritual dissipation is futility and misery. True religion is pure selflessness, and you cannot pursue pure selflessness for the sake of anything else beyond it; that would be a contradiction. Pure selflessness can only be sought for its own sake and as being intrinsically valuable. So religion, on the Buddhist account, cannot be dependent upon metaphysical facts like the existence of God. Within Buddhism the typical apparatus of other faiths has often developed – worship, belief in gods and spirits, the cult of Buddhas – but it seeks to keep such tendencies in check. The spiritual discipline comes first, and the worship of gods and Buddhas is only justified in so far as it helps the disciple to attain his spiritual objectives.

So in Buddhism spirituality comes first, and has the authority to determine what is right and wrong in the way of belief in and the worship of gods. The gods are for the sake of the spirituality, and not vice versa as in the Abrahamic faiths that we know best. Thus Buddhism presents us with the challenging suggestion that our usual ideas about religion are the wrong way round and need to be reversed.

Prospect

Through their new experience of learning to live together as minority faiths in pluralist societies that no longer tolerate discrimination or even segregation, the world religions are beginning to change. They are not altogether happy about this change, because they all share a sense of exile and of nostalgia for the old days when the faith was a dominant force in the public life of an integrated religious culture; but it is happening none the less. Now that they are becoming accustomed to the idea that others walk in other paths and have other values, they are becoming less exclusive in outlook and more tolerant. Doctrine begins to be seen in a new way: instead of having all-encompassing public authority, it comes to be regarded as being something more like a musical notation, a device for communicating the real stuff of religion, which is its *life*, its ethic and spiritual values.

With these changes comes increasing eclecticism. The boundaries between the faiths become less sharply defined, and people and ideas move readily across them. In some places already, the splintering of sects and the tendency for each individual to invent his own religion has gone so far that the ancient organisations have largely broken down. Parts of California are a case in point, and those who are attracted to C.G. Jung's view of religion do not deplore it. Jung, one might say, made one-man religions respectable by inventing his own and living it himself. He thought that we each need to evolve a religion of our own because a man's religion is simply his personal myth, spontaneously generated by his own psyche in the course of its development.

Jung represents religion at its most privatised. At the opposite extreme it is possible for a whole religion to become secularised and transformed into a predominantly political movement, in which solidarity with my people takes precedence over piety towards my God. Among Jews, Zionism may now draw more people together more effectively than the common practice of traditional piety; and something similar may be occurring in Islam. The very word 'Islam', which originally meant submission to God, has instead come to be used to mean a great cultural bloc, a community of people to whom one owes prime allegiance.

If modern secular culture tends to privatise religion at the personal level and to secularise it at the communal level, then a third possibility may present itself: a fundamentalism which rejects modern Western culture and seeks to restore the old order both at the personal level and at the social. The fundamentalist movements that have arisen in several faiths during this century owe their strength to the fact that they are both pietistic and political. But can they succeed? The evidence from Iran and elsewhere suggests that fundamentalism is too romantically reactionary. It cannot understand the spirit of science or the modern concern for human rights, but neither can it get rid of them; so it proves itself unable to govern a modern state successfully. When it fails the people seek scapegoats, and begin to lynch deviants and demand wars.

Yet fundamentalism has one interesting insight. It perceives the science-based, libertarian, humanist culture of the modern era as being itself a kind of new religion – and its deadly enemy. We do not see this because we are immersed in it, it dominates more than nine-tenths of our lives, and it is so amorphous. It has no officially recognised scriptures, creeds, prophets or organisation. It is a loose coalition of many different forces: science and technology, critical thinking, humanism, modern industry, economics and politics; the whole being kept on the move and in constant self-criticism and self-correction by an active and striving ethic derived from Protestantism. So far as this new faith – if that is what it is – has theologians, priests and prophets they are, respectively, the scientists and scholars whose business it is to criticise and increase knowledge, the artists who refine our perceptions and open up new life-possibilities, and the armies of idealistic campaigners who urge us to ban the Bomb, struggle for human rights, protect the environment, help refugees and generally become active in hundreds of good causes.

So seductive and compelling is this new faith – again, if that is what it is – that it is somehow impossible to avoid adopting its language and its way of thinking. They are everywhere, and irresistible. That is what makes it like a religion: because we are in the midst of it and do not appreciate how strong and distinctive a flavour it has, we are largely unaware of its awesome, unstoppable, disruptive evangelistic power. Far more even than Islam in the later seventh century, it annihilates everything that stands in its path. To appreciate this, we have only to step outside it awhile and go to some beautiful old traditional culture in the Third World which is just beginning to feel the impact of 'Westernisation' (for that is what its evangelistic outreach is called, though sometimes people use other expressions like 'Americanism'). We will not need to stay there for long to be convinced that Westernisation is inevitable and that it will destroy everything these people now hold dear. It can be sensed coming, and its smell is unmistakable. What people say of the Americans – that they do not understand or respect other cultures, that they carry their own very strong culture with them wherever they go and that they do not realise how unpopular this makes them – is really something that is true of Westernisation in general, and therefore of all of us who are part of this strange new faith that we ourselves do not fully understand. Not only the

ιcans (who probably take an unfairly large share of the blame), but
ί us in the West are the unconscious missionaries of a devastatingly
ｐｏｗerful new creed which threatens to destroy all the older faiths by
reducing them to the status of tourist attractions and ethnic folkways.

Yet, *is* it a new faith? It is oddly unconscious of itself, as if it were
slightly ashamed of itself. It often lives within a hollowed-out shell of
Christianity, as if eager to conceal its true identity. Thus, Americans in
the Third World do not seem to the people they move among to be
Christian or in any customary sense to be religious at all; they seem
merely to be apostles of Americanism. Yet to themselves these same
Americans may appear to be twice-born Protestants, or whatever. If we
really supposed that our modern Western culture in some way constitutes
a new secular faith destined to replace traditional faiths, we should surely
be more proudly conscious of it. In fact, though, we seem to be uneasily
aware of its hollowness, its lack of spiritual roots, its potential violence
and its insubstantiality. Historically, it is very urban in character, and it
tends to spread everywhere the disaffection and restlessness always typical
of the urban masses. We find that it is very difficult to hold our vision of
human life steady, when it is lived in continual flux without any stabilising
vision of a transcendent order. When we compare our modern secular,
urban and industrial culture with what preceded it, we have an uneasy
sense of loss, so that even today the majority of the human race still
prefers to retain some degree of allegiance to the old faiths of the
agricultural civilisations, faiths that were born between one-and-a-half
and three millennia ago, faiths which are in many ways preposterously
out of touch with modern knowledge and our present way of life – and yet
faiths which have something irreplaceably valuable that we cannot and
dare not relinquish altogether.

What is that something? It seems to involve a sense of the transcendent,
a discipline of the spirit, and the power to create a stable public moral
reality that people can live in and by. To put it bluntly, one might say
that in the past reality itself was a religious postulate. That was what was
meant by the belief that God had created the world: the sense of God, the
various disciplines of the spirit that the relation to God involves, and the
underwriting of all public activity by the rubric 'To the glory of God' –
all this combined to establish the reality that people lived in and by. The
function of religion was to set standards by which to measure things, or to
provide the co-ordinates by reference to which individuals could plot
their life-paths. Critics used to claim that the transcendent ideal world
robbed this present world of value and reality, but now that the transcendent world has been abolished we see that the truth was rather the

other way round; for where the transcendent is wholly lost, life becomes an insubstantial dreamlike flux.

If so, then the religious problem today is: how can the older faiths transmit or bequeath something of their spiritual values, and in particular their power of creating a durable home for the spirit, to the new secular age? They should not aim merely to accommodate themselves to modern reality just sufficiently to ensure their own survival (though that is itself no doubt a difficult enough task); they need to go further and ask in what way they can actually give to modern culture the spiritual substance that it so evidently lacks.

Chapter 7
THE NEW WORLD

In the chief cities of Europe works of art are commonly segregated into different types of gallery in a way that provides an interesting epitome of the recent history of our culture. There are three different galleries, the Art Gallery, the Gallery of Modern Art and the Gallery of Contemporary Art, and they house three different types of work that can be roughly labelled public, bourgeois and modern respectively.

In the Art Gallery proper – often appropriately housed in a converted Baroque palace – most of the works hung use a publicly recognised symbolic language and were produced for public display in such places as churches, civic buildings and the residences of great public figures. These works glorify or celebrate the great public myths, institutions and persons, both religious and secular. However, when introducing Kierkegaard we noted how Friedrich Schiller was already complaining in 1795 that the commercialisation and industrialisation of modern society were leading to a decay in the glory (the right word: it originally meant something like weight or substance) of the public realm; and we might go on to see Napoleon and Hegel as two figures who in their different ways made the last grand attempts to save that glory of the public realm. After the waning of their influence the new kind of society, a society without glory, became dominant. Thus, in retrospect it seems that the age of Napoleon may have been the last in which the conception of the public realm still had the grandeur, confidence and spiritual spaciousness that made it possible for great artists to inhabit it, and produce major works celebrating it. In Central and Eastern Europe the divorce was finalised only in the 1890s, when the leading artists at last seceded from the Academies and the older forms of patronage, but by then it was clear that the relationship had in fact been dead for some time. Henceforth art would not exist to serve and to glorify the public realm in quite the old way any longer; it would attain to public significance only on scattered occasions when it voiced a widely-felt public mood of protest or sorrow.

The kind of art that was to succeed the old public art had already been developing for some time, for in the Art Gallery there hang a number of smaller works of a kind that began to be produced especially in the Low Countries after the Reformation. These works are private, made to please and divert private persons and to be hung in private rooms. They include landscapes, still lifes, family portraits, scenes of domestic piety, scenes of low life, flower paintings and so forth, and they do not make the old kind of grand public symbolic statement. During the nineteenth century this kind of bourgeois art, sold to private persons, became dominant, and special galleries of 'modern' art were created to house it. However, it proved to be merely transitional, for in the Gallery of Contemporary Art the spectator is confronted by works produced especially in the last three to six decades, works that seem to proclaim a wholly new era quite discontinuous with anything that has gone before. Tradition is dead, and the world has to be recreated from scratch. It is notable that whereas the Art Gallery can combine public art with bourgeois art, because the new middle classes were keen to have for themselves smaller versions of works produced for the Church and the aristocracy, genuinely modern art is so different from anything that preceded it that it cannot easily be hung alongside it.

Whether fearsome, exhilarating or confounding, the sense of having come to a quite a new era has been felt over and over again during the past hundred years, and with fresh force on each occasion. In art we witness the progressive dissolution of all the great public realities within which human life used to be contained: not only religion, the State and its institutions, and the public moral order, but also, by the end of the nineteenth century, the objective physical world and the human being. The painting ceases to be a public symbolic communication celebrating public myths, it ceases to be a representation or a framed window, and finally it comes right out of its frame (and here we should note carefully the point at which a traditional type of frame becomes inappropriate) until it stands before us as a pure creative expression that has become quite unhistorical and owes no allegiance to anything. In extreme cases it may even cease to be a fashioned object.

What is modernity? Surprisingly, for one who lacked artistic feeling and who became in his last years such a strong, if idiosyncratic, traditionalist, C.G. Jung at one stage in his career could describe the experience of the modern very well. In an essay of 1930 on 'The Spiritual Problem of Modern Man', he emphasises its unhistorical character.

Because it is highly conscious, it is unguided by tradition. As yet, only a few people have attained it:

> The modern man – or, let us say again, the man of the immediate present – is rarely met with. There are few who live up to the name, for they must be conscious to a superlative degree. Since to be wholly of the present means to be fully conscious of one's existence as a man, it requires the most intensive and extensive consciousness, with a minimum of unconsciousness. It must be clearly understood that the mere fact of living in the present does not make a man modern, for in that case everyone at present alive would be so. He alone is modern who is fully conscious of the present.
>
> The man whom we can with justice call 'Modern' is solitary. He is so of necessity and at all times, for every step towards a fuller consciousness of the present removes him further from his original 'participation mystique' with the mass of men – from submersion in a common unconsciousness.
>
> Only the man who is modern in our meaning of the term really lives in the present; he alone has a present-day consciousness, and he alone finds that the ways of life which correspond to earlier levels pall upon him. The values and strivings of those past worlds no longer interest him save from the historical standpoint. Thus he has become 'unhistorical' in the deepest sense and has estranged himself from the mass of men who live entirely within the bounds of tradition. Indeed, he is completely modern only when he has come to the very edge of the world, leaving behind him all that has been discarded and outgrown, and acknowledging that he stands before a void out of which all things may grow.

Because modernity is so unhistorical and unsustained by the presence of tradition, it is both impoverished and sinful:

> An honest profession of modernity means voluntarily declaring bankruptcy, taking the vows of poverty and chastity in a new sense, and – what is still more painful – renouncing the halo which history bestows as a mark of its sanction. To be 'unhistorical' is the Promethean sin, and in this sense modern man lives in sin. A higher level of consciousness is like a burden of guilt.

Never has it been so difficult to live fully in one's own time as it is today. Whole classes of the population prefer to reject modernity and instead to haunt metaphorical antique shops, attempting to create for themselves a habitable *pastiche* reality assembled from scraps of earlier forms of consciousness and ways of life. Naturally they require religious institutions to function as spiritual antique shops, purveying the picturesque mementoes of earlier times that they need to surround themselves with before they can feel at ease in their homes.

The pressure of the marketplace against modernity and in favour of nostalgia has virtually taken the modern off the shelves in all those arts that depend for survival upon selling their wares to a fair-sized public. Thus, in the novel, technical innovation almost ceased with Joyce. It is not surprising that religion has also been forced into the nostalgia business and has had very great difficulty in coming to terms with modernity. Where most of our culture has become an apparatus of protective illusions, religion shares in the general corruption. With a very few honourable exceptions, even the most avant-garde religious thought now scarcely dares to venture even so far as the positions explored by Matthew Arnold in the 1870s. To the churches at large modernity proper, that strange new condition that first appeared in the last generation or so before 1914, remains unexplored territory, forbidding and desolate, barely habitable.

Yet sooner or later we will have to come to terms with it, for it was not simply an ephemeral and now-superseded movement in the arts, but a profound cultural transformation which is permanent. What makes it so hard to grasp is that it is so many-faceted. Our first chapter has suggested that about a century ago the process of secularisation reached a certain completion; chapter 2, that mathematical-mechanistic thinking finally dissolved away the last shreds of belief in progress or a moral providence in the world-process; chapter 3, that Darwinism compelled people to see that the thinking subject is not a metaphysical entity somehow occupying a privileged position outside nature, but is itself merely a product of nature and immersed in nature, so that all human thinking is in the end practical; chapter 4, that the belief that there could be in history a revelation transcending history, and providing historically immutable guidelines for all human life thereafter, became at last untenable; chapter 5, that people came to realise that we can see the world only from a human point of view, and that there is no sense in the suggestion that we could have any other point of view than our own, or that there could be any other world for us than our human world; and chapter 6, that people came to see religion itself as a multifarious, ever-changing human product, and that *many* religions must therefore be true in the only sense in which any *one* religion can be true.

Somehow, about a century ago these various realisations began to coalesce with each other, and with others too. Thus, until late in the nineteenth century the Newtonian reconstruction of the physical world still held pretty firm. Aristotelian logic, Euclidean geometry, and Newton's conceptions of time, matter and physical law were all felt to be constitutively true of reality. The world was solid, with a constitutive intellectual structure. Kant's critical philosophy had indeed taken away the objectivity of this structure and had made it instead ideal, but for

Kant it nevertheless remained compulsory, and there was not any alternative way of constructing reality. Like the realists, the Kantians still saw the world in terms of Aristotle, Euclid and Newton: the only difference was that the realists said that the principles taught by those thinkers were objectively valid and therefore compulsory, whereas the Kantians said that they were subjectively necessary as conditions for knowledge – and therefore also compulsory.

However, by the end of the nineteenth century the development of new geometries had overthrown Euclid's monopoly, and a revolution in logic brought about by Gottlob Frege and others had rather similarly overthrown Aristotle's. Then the great revolution in physics overthrew the Newtonian conceptions of space, time, matter and so forth. The long-established belief that there is an objective world-order that embodies just one intellectual structure, or (in the Kantian version) that the world can only be known as objective in so far as it is made to conform to the requirements of just one intellectual structure, at last broke down. It became increasingly clear that all theories are not discoveries but inventions, human imaginative constructions that are imposed upon experience and can be described as 'true' only in the sense that , and for so long as it is found that, they work usefully. To put it brutally, there *is* no ready-ordered objective reality any more: there is only the flux of becoming, and the continuing ever-changing human attempt to imagine and impose order. We have to *make* sense; *we* have to turn chaos into cosmos.

A spectrum of opinions is possible at this point. A thoroughgoing voluntarist will say that every 'reality' that human beings have ever inhabited or ever will inhabit is inevitably wholly of their own construction, whether they recognise the fact or not. It is a truism that the only world there can possibly be for us is our world, that we are fully responsible for our world, and that according to the record human beings are evidently capable of creating a wide variety of worlds. The world is a social postulate, and the quality of the world we together make is a reflection of our own inner quality: the external world is the mirror of our inner lives and a judgment upon them. The measure we have meted is the measure we have got. To make a better world we must first become better people: there lies the challenge to our moral will, our courage and our creativity.

Others will not wish to go so far. They will say that there is no evidence for nihilism, that there is evidently *some* reality out there of which we have experience, and that therefore human beings can gain some (albeit only provisional and fallible) empirical knowledge. Such a moderate critical realism, typical of many philosophers in the English-speaking world, is neatly summed up in J.L. Mackie's formula for the human situation: 'fallible knowledge and invented ethics' – and, by implication, nothing more.

This cautious realism, however, is not so very far from the more radical view, and continually tends to slide towards it as we consider the problems that David Hume ran into, the difficulty of proving that raw experience already has some objectively given order in it prior to and independent of the constructive activity of the human understanding, and the historical fact that all human values and knowledge systems are in a process of constant change which is nowadays very rapid.

Thus although there is today a spectrum of possible views ranging from nihilism to critical realism, its opposite ends are not quite irreconcilable. Nihilists must acknowledge some constraints on human creativity in order to get going at all, in order to find reason for preferring one human creative expression to another. Realists cannot deny that all our knowledge is human and fallible, and in fact is constantly failing and being reformulated. The chief remaining difference is that those who stand at the nihilist end of the spectrum put ethics first, regarding 'reality' as created by the will, whereas those at the realist end put knowledge first, fallible though it be, and invent the ethic that makes the best of life in the world as it is presently thought to be.

Yet, once again, further consideration does something to close even this remaining difference; for the older realist attempt to keep evaluation and description separate has failed, and it cannot now be denied that the values we posit and choose to live by profoundly affect the way we apprehend and describe the world of experience. Even if the realist wishes to say that facts come first, he cannot but concede that they come to us inextricably intertwined with our values. At the same time the nihilist or voluntarist must have some conception, if not of nature at large then at the very least of human nature, which he will see as making it appropriate to claim that some values are more life-enhancing than others. Thus although the flamboyant Continental nihilist or existentialist may seem at first sight to be very different from his more sober and cautious Anglo-Saxon colleague, reflection and analysis tends to close the gap between them and to present us with something approaching a consensus view of the human situation today.

As our whole argument has been tending to show, it is a view that is profoundly post-metaphysical and anthropocentric, and challenges us to freedom and creativity. To continue nowadays to lean on the old mythological idea that there is out there a pre-existent and eternal intellectual order laid on for us is to delude ourselves, to live in an imaginary house when the requirement is to build a real one. People, and especially religious people, dread modernity because it threatens to make faith hard work again. Before modernity arrived, belief in God expressed the comfortable and pious confidence that we live in a ready-made family home with everything provided for us. We did not need to make the rules, but only to keep them, and then all would be well. But when modernity arrives, then belief in God becomes something quite different. It becomes an expression of deep discontent with the world and human nature as they are at present constituted in this sinful age, and a judgment upon them. To believe is to have become an alien in this present world, to flee from it, and passionately to fix one's hopes upon and to direct one's strivings towards a new and better world and a new and better kind of human being that are yet to come. After centuries of being lazy and cosmological, faith becomes more demanding again, more a matter of the will, less a matter of serving a pre-established order and more a pilgrimage towards a new one. It becomes more eschatological, in that it is directed towards a new world and a new human nature which this present era thinks impossible. It no longer sees (or rather, fancies that it sees) its objects. They become invisible, things unseen, ideals and things hoped-for. Do not tell me that this complete loss of objectivity is hard, for nobody knows that better than I do. It is hardest of all to give up the last slivers and shreds of objectivity, but only by doing so can faith finally free itself from all that is outworn and become as fully voluntary, creative and courageous as it is required to be today.

Nothing less than that is the challenge of modernity; and if we today think it hard, then there were a few others of generations earlier than our own from whom it was harder still, for they were the first to grasp it. To one of them, Schweitzer, we have already paid tribute. But behind him stands a still greater and more extraordinary figure.

Nietzsche

After a century, a double barrier still blocks our view of Nietzsche. When we have overcome the prejudice caused by his fearsome and misleading popular reputation and have brought ourselves to tackle the man himself, we then find ourselves confronted by a talent, a tragedy and an eloquence that are almost unbearable:

> The last philosopher I call myself, for I am the last human being. No one converses with me beside myself and my voice reaches me as the voice of one dying. With thee, beloved voice, with thee, the last remembered breath of all human happiness, let me discourse, even if it is only for

another hour. Because of thee, I delude myself as to my solitude and lie my way back to multiplicity and love, for my heart shies away from believing that love is dead. It cannot bear the icy shivers of loneliest solitude. It compels me to speak as though I were Two.

Friedrich Nietzsche (1844–1900) was spiritually a Protestant. His background in a Lutheran parsonage and in a strict classical education gave him a titanic seriousness of purpose, a driving will to inner truthfulness, self-conquest and self-transcendence, and a great love for the Greeks. He became caught in a circle, for the more honest and truthful he became the lonelier he became until in his loneliness, with nobody to speak to but himself, he turned the full power of his intellect against himself and by ceaseless self-criticism forced up his own self-awareness and spiritual tension higher and then higher again. This internal chain-reaction led him, as Freud once remarked, to a degree of introspection never previously achieved by anyone else and not likely ever to be achieved again, but at a price that his readers find frightening.

The fierce ambition showed itself early. We are told that when he was eight his six-year-old sister was already filing away his literary output, that by the age of twelve he was already rising before dawn and studying far into the night, and that at fourteen he reviewed his poetic development and divided it into three phases. He strove to find a satisfactory philosophy of life, working his way through Christianity and Romanticism, absorbing Darwinism, and then coming to a temporary rest in his enthusiasm for the philosophy of Schopenhauer and the music of Wagner; while in the same period under the guidance of the classicist Erwin Rhode he made such rapid progress that he was appointed to a professorship at Basel in 1869 at the age of twenty-four. There he found sympathetic colleagues of high standing such as Jacob Burckhardt and Franz Overbeck, and his own passion for the classical philosophers, for education, for art and for cultural renewal made him a popular lecturer. He seemed to have reached a plateau, and to have reached it early.

Yet in other ways Nietzsche was less precocious. For a man who was to have so much to do and so little time to do it, it seems extraordinary that he should have spent no less than seven years (1869–76) as the protégé of Richard Wagner, and then after that a further three or four painful years during which he cut his ties with the University, with Germany and with Schopenhauer, and struggled to reach his own mature outlook. By then he was already in his mid-thirties, with his health weakened by eyestrain, by his experience in the Army at the time of the Franco-Prussian War, and by the extreme psychological stress that he imposed upon himself. The University granted him a modest pension, just sufficient to support him in his new life as a 'free spirit', wandering in search of better health from one cheap hotel to another in Italy, the south of France and Switzerland. Everywhere he stayed the way of life was much the same:

> Carefully the myopic man sits down to a table; carefully, the man with the sensitive stomach considers every item on the menu; whether the tea is not too strong, the food not spiced too much, for every mistake in his diet upsets his sensitive digestion, and every transgression in his nourishment wreaks havoc with his quivering nerves for days. No glass of wine, no glass of beer, no alcohol, no coffee for him, no cigar and no cigarette after his meal, nothing that stimulates, refreshes, or rests him; only the short meagre meal and a little urbane, unprofound conversation in a soft voice with an occasional neighbour (as a man speaks who for years has been unused to talking and is afraid of being asked too much).
>
> And up again into the small, narrow, modest, coldly furnished *chambre garnie*, where innumerable notes, pages, writings, and proofs are piled up on the table, but no flower, no decoration, scarcely a book and rarely a letter. Back in a corner, a heavy and graceless wooden trunk, his only possession, with the two shirts and the other worn suit. Otherwise only books and manuscripts, and on a tray innumerable bottles and jars and potions: against the migraines, which often render him all but senseless for hours, against his stomach cramps, against spasmodic vomiting, against the slothful intestines, and above all the dreadful sedatives against his insomnia, chloral hydrate and Veronal. A frightful arsenal of poisons and drugs, yet the only helpers in the empty silence of this strange room in which he never rests except in brief and artificially contrived sleep. Wrapped in his overcoat and a woollen scarf (for the wretched stove smokes only and does not give warmth), his fingers freezing, his double glasses pressed close to the paper, his hurried hand writes for hours – words the dim eyes can hardly decipher. For hours he sits like this and writes until his eyes burn.

He had a few solicitous friends who would occasionally seek him out. Rather less frequently, he might himself seek them out, and there were even a few tentative and hastily-retracted overtures to women. But on the whole this man, who so devastatingly exposed the psychology of asceticism and who taught that we should say Yes to life, said No to it himself and was a pitifully severe ascetic. One of the very greatest of writers, a writer's writer as Cézanne is a painter's painter, his whole life was given to the written word – and yet remained littered with uncompleted projects and promises unfulfilled. Hegel had implanted in the great German tradition the idea that it was each generation's task to go beyond its predecessor, and although Nietzsche was always a strong opponent of historicism and the belief in progress, he ardently embraced that challenge to 'go beyond', pressing the method of critical thinking by questioning

Top The copy of the Greek Testament – open at St Matthew chapter x – which Schweitzer took with him on his military manoeuvres in 1894, with the original annotations;

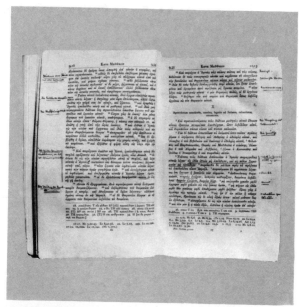

below Schweitzer building at Lambaréné

Top The bedroom in
'the Doctor's bungalow'
at Lambaréné;

below Schweitzer at
work

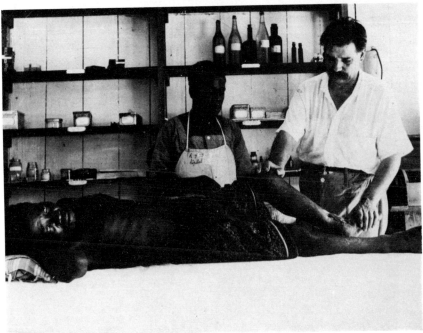

William Blake, 'Satan
and the Rebel Angels'.
After the Renaissance
Satan increasingly
symbolised human
beauty, intelligence and
pride – and attitudes to
him became ambiguous

Georg Wilhelm
Friedrich Hegel,
from a portrait by
Jacob Schlesinger

Immanuel Kant,
by Dobler

Paris 1844: Karl and Jenny Marx in the rue Vaneau with Heinrich
Heine (seated)

The surviving portraits
of Kierkegaard are few
and of poor quality.
They are all either
idealisations or
caricatures

Christianity in Asia: the Jesuit father Matteo Ricci, portrayed in about 1600 with the first Chinese convert, Li Paulus

Arthur Schopenhauer
at 21. His unhappy
relationship with his
mother Johanna *below*
may underlie the
pessimism and misogyny
of his thought. She
became a society hostess
and popular novelist;
he, a recluse

and self-questioning so hard that it was impossible that his self-tormenting spirit could ever come to rest:

> I want to make things *as hard* for myself as they have ever been for anybody: only under this pressure do I have a *clear* enough *conscience* to possess something few men have or have ever had – *wings*, so to speak.

He resembled Kierkegaard in that, precisely by making things so very hard for himself, he cut himself off from attaining in his own person the Promised Land to which he seeks to lead his readers. He climbs his Mount Pisgah to look over it, but there he comes to an end:

> I do not wish for life again. How have I borne it? By being creative. What makes me able to bear the sight of life? The vision of the Superman who affirms life. I have tried to affirm it myself – ah!

The best starting-point for understanding the mature Nietzsche is the scepticism and the self-examination of the years 1876–81, during which he laboured over *Human, All Too Human* and *Daybreak*. In breaking with Wagner he had lost his early idealism, his romanticism and his faith in the redeeming power of art:

> ... after this disappointment I was doomed to mistrust more thoroughly, to despise more thoroughly, to be alone more thoroughly than ever before. My task – whither had it flown?

Nietzsche was religious in the sense that he had to have a mission in life and a gospel to proclaim:

> That hidden masterful Something, for which we have no name until at last it shows itself as our task – that tyrant in us exacts a terrible price for every attempt that we make to escape him or give him the slip, for every premature act of self-constraint, for every reconciliation with those to whom we do not belong, for every activity, however reputable, which turns us aside from our main purpose, yes, even for every virtue that would fain protect us from the cruelty of our most individual responsibility.

Returning then to his task after what he now saw as having been an aberration, Nietzsche sought to correct his course. If he had succumbed to idealism, then the remedy must be to study positive science and make his own thinking more stringently naturalistic. The results went into *Human, All Too Human* (1878–81). And if he had been too credulous, then he must carry out a rigorous self-examination and critique of his own thinking. The results of this went into *Daybreak*.

Human, All Too Human is a reminder that Nietzsche was deeply influenced by Darwinism. Not that he particularly loved Darwin, whose views he regarded as being obviously true but dangerous, not good news but rather a threat to be overcome. The method of overcoming was, as usual, to trace out and to experience within himself the furthest sceptical implications of Darwinism. If the human mind together with all its capacities and products is simply a part of nature, then Nietzsche must work out thoroughly naturalistic interpretations of morality, of art, of religion, of genius and even of the will to truth itself. So he worked them out, and in the process found himself moving towards nihilism.

At the earliest and simplest stage, every organic being surrounds itself by a little world which it creates by projecting out its strength, its desires and its habitual experiences. This aptitude that every living creature has for simulation, for inventing, modelling and projecting out, is the primary aptitude that enables it to survive. It generates a little world by means of which it orients itself so that it can fulfil its desires. In man, who is a social and language-using animal, this is done collectively. All our knowledge is crowd-knowledge, all our meanings are crowd meanings. Crowd-survival is the name of the game, and the dissenter, the exceptional individual, has always been elbowed aside as a madman who is unfit to survive – unless haply the crowd should see fit to appropriate fragments of his teaching and put them to its own use.

Thus all the categories of our thinking, all the structures of our language, and even the perceived external world itself, are crowd-products, fictitious projections of the masses refined by natural selection and the struggle for survival. All our knowledge is practical and perspectival, evolved in the service of group life. There are no facts, only interpretations, and no truths, only useful fictions. The best science of the future will be genealogical: it will display the evolution of the fictions men live by, and the story it tells will inevitably be – yet one more fiction.

Then in *Daybreak* Nietzsche, in dialogue with such predecessors as Montaigne, Pascal and Schopenhauer, applies the same tools of sceptical and reductive analysis to introspective psychology. Indeed, the book roughly corresponds to Freud's *Interpretation of Dreams* (1899) and actually anticipates most of the main insights of psychoanalysis. Our conscious, rational and ethical self is largely a system of inherited protective illusions: the real self is the dreamer, who reveals himself as a fantasiser, an archaic symboliser struggling to express and to reconcile the dense tangle of his own conflicting irrational drives. Nietzsche is led to deny the freedom of the will, and to insist that rationality cannot be more than instrumental. The self really is a natural product, and the ultimate springs of our own action are quite mysterious to us:

. . . perhaps there exist neither will nor purposes, and we have only imagined them. Those iron hands of necessity which shake the dice-box of chance play their game for an infinite length of time: so there *have* to be throws which exactly resemble purposiveness and rationality of every degree. *Perhaps* our acts of will and our purposes are nothing but such throws – and we are only too limited and too vain to comprehend our extreme limitedness: which consists in the fact that we ourselves shake the dice box with iron hands, that we ourselves in our most intentional actions do no more than play the game of necessity. Perhaps!

For Nietzsche that 'perhaps' is sufficient fatally to undermine our confidence in traditional ideas about reason, truth and freedom. His investigations lead him towards a doctrine of psychological egoism. All our actions are determined: in our deliberations we experience the conflict of our motives, and in our choices merely the victory of the strongest among them. The self seeks simply to affirm itself and to gratify its desires. Thus one might have expected *Daybreak* to be another pessimistic and nihilistic book; and yet it is not. The key insight is that *if everything is necessary, then everything is innocent*. No ground remains for feeling guilty, for accusing ourselves, or for wishing that we were other than we are. We can learn to stop blaming ourselves, and to start understanding and accepting ourselves. The old sadistic moralities which branded the passions as evil and taught us to struggle uselessly to punish ourselves and to conquer ourselves are dispelled like nightmares when the dawn comes. Nietzsche proclaims the sacred purity and innocence of an egoistic ethic:

> *Ideal selfishness.* – Is there a more holy condition than that of pregnancy? To do all we do in the unspoken belief that it has somehow to benefit that which is coming to be within us! – has to *enhance* its mysterious worth, the thought of which fills us with delight! In this condition we avoid many things without having to force ourselves very hard! We suppress our anger, we offer the hand of conciliation: our child shall grow out of all that is gentlest and best. We are horrified if we are sharp or abrupt: suppose it should pour a drop of evil into the dear unknown's cup of life! Everything is veiled, ominous, we know nothing of what is taking place, we wait and try to be *ready*. At the same time, a pure and purifying feeling of profound irresponsibility reigns in us almost like that of the auditor before the curtain has gone up – *it* is growing, *it* is coming to light: *we* have no right to determine either its value or the hour of its coming. All the influence we can exert lies in keeping it safe. 'What is growing here is something greater than we are' is our most secret hope: we prepare everything for it so that it may come happily into the world: not only everything that may prove useful to it but also the joyfulness and laurel-wreaths of our soul. – It is in this *state of consecration* that one should live! It is a state one can live in!

Those words were written at Genoa in the winter of 1880–81, and they show Nietzsche's spirits rising. After pressing naturalism and scepticism to their furthest limits he finds something new and beautiful coming to birth in him, the gospel of his mature thought. It contains a whole series of interconnected ideas. Everything is necessary; therefore everything is innocent. Every form of idealism is exposed as a damaging illusion that makes us hate ourselves and hate life. Instead, Nietzsche offers 'the innocence of becoming'. When we really know ourselves and our own desires, then it is innocent and necessary and right that we should choose our own values on the basis of our own desires. We consciously and innocently accept the self-affirmation of our own desires, and say Yes to life. And the very fact that this new life-affirming egoistic ethic is itself also yet another rationalisation, and knows itself to be such, makes it playful and irresponsible. It is the Joyful Wisdom, the *gaya scienza*: it is *amor fati*, the love of necessity.

Daybreak was published in July 1881, as usual without attracting any attention at all: 'Nothing has happened to anyone because of me; no one's given me any thought.' In the same month Nietzsche arrived for the first time at Sils Maria, in the Upper Engadin some miles south-west of St Moritz. In the room where he was to spend most of his remaining summers he began by taking to his bed for three days of migraine and vomiting. Then as his condition began to improve he studied Spinoza once more, and joyfully recognised an affinity. Spinoza had also been a naturalistic thinker who had denied any moral world-order, had been sceptical about the freedom of the will and about altruism, and had seen that ethics must be based on an egoistic psychology. What was more, he, like Nietzsche, had converted naturalism into mysticism; for Spinoza had identified the acceptance of necessity with 'the intellectual love of God', and Nietzsche taught that one who accepted necessity, and therefore the innocence of becoming, could learn 'to look upon the world as upon a god'.

That August at Sils Nietzsche reached a climatic joy and exaltation:

> On my horizon thoughts have arisen, the like of which I have never seen before. Sometimes I think the life I am living is really dangerous because I am one of those machines that could *explode*.

At this time he was beginning to make notes that would go into *The Joyful Wisdom* (1882) and *Zarathustra* (1883–85). He would need all his literary powers to formulate the new message in a way that would be intelligible, for there is no doubt that his teaching is so novel and strange that it is hard to understand. *The Joyful Wisdom* would need to include a thorough critique of all morality hitherto and then point the way to 'the trans-valuation of all values' and the creation of a new morality. The new ethic was not simply an egoistic ethic of naturalistic humanism. It would not be joyful if it were merely that: the joy came from its amused self-mockery. There *is* no essence, only appearances:

> Appearance is for me the operating and living thing itself, which goes so far in its self-mockery as to make me feel that here there is appearance, and Will o' the Wisp, and spirit-dance, and nothing more – that among all these dreamers I also, the thinker, dance my dance, that the thinker is also a means of prolonging further the terrestrial dance, and so is one of the masters of ceremony of existence. . . .

It has often been said that the twentieth century came to birth in Nietzsche's mind in the 1880s. *Daybreak* contains not only Freud's ideas but also, in the passage about pregnancy, Jung's idea that the little ego must stand aside and allow the greater Self to come to birth. The existentialist idea of the absurdity and meaningless of human existence, and the need for us to assume full responsibility for the creation of new values, is Nietzsche's; but so also is the stranger and more exalted idea that in and through a complete acceptance of absurdity we can find an 'ultimate emancipation and irresponsibility'. The dream and the dance ran on, maintained by their high-spirited recognition of their own absurdity, 'the union of laughter with wisdom'.

Rather as Kant devised the Categorical Imperative as the sure test of whether our principles of action are truly moral, so Nietzsche devised his own test by which we can find out whether we are really willing to say Yes to life. Suppose a little gnawing demon creeps into your heart at your loneliest moment and says to you, 'You must live your whole life just as it has been, with every pain and joy and thought and sigh, over and over again. In the endless permutations of the world the sand-glass of existence will be turned over, and you with it, you speck of dust.' How will you reply to the demon? Will you curse him? Or has there been a moment in your life so great that it redeems everything else and enables you to reply, 'You are a god, and I never heard anything more divine!' If you can say that, then indeed you are able to say Yes to life.

For Nietzsche himself 'the Great Noon', the supreme moment of his life, arrived with the discovery of this test and his realisation that he could now pass it:

> I shall now tell the story of Zarathustra. The basic conception of the work, the idea of *eternal recurrence*, the highest formula of affirmation that can be attained – belongs to the August of 1881: it was jotted down on a

piece of paper with the inscription: '6000 feet beyond man and time.' I
was walking that day through the woods beside the lake of Silvaplana; I
stopped beside a mighty pyramidal block of stone which reared itself up
not far from Surlei. Then this idea came to me.

As long as his mind lasted Nietzsche believed that this revelation was a
major historical event. One might compare it with Luther's discovery of
justification by faith, and Nietzsche was honest enough to wonder if it
was evidence that an unseen Providence had after all guided his life
hitherto and had led him at last through all his conflicts to this resolution.
He dismissed the idea on the ground that it was only by following out the
implications of a thoroughgoing scepticism and atheism that he had been
able to reach his new position. Even so, had he not therefore himself
passed through death to a new life on the far side? Yes, he had; but *his*
dying-and-rising God was not to be Christ but Dionysus, a nature-god.
Following Schopenhauer, he saw Jesus as a fundamentally world-re-
nouncing figure whose kingdom of heaven is a state of dissociation from
life, whereas Dionysus stands for the affirmation of life. In Nietzsche's day
the return of Christianity to the body and this world, observable not very
long afterwards even in such minor figures as the English artist Eric Gill,
had scarcely begun: he himself took it that his discovery was radically
anti-Christian. It dispelled the last remaining shadows of God, the last
lingering nostalgia for anything at all that transcended this world and
this life. He now felt able to proclaim himself the Antichrist, to launch
into increasingly violent attacks on Christianity as a life-denying faith,
and above all to announce the death of God.

Fierce though his polemic against Christianity became, his affinity
with figures like Pascal had taught him that there is in Christianity itself,
at its very heart, a passionate longing for truth and for inner integrity.
Had he not himself been taught this very thing by Christianity? But by
the same token he had learnt through years of struggle and suffering that
the will to truth, the principle of critical analytical reason, when pressed
to its furthest limit, comes at last to the ironical conclusion that there is no
absolute truth, and is forced to pass over into the Superman's joyful
wisdom of 'goodwill towards appearance'. Nietzsche did not think
Christianity would ever be able to make that final spiritual movement.
Rather, he saw in nineteenth-century critical theology Christianity's
heroic act of self-cancellation.

> All great things perish of their own accord, by an act of self-cancellation:
> so the law of life decrees . . . Thus Christianity as dogma perished by its
> own ethics, and in the same way Christianity as ethics must perish; we are
> standing on the threshold of this event. After drawing a whole series of

conclusions, Christian truthfulness must now draw its strongest conclusion, the one by which it shall do away with itself. This will be accomplished by Christianity's asking itself, 'What does all will to truth signify?'

The point being made here recalls Schweitzer's verdict on the achievement of nineteenth-century liberal theology, and his subsequent passing-over into the religion of love and Reverence for Life. When Christian scholars have pushed their critical thinking to the point where the will to truth itself questions itself and so becomes critically conscious of itself – the point Nietzsche had been the first to reach – then Christianity would be at an end. He continues:

> It is by this dawning self-consciousness of the will to truth that ethics must now perish. This is the great spectacle of a hundred acts that will occupy Europe for the next two centuries, the most terrible and problematical but also the most hopeful of all spectacles.

The apocalyptic crisis in European culture that Nietzsche calls the death of God had begun long before. He did not think of himself as bringing it about. Rather, he was trying to warn his generation that it was so great an event that it was still on its way: its full implications were only just beginning to be apparent.

> Have you not heard of that madman who lit a lantern in the bright morning hours, ran to the market place, and cried incessantly, 'I seek God! I seek God!' As many of those who do not believe in God were standing around just then, he provoked much laughter. Why, did he get lost? said one. Did he lose his way like a child? said another. Or is he hiding? Is he afraid of us? Has he gone on a voyage? Or emigrated? Thus they yelled and laughed. The madman jumped into their midst and pierced them with his glances.
> 'Whither is God?' he cried. 'I shall tell you. *We have killed him* – you and I. All of us are his murderers. But how have we done this? How were we able to drink up the sea? Who gave us the sponge to wipe away the entire horizon? What did we do when we unchained this earth from its sun? Whither is it moving now? Whither are we moving now? Away from all suns? Are we not plunging continually? Backward, sideward, forward, in all directions? Is there any up or down left? Are we not straying as through an infinite nothing? Do we not feel the breath of empty space? Has it not become colder? Is not night and more night coming on all the while? Must not lanterns be lit in the morning? Do we not hear anything yet of the noise of the gravediggers who are burying God? Do we not smell anything yet of God's decomposition? Gods too decompose. God is dead. God remains dead. And we have killed him. How shall we, the murderers of all murderers, comfort ourselves? What was holiest and most powerful of all that the world has yet owned has bled to death under our knives. Who will wipe this blood off us? What water is there for us to

clean ourselves? What festivals of atonement, what sacred games shall we have to invent? Is not the greatness of this deed to great for us? Must not we ourselves become gods simply to seem worthy of it? There has never been a greater deed; and whoever will be born after us – for the sake of this deed he will be part of a higher history than all history hitherto.'

Here the madman fell silent and looked again at his listeners; and they too were silent and stared at him in astonishment. At last he threw his lantern on the ground, and it broke and went out. 'I come too early,' he said then; 'my time has not come yet. This tremendous event is still on its way, still wandering – it has not yet reached the ears of man. Lightning and thunder require time, the light of the stars requires time, deeds require time even after they are done, before they can be seen and heard. This deed is still more distant from them than the most distant stars – *and yet* they have done it themselves!'

The death of God is more than simply dogmatic atheism. Nietzsche had after all been an atheist since his youth, long before he felt able to announce the death of God. Rather, it means the final loss of belief in any external reality at all that might guide and sustain human life, including even an ordered objective world: it means nihilism.

In *The Twilight of the Idols* (1880) Nietzsche has an extraordinary short chapter called 'How the "Real World" at last became a Myth', in which he traces the dissolution of the world and shows just how far he was ready to take the idea. At first the real world was simply the present world of the wise, the pious and the virtuous man. Then it became unattainable for the moment, but at least promised. It became a world above or beyond, as in Christianity. At the next stage, roughly corresponding to Kant's philosophy, it became an unattainable idea, a guiding star. Then people said, 'Unattainable? – therefore unknown, and practically negligible', and they turned to empiricism and positive science. The next step was to declare the whole idea of a 'real world' redundant and refuted; and here we might have expected Nietzsche to stop, with the goodwill towards appearances and the high comic spirit of the Gay Science. But he goes on: 'What is left? the apparent world perhaps? . . . But no! *with the real world we have also abolished the apparent world!*' In parentheses he adds a string of phrases: 'Mid-day; moment of the shortest shadow; end of the longest error; zenith of mankind; ZARATHUSTRA BEGINS.'

Here Nietzsche runs out into what on the reverse side is nihilism, but on the obverse a pure voluntaristic idealism which says, 'Nothing constrains you: you can, you must, fashion whatever your heart desires!'

At this point we begin to wonder what can have happened to the naturalism from which Nietzsche had begun a decade earlier, in the late

1870s. Has he not sawn off the branch on which he stood? He had set out on his journey into scepticism with the Darwinian idea that the human mind with all its capacities is wholly a product of the chances and necessities of the evolutionary process in nature; and this starting-point itself presupposes a world, the biological world, and assumes some knowledge of its contents and its laws. Up to 1881 Nietzsche's conclusions remained broadly consistent with this starting-point, for he could follow Kant and Schopenhauer in teaching that science does no more than order the world of appearances, and then argue that the Gay Science consists in the recognition that the world is nothing but appearance, that we as products of it are also appearance, and so are all our theorisings about it. So man 'the visionary animal' who likes to believe in his dreams can attain at least to a modest biological self-understanding, enough to enable him to laugh at himself and it, and to dance as he says Yes to life.

Thus far Nietzsche the naturalistic thinker is consistent with himself, and those who interpret him as a man of the Enlightenment and a follower of Goethe (really quite a moderate fellow, in fact, and not so frightening as you all think) are able to interpret him along these lines. But it cannot be the whole story, for there is also Nietzsche the nihilist, the really radical sceptic who abolishes not only the real world but also the world of appearances – including biological appearances. Yet when words like life, desire and dream lose their foundation in biology, they seem to lose meaning and nothing remains to say Yes to. The Superman has to create his new world, not out of biological materials, but *ex nihilo*, truly *ex nihilo*.

So there is a serious conflict between naturalism and nihilism in Nietzsche's thought. My own belief is that the nihilism is the more interesting, and in the end prevails That is why Nietzsche becomes such an inspiration to the Modern movement in the arts. And although the naturalism was used to banish Christianity, the nihilism must readmit it as a possibility, for it brings us back to a position like Kierkegaard's: in the end nothing exists except the range of possible forms of consciousness before us, and the need to choose what to make of our lives.

Nietzsche, infuriatingly clever, misses so little that he has seen even this. If all truth is invented and not discovered, and all knowledge systems are works of art; if all philosophies are poetry, then indeed the task of the man of the future will be to accomplish consciously and in a spirit of self-mockery what earlier ages did unconsciously. So why would we not be just as much entitled to will and create a future Christian reality as any other? Nietzsche's reply shows that he can envisage artist-philosophers, but not artist-theologians:

The creation of a religion would consist in this, that one awakened *faith* in the mythical construction he had erected in the void: i.e., that it corresponded to an extraordinary need. It is *unlikely* that this will ever happen again, after the *Critique of Pure Reason*. On the other hand, I can imagine an altogether new kind of artist-philosopher.

Since I hold that the age of the artist-theologian has actually arrived (and we all know in our hearts that it has arrived: Kierkegaard, who called himself a poet, was one, and Karl Barth knew in his heart's heart that he was another), I want to know on what ground Nietzsche rules out the artist-theologian, while admitting the artist-philosopher. His answer is that for there to be religion there must be faith; and for there to be faith there must be assent to dogma, belief in some absolute metaphysical reality out there. But Kant (Nietzsche is saying) has shown that dogmatic metaphysics is impossible, and therefore faith is henceforth impossible, or at any rate – unexpectedly cautious word – 'unlikely'.

Nietzsche was well aware of the many post-Kantian theologians who accepted the end of metaphysics and accordingly described faith as consisting not in assent to dogmas but in commitment to ideals; but he declared himself unimpressed by them. The ideal God of post-Kantian theology was a mere shadow of God, a stopgap, a piece of nostalgia and a device for fending off the realisation that we must now create our own values. Faith for Nietzsche must always be dependent, receptive, other-centred; he could not imagine it ever attaining to the ironical, amused lightness and self-mockery of the Joyful Wisdom. He liked to insist that Christianity is an integral system with every part interlocked in such a way that if just one element is removed the whole collapses. In short, he used the same tactics as Freud, setting up a block-Christianity, monolithic and necessarily pre-conscious, as being the only genuine article, and then claiming that since it was unconscious of itself whereas he was conscious of it, then he had transcended it and could leave it behind, sure in the knowledge that it could never again catch up with him.

Here at last in our long struggle with Nietzsche, the best foeman, we begin to feel we have the upper hand. Has he not heard of Zen, of the Hasidim, of Eckhart? Does he not know that the Joyful Wisdom was attained and taught by religious mystics long before he discovered it? There have been occasions in the past when religion has become self-mockingly conscious of itself; not many perhaps, but enough to encourage those of us who believe that it can and must become so today. That God is radically unknowable, that the eye with which he looks at us is simply the eye with which we look at him, that religious ideas are inescapably and *rightly* human and full of human absurdity, that they exist not to describe

God nor to constrain us but simply to liberate the spirit – all this was known once, however completely it has been forgotten since. Nietzsche could see that a movement towards non-realism in religious thought had been slowly going on for centuries, and had been especially stimulated by Kant's philosophy. But he could not see that it might eventually lead to religion's becoming at last fully self-conscious and regaining the Joyful Wisdom. Why could he not see this? – because in such early exponents as Luther, Pascal and even (one might add) Kierkegaard, the first moves appeared to be in the direction of an authoritarian and gloomy irrationalism that Nietzsche diagnosed as 'the suicide of reason'. Christianity had perforce to develop in the modern period through the stages we have been describing – Protestantism, fideism, existentialism, tragic Christianity – before it could break through to the Joyful Wisdom, and those early stages were indeed somewhat harsh and difficult. Yet this was no more than had happened in the course of Nietzsche's own development, as he struggled through Romantic pessimism, naturalism, scepticism, nihilism. The law in these matters is that you have to go through a great many Noes before you can reach the Yes, as he well knew.

However, we have as yet little reason to pride ourselves on having exceeded Nietzsche's insight, or even on having equalled it. If Christian thought is, as I believe, on the verge of breaking through first to conscious non-realism and then to a rediscovery of the Joyful Wisdom of the mystics, it must be confessed that there are as yet all too few signs of it; and Nietzsche's polemics against the corruption that he diagnosed in Christian thought and ethics remain very telling. In his book on Nietzsche, Walter Kaufmann sums them up elegantly by quoting from Goethe's *Conversations with Eckermann.* Asked to comment on the charge that his books were too pagan, the old man replied, 'I, pagan? I let Gretchen be executed and Ottilie starve to death; don't people find that Christian enough? What do they want that would be more Christian?'

That says it all: everyone who has ever felt that he has seen just too many graphically-depicted martyrdoms in Italian frescoes, everyone who has sat through a hundred operas in which the reaffirmation of the moral order requires the heroine to suffer and (usually) to die, knows just what Goethe means. There is a small-town moralism which is prying, envious and vindictive, which is little more than a conspiracy of sadism, and which has in the past all too often succeeded in passing itself off as Christian. It has been able to do so because when religious beliefs are understood in a realist and objectified way they do indeed become tools of oppression, producing first a religious psychology that is self-punishing and self-mutilating, and then an ethic that is determined to give others as bad a time as we have given ourselves. If we are nowadays beginning to rid ourselves of all these horrors, then we owe a debt to Nietzsche and may one day turn the tables on him in a way he would have appreciated, by saluting him as a great reformer of Christianity. Inevitably, he anticipated that fate, and warned that he did not want to be a saint: he would rather be a clown. Always his formula for would-be disciples was 'Follow me – by following yourself.'

His end was terrible. Early in 1888, still only forty-three, he was working on notes for the never-completed *Transvaluation of All Values*. Then he went on to *The Wagner Case*. At Sils in July and August he wrote *The Twilight of the Idols* and then went straight on to *The Antichrist*. On 20 September he left for Turin where he completed *The Antichrist* and began *Ecce Homo*. The productivity seemed unstoppable, but his delusions were getting the better of him:

> Here in Turin I exercise a perfect fascination. Everybody glances at me as if I were a prince. . . . Everything comes easily to me, everything succeeds, although it is not likely that anyone has ever had such great things on his hands . . . there is a special distinction in the way doors are held open for me, meals set out.

In December came the last piece of good news, a warm salute from Strindberg. By this time he had lost control of his facial muscles and his handwriting was deteriorating. The final breakdown – more or less coinciding with Van Gogh's – came on 3 January.

Nietzsche, who had taught that one should die like Socrates, quickly, freely and at the right moment, lingered on for ten wretched years. Two of his oldest and most faithful friends, Peter Gast, the composer who acted as his copyist, and Franz Overbeck, his former Basel colleague, both entertained a suspicion that his madness was feigned. Others might point to the fact that his father had died mad at thirty-five, or suggest that his breakdown was the poetic culmination of his teaching or the consequence of the prolonged strain to which he had subjected his mind, or even that it was the revenge of the gods for his impieties. The most probable answer is that its cause was purely physical; he had perhaps become infected with syphilis in his student days at Bonn. We shall never know for sure.

Nietzsche's explosive literary style, the grimness of his last years and the damage done to his reputation by his sister during the period in which she managed his literary affairs have combined to create an impression of overheating and excess. Yet the real Nietzsche was a quiet, sensitive and unassuming man. As a creative person with a sense of mission but plagued by ill-health, he had to nurse his gift and was engaged in a race against the clock; but until the last months before his collapse he cannot be called psychologically abnormal. He thought he was 'the last philosopher' in the sense that in him metaphysical realism and idealism both came to an end, and the human race arrived at a new situation. The process by which European thinking had been becoming more and more anthropocentric ever since Luther and Descartes was now complete, and Nietzsche's thought expresses the sense of shock and challenge when this was realised. One might object that Feuerbach and Marx had come to almost the same point fifty years earlier, but Nietzsche's view was that they and others like them had failed to grasp the full gravity of what had happened.

Nietzsche's main achievement is in ethics, in which he is one of the very few great originals. In other areas, he portends a revolution in philosophy rather than actually carrying it out. He did after all belong to the nineteenth century rather than the twentieth, and used the language of the old order to announce its dissolution. This makes his message the more alarming and urgent, for it emphasises how much is being lost; but at least it makes him relatively easy to understand.

The situation changes as we turn now to a thinker who is very much of the new century. He was a man who resembled Nietzsche in many ways, for he was another wanderer and ascetic, driven by an extreme need for freedom and a passion of doubt. Because in him the shift to an entirely new outlook actually took place, leaving older ways of thinking not as enemies to be combated but rather as persistent illusions to be cured, he can seem both cooler and more difficult to understand. Beneath the surface, though, the sense of inner strain and the fragmentation remains very acute.

Wittgenstein

Ludwig Wittgenstein (1889–1951) was the ninth and last child of Karl and Leopoldine Wittgenstein of Vienna. The father was a very successful steel magnate, immensely rich and an active patron of the arts. The leading musicians of the day, including Brahms, Mahler, Bruno Walter, Joachim and the young Casals, frequented the house, and most of the children became highly musical. Ludwig – himself a clarinettist – was once heard to say that in his childhood home there had been seven grand pianos.

The Wittgensteins prided themselves on being racially Jewish, associating Jewishness and aesthetic idealism, high achievement and a touch of intellectual dissent. In fact though, the father had been baptised a Protestant, and the mother and children were Catholics.

213

The household was something of a microcosm of Viennese life at that time. The Habsburg monarchy lingered on, and through the Academies and the system of patronage still endeavoured to keep intellectual and artistic life tied to the service of the regime and to a preposterously overblown and decadent version of the Baroque style. Among a highly gifted younger generation there was a sense of malaise, articulated in the fiction of men like Arthur Schnitzler and Robert Musil and rising to open revolt among admirers of the great satirist Karl Kraus. Looking today at the last monuments erected by the Habsburgs one can see why the rebels felt that all the symbol-systems through which that society expressed to itself its sense of itself had become bankrupt and meaningless.

In 1897 the painter Gustav Klimt led the Secession of artists from the Academy, and Hermine Wittgenstein, Karl's oldest child, who was herself a painter and an admirer of Klimt, persuaded her father to pay for the Secession building designed by Josef-Maria Olbrich. At first the Secession was aesthetically a mess, as Olbrich's bizarre structure makes all too clear; but two years later Oscar Wagner joined the movement and architecture began to change. A cultural revolution advanced on many fronts: architecture moved from Olbrich and Wagner to Adolf Loos, painting from Klimt and Schiele to Oscar Kokoschka, and music from Mahler to Schönberg. The Modern Movement had arrived.

Viennese society in those days was small and highly interconnected. Bruckner gave piano lessons to the physicist Boltzmann, Mahler took his problems to Freud, and the young lyric poet Hugo von Hofmannsthal went to lectures by the philosopher of science, Ernst Mach. In later life Ludwig Wittgenstein was to lament more than anything else the loss of that kind of cultural coherence and interconnection, and certainly in his youth it had made very rapid advances possible. The common theme among a whole generation of artists and thinkers was a concern for rigorously honest and truthful communication. The age of Freud was an age of demythologising, of unmasking illusions and of open war against every kind of hypocrisy and falsity. In the arts, unnecessary ornamentation and outworn symbolism were rejected in favour of austere functionalism.

In religion and philosophy the corresponding movement of the spirit turned away from idealism and from the affirmation of the images in Baroque Catholicism towards silence and purity. Philosophy emphasised the limits of thought, moving towards empiricism and logical positivsm. Many thought that to be really pure it should restrict itself to defining how empirical knowledge and fact-stating language were possible. In religious thought there was interest in Kierkegaard's rejection of 'Christendom', and his doctrine that religious truth could be communicated only indirectly, as in the use of parables to bring about an inner shift within the hearer. The moralism and asceticism of the later Tolstoy was a potent influence, and Wittgenstein treasured his *Twenty-three Tales* and *What I believe*. Schopenhauer's doctrine that 'the mystical' is ineffable – that the highest truths about salvation and the ultimate goal of life cannot be expressed in language – was interestingly taken up and developed by the linguistic philosopher Fritz Mauthner.

All these currents of thought were duly reflected in the Wittgenstein household. The entire family shared a common strenuousness and seriousness of purpose, but there was some conflict between the capitalist father and the aesthete children in that where the father was able to combine his financial interests and *haut-bourgeois* social position with his active cultural concerns, many of the children were not. The conflict led to the suicide of two of the sons, Hans and Rudi. A third son, Kurt, committed suicide to avoid capture during the War. Wittgenstein was thus to be cut off from the world of his childhood by family tragedies as well as by vast political upheavals.

All the children were tutored intensively at home. Ludwig went on to the Linz *Realschule* in 1904, and there got a good grounding in mathematics and physics. His talent for making models, and his understanding of the way nature is modelled in mechanics, were to be reflected in his later attempt to show how language can model or represent reality.

By 1908, when he left school, Wittgenstein had become interested in aeronautical engineering. That summer he was testing kites at the upper atmosphere kite station at Glossop in Derbyshire, England, and in the autumn he became a research student at Manchester University, where he worked on aero engines and explored the idea of a jet-reaction engine which could deliver the thrust through nozzles at the tips of the propeller blades.

Although at this stage of his life Wittgenstein is reported as having been cheerful, wealthy and excitable, there were already some signs of his later character. He was exceedingly fastidious about matters of furnishing. He complained about inability to concentrate, and once attempted to have himself questioned about points of logic while under hypnosis – an experiment which was a resounding failure.

The story of how he discovered his vocation is well known. His engineering work required him to solve mathematical problems, and this led to an interest in the foundations of mathematics. What was the nature of mathematical truth; did anybody study such a subject? Happily, he was directed to the two best philosophers alive, Frege in Jena and Russell in Cambridge. He arrived in Cambridge at the end of 1911, became

Russell's pupil, and made such extraordinary progress that in less than two years he was ready to disappear to a hut in Norway in order to work on a book.

Completion of the book was delayed by the outbreak of war. Although technically exempted from military service on medical grounds, Wittgenstein insisted on volunteering for the Austrian Army in the hope that the hardships and dangers of military life would make him a better human being. Like Nietzsche he needed to make things hard for himself in order to have a clear conscience, but unlike Nietzsche he put the point in religious terms:

> Perhaps the nearness of death will bring light into life. God enlighten me.
> Be at peace within yourself. But how do you find this peace in yourself? *Only* if I live in a way pleasing to God. *Only* so can one bear life.

In the jargon, Wittgenstein was a highly inner-directed person who needed before all else to satisfy his own conscience. To such a person believing in God and doing God's will means the same thing as being inwardly free from falsity, having a right sense of oneself and one's own life, and living a life that is both free and dedicated. Intellectual truthfulness must spring from and rest upon something more fundamental, moral truthfulness.

During the war Wittgenstein carried his manuscript with him, along with a volume of Tolstoy. He was discharged from the Army in 1919, trained as a teacher, and then spent the years 1920–1926 as a village schoolmaster in Lower Austria.

Meanwhile the book, the *Tractatus Logico-Philosophicus*, was published in German in 1921 and in an English translation in 1922. Brief, and written in an exalted aphoristic style, it immediately became famous. Wittgenstein himself, though, had vanished from view: he believed that he had completed the task of philosophy and could therefore abandon the subject, and the fact he felt the book was being misunderstood did not encourage him to emerge from obscurity.

At first sight the book seems to be a manifesto of logical positivism, designed to show how language should be used solely for the purpose of describing reality precisely. The propositions of logic are all tautologies, empty truths which Wittgenstein uses to mark out the field of all that there can possibly be. Within this abstract framework of logical space lies the actual world, which is an assembly of simple objects. All true fact-stating language can be analysed down into simple propositions that name these objects and make assertions about them whose logical structure corresponds to objective structures in reality.

The *Tractatus* draws the limits of meaningful language so tightly and is so puritanical that it makes nonsense even of itself, for the statements it contains are not themselves factual. Wittgenstein recognises this: 'Anyone who understands me eventually recognises them as nonsensical.' You cannot state in language how language is related to reality. The relation can only be *shown*, and once the book has done the showing you could discard it. In addition the book leaves out the human self, the subject of knowledge and user of language. He is transcendental, outside the world of fact. And since the world consists of nothing but simple objects, everything to do with value – religion, morality, art – is also left out. These things do not appear in the world, and what they are about therefore cannot be put into words. It too can only be shown, not said.

Wittgenstein, with his intense moral and religious seriousness, was distressed that the book was read by many as being simply a work of reductive positivist metaphysics. He himself saw it was an essay in Kierkegaardian 'indirect communication':

> *The book's point is an ethical one* . . . . My work consists of two parts: the one presented here, plus all that I have *not* written.
>
> The correct method in philosophy would really be the following: to say nothing except what can be said, i.e. propositions of natural science – i.e. something that has nothing to do with philosophy – and then whenever someone else wanted to say something metaphysical, to demonstrate to him that he had failed to give a meaning to certain signs in his propositions.
>
> In ethics people are forever trying to find a way of saying something which, in the nature of things, is not and can never be expressed.

In short, Wittgenstein's purpose was much the same as Kant's had been: by fixing the limits of knowledge he would secure room for faith. The task of philosophy is to define the nature and limits of scientific knowledge, and then bow out. Everything to do with values and the meaning of life is thus proved to be beyond the scope of science, and cannot be encroached upon by it. The 'truths' of religion and morality cannot be put into words: they can only be shown indirectly by art, and felt and done by the individual. Thus religious truth could be *conveyed*, as in a tale by Tolstoy, but it could not be theorised about. Any attempt to theorise about religion and morality, and any attempt to do speculative metaphysics, must fail because it would represent our beliefs in those spheres as being of a factual kind – which they are not.

Wittgenstein's point here was typically modern, and yet it remains controversial and hard to grasp. By drawing a sharp line between the sphere of factual knowledge and the 'ethical' sphere (which includes religion) he had gained a protected status for religious belief – but at the price of making it non-factual. Throughout his life it could be said of him that he believed in God, in the sense that the thought of God was constantly with him, guiding him and influencing his life; and yet he did not think that it is factually the case that there exists a god. Thus in 1931 he wrote:

> If I, who do not believe that somewhere or other there are human-superhuman beings, which we might call gods – if I say 'I fear the wrath of the gods', then this shows that with these words I can mean something or express a feeling that need not be connected with that belief.

Faith in God can shape your life, without its being necessary to suppose that God exists objectively 'out there'. Indeed, Wittgenstein considered that it was a mistake to think in such a way. He is reported as having said in 1930:

> It is a dogma of the Roman Church that the existence of God can be proved by natural reason. Now this dogma would make it impossible for me to be a Roman Catholic. If I thought of God as another being like myself, outside myself, only infinitely more powerful, then I would regard it as my duty to defy him.

At some stages in his life Wittgenstein prayed a good deal, and he had a strong sense of the sacredness and fearsomeness of the idea of God: 'Never allow yourself to become too familiar with holy things!' But for that very reason God ought not to be objectified or turned into some kind of factual entity, for that would be a profanation. Rather, the thought of God ought to be kept holy and used in self-examination, as when we think of God as a Judge whose eye sees everything, and use that image to guide our self-assessment. Nor is Wittgenstein's doctrine so far particularly strange. It may be seen as corresponding to the typical modern layman's extreme reticence about his private religious beliefs.

In the later 1920s Wittgenstein was given an opportunity to express his message in artistic terms. In 1926 he had left school-teaching after an incident in which he had struck a child. He was always highly strung and irascible, but the exact circumstances are obscure. At any rate, the episode left him almost suicidally pessimistic about his own chances of 'becoming a better person'. His sister Gretl (Margarete Stonborough-Wittgenstein, whose portrait by Klimt can be seen in Munich) was the only member of the family still with money, and she drew him into the project of designing a new house for her in Vienna. He became absorbed in the aesthetic and technical challenges of the task, and the result was a masterpiece. Down to the smallest details it is immaculately engineered, and represents perhaps the furthest extreme of pure functionalism that architecture has reached. After exploring and digesting it for a while, the visitor begins to be reminded of a mosque: what can be said is said with such austerity that it indirectly makes one aware of the brooding presence of that which cannot be said, but only shown. Such was Wittgenstein's negative or indirect theology. The nearest he will come to any kind of argument from the world to God is this, from the *Tractatus*: 'Feeling the world as a limited whole – it is this that is mystical.' Drawing the limits, whether in architectural or in linguistic terms, as tightly as possible heightened the sense of the world as a limited whole and therefore indirectly helped 'the mystical' to make its presence felt.

Gretl's therapy worked, and Wittgenstein decided that he could return to philosophy and do creative work again. In 1929, forty years old now and after a sixteen-year-absence, he returned to Cambridge. He enrolled, rather incongruously, as a research student but quickly became in succession a Fellow of Trinity College, a University lecturer and then, just before the War, a professor.

It is greatly to Cambridge's credit that it recognised his ability generously and was singularly tolerant of a man wholly unsuited to academic life – a man indeed whose view of it was no more favourable than Schopenhauer's or Nietzsche's had been. For his part, he was able to find in Cambridge freedom, a haven, and the very small group of friends he needed. There were several absences, long and short, but he returned to die in 1951. The almost unprecedented spectacle of a major genius at large in English society has its comic side, but the anecdotes and legends are all sufficiently well known by now: what is alone important is that he was almost continuously productive during his last twenty years, though he published nothing. His output was confined to oral discussion and vast numbers of carefully-stored manuscript notes. His literary executors were left with a daunting task. So far they have issued over a dozen volumes from his remains, but their slow publication and their piecemeal nature have meant that the full impact of his later philosophy is being felt only gradually.

What is clear is that by 1933 Wittgenstein had already rejected most of the basic principles of his early philosophy and was developing something so novel, strange and hard to understand that he himself thought he was inventing a new subject. It may be that he was changing the whole course of Western thought; but if so the change was not from one system to another, but rather from system to method. It is a change that needs to be learnt as a skill and studied in process in a large number of particular cases. It is a change for which one needs an apprenticeship: that is what makes it so hard to understand. My attempt to give a summary description of it as if it were a metaphysical shift would have incurred his instant wrath. So the account, once given, must negate itself.

Roughly, then, Wittgenstein renounced the idea that the chief function of language is to copy or trace the structure of a pre-existing independent reality out there. Language does not gain its meaning by referring and copying in that way. Instead, language has to be seen as embedded in and interwoven with human practices. It is highly rule-governed, and it gets its meaning from the various jobs it does in furthering human language-games and forms of life.

To take a very simple example, the cry 'Owzat!' is to be heard rising from cricket-pitches in summertime. What does it mean? Its meaning is to be explained in terms of the Laws of Cricket, the playing of an actual game of cricket, the aims of the fielding side, rules defining the sort of moments at which it is appropriate to utter this cry, and the umpire's duty to decide how to respond to it. All the simpler uses of language – all the 'restricted communication codes', as they have been called – are of this ritualised kind, and can be observed in such places as lawcourts, operating theatres, the army, work-places, church services, restaurants and so forth. Wittgenstein holds that these obviously ritualised utterances give us a vital clue to the nature of language generally, for, as everyone who has struggled with a foreign language knows, to understand what people are saying you have to understand – and more than that, to be able to play your part in – a whole social world. You have to 'know the ropes'. The meaning is the use in a certain social context. Wittgenstein thinks that language can be fully explained in these terms, and sets out to show that nothing can be gained by appealing to any external points of support for it. Language comes first, for it prescribes the shape of the various 'realities' amongst which we move, and not the other way round. Reality does not determine language: language determines reality. Most people simply use language without being aware of it, but when we have become conscious of language (a most rare and difficult feat, which Wittgenstein achieved because his unusual personal history had predisposed him to be able to do it) then we see that language is the creator of everything. In the beginning was the Word. And this doctrine is positivistic in the sense that when we have managed to achieve in some particular instance a clear overview (*Ubersicht*) of how the language works, then we grasp that no further justification of it is either needed or possible.

In the case of religion there was some precedent for this insight, for even in ancient times subtle religious thinkers had already grasped that all our language about God is metaphorical, symbolic or analogical; that is, that all our religious ideas are human. What then can be the point of them? The crucial insight is that, just as fiction about animals or extra-terrestrials has to humanise them in order to allow a novel about them to be written, for if they were inhuman they would be unintelligible to us, so our religious imagery must be human if it is to evoke our affections and guide our responses and our behaviour. Just as rabbits or science-fiction aliens have to be humanised in novels, so every God has to be incarnate to be a god to us, for the non-human is nothing to us. To think of God as a heavenly father is to adopt and to carry about with us wherever we go an image that inclines us to to behave as if an unseen paternal eye watches over us, so that we get the habit of trusting life and acting as people who have something to live up to. In short, the more we become conscious of the merely-human character of religious language, the more clearly we see that all our religious 'knowledge' is – and has to be – simply practical. We give up gnostic metaphysical dreams and are returned to the human realm; to a sense of reverence, to trust in life, and to love of our neighbour.

Thus religion has to be merely human in order to work as religion, a paradox which brings religion within a hairsbreadth of merely secular humanism. This profound insight Wittgenstein expresses in the aphorism:

> An honest religious thinker is like a tightrope walker. He almost looks as though he were walking on nothing but air. His support is the slenderest imaginable. And yet it really is possible to walk on it.

The movement of the spirit whereby we become conscious of the limits of language and are forced to give up the illusions of metaphysics, renounce objectivity, and return to the human world and the primacy of the practical, is of religious origin. Wittgenstein learnt of it in Augustine, saw it confirmed by Kant, and above all found it taught (as we saw earlier) most explicitly by Kierkegaard. He applied it quite generally, in such a way that it came to pervade his whole philosophy. I suspect that this may be the meaning of some of his reported remarks such as:

> I am not a religious man but I cannot help seeing everything from a religious point of view.
>   Your religious ideas [Drury] have always seemed to me more Greek than Biblical. Whereas my thoughts are one hundred per cent Hebraic.
>   The religion of the future will have to be extremely ascetic; and by that I don't mean just going without food and drink.

For 999 people out of every 1000, religion has to do with metaphysical yearnings and a desire to be reassured about God's existence and a real life after death, and suchlike. Since Wittgenstein's later philosophy is designed to cure us of just this kind of metaphysical longing and of every other sort of objectivism or realism, it must seem to most people to be radically anti-religious. He seems determined to push us into accepting that it is futile to try to go beyond the human realm and the limits of language. Philosophy, in his view, is a sustained attempt to cure ourselves of transcendent illusions and persuade us to be content with what is – and what *is*, is language and the human realm, and nothing else. Wittgenstein's mature outlook is linguistic naturalism (there are in the end only the facts about language), voluntarism (we, through language, constitute our world), and radical humanism (there is no sense in supposing that we humans might be able to transcend the limits of our own humanity, while yet somehow retaining it). And Wittgenstein extends these doctrines to cover even logic, mathematics and natural science. Everywhere he is a thoroughgoing constructivist and voluntarist: logical necessity is created by the rules governing language. If he is a non-realist about religion, he is also a non-realist about everything else.

Yet these features of his thinking, which seek to cure us permanently of any temptation to metaphysics, or realism or solipsism, and which to all right-thinking people seem radically anti-religious, were for Wittgenstein himself evidence that he indeed approached all problems from a religious point of view. 'The last and highest parting', as Eckhart calls it, the most difficult movement of the spirit to make, is the one that returns from theory to practice, from heavenly yearnings to common human life, from realism to voluntarism. It is not enough always simply to have been immersed in common life, because you can enter the new kind of relationship to it only after you have passed through Wittgenstein's new discipline. It is not enough merely to be innocent; you must have sinned and been forgiven. So Wittgenstein wished his new position to be understood against the background of the various forms of realism for which it is the cure.

In a way the new position is very simple. Pick up something yellow and look at it. What *justifies* you in calling this thing yellow? There are well-known difficulties in the supposition that yellowness is an objective physical property of material bodies out there in the world. Is yellowness then a subjective sensation in you? If so, then how do you identify it to yourself as yellow? What criterion do you use; and by what criterion could you ever hope to establish that your own subjective sensation of yellowness is the same as someone else's? Wittgenstein shows us the way out of these puzzles by reminding us that the dictionary defines 'yellow' as 'of the colour of gold, butter, egg yolks, etc.' In English there are publicly agreed rules for using the word. If you follow them and use the word as it is commonly used, then you understand what 'yellow' means.

horizontal reference

If you have the skill of using colour-words in accordance with the public consensus, then you will be able to pass any imaginable test of your colour vision, and reference either to your private sensations or to the question of what colour things 'really' are adds nothing, and is redundant.

There are indeed different domains within language. As well as the common language which ascribes yellowness to gold, butter, egg yolks and the rest, there is also a language-game in which we do ascribe private sensations of yellowness to ourselves, and a scientific language in which yellow light is defined as a certain frequency-range of electromagnetic vibrations. But these language-games need to be distinguished, for they have different rules, and needless metaphysical puzzles will arise if we speak in a way that tries to straddle the boundaries between them. It is a confusion to wonder if I might perchance be able to see your sensation of yellowness in the same way that I can undoubtedly see and admire your daffodils; and the remedy for this confusion lies in gaining a clearer overview of our colour-words and the rules governing their use in different language-games.

Yes, it *is* simple. Wittgenstein's method is to struggle for such an 'overview' in thousands of particular cases. It corresponds to the feeling for the world as a limited whole in his early philosophy: it is the only bit of transcendence he allows, and he uses it to persuade us to accept his linguistic naturalism, his radical humanism and voluntarism without repining or feeling that we have lost anything. His motive is religious in that he is indeed bringing us back to Jewishness, away from gnostic fantasies and metaphysical illusions and back to common life and the primacy of the practical and the ethical. The resulting view of the world is not flat and dull like the Marxist one, for Wittgenstein is second to none in his capacity to provoke wonder; and it is not sceptical, for in his last writings he develops a novel and subtle critique of scepticism. Nor should it too hastily be described as religiously inadequate. Until quite recently an immense amount of discussion of Wittgenstein's religious views had taken place on the basis of very little evidence: some rather garbled and obscure notes on three lectures of about 1938, the 'Remarks on Frazer's *Golden Bough*', and a few other scraps. On the whole, Wittgenstein's strictly philosophical work says rather little about religion. But in *Culture and Value* (1980) there has appeared a collection of personal notes in which he does express religious views, and they show him as standing firmly in the tradition of Kierkegaard:

> It strikes me that a religious belief could only be something like a passionate commitment to a system of reference. Hence, although it's *belief*, it's really a way of living, or a way of assessing life. It's passionately

seizing hold of *this* interpretation. Instruction in a religious faith, therefore, would have to take the form of a portrayal, a description, of that system of reference while at the same time being an appeal to conscience. And this combination would have the result in the pupil himself, of his own accord, passionately taking hold of the system of reference. It would be as though someone were first to let me see the hopelessness of my situation and then show me the means of rescue until, of my own accord, or not at any rate led to it by my instructor, I ran to it and grasped it.

Wittgenstein is still a clear non-realist in theology:

The way you use the word 'God' does not show whom you mean – but, rather, what you mean.
God's essence is supposed to guarantee his existence – what this really means is that what is here at issue is not the existence of something.

Since most people have not yet moved over to the new point of view, most people will doubtless judge Wittgenstein to be an 'atheist', a word which historically has been used as a quasi-political smear-word to brand innovators – including, at one time, the early Christians. But study of his now-published thoughts on religion will, I think, show that although he always insisted that his own religious level was very low one, he does carry a great deal of what is most precious in religious belief through with him into his new outlook. If faith was able to survive past transitions, from Hebraism to Platonism, to Aristotelianism and to Kantianism, then why should it not be able to survive a similar mutation today?

The human being is the best picture of the human soul.

When Plato looked at the world, the thought uppermost in his mind was that of *Being*. He saw reality as a hierarchy of different levels of being, and thought that since man is naturally oriented towards being, there must be a distinct mode of knowledge appropriate to each of its grades. The supreme goal of life was the contemplation by the highest means of the highest Being. When Descartes looked about him his first thought was of *knowledge* and how to gain it, so that he constructed the world as the object of his knowledge. But when Wittgenstein looks about him he sees a word of *meaning*. It is not an easy viewpoint to reach without long training in philosophy. Not many people see that in everything that matters questions of meaning come first, but for Wittgenstein it is so. Astonishingly, he overcomes existence: it ceases to be the first question. For him the world of objective beings out there does not come first, nor does the individual knowing subject come first, but questions of meaning and the struggle for understanding come first. Existence is ascribed and knowledge-claims are made only *within* language-games, whose rules must first be understood: and because meaning is not privately but publicly established, Wittgenstein finds himself already in a common world, the marvellous world of language. Nietzsche also saw this far, but then as a heroic individualist he rejected crowd-meaning and crowd-truth and set out to create new meanings and truths of his own; whereas Wittgenstein as a religious man respects the world of public meanings in which he finds himself and struggles, not for Being or for knowledge, but simply for – understanding. He is not a behaviourist or a materialist for whom an objective physical reality comes first, nor is he an empiricist or idealist for whom private sensations or mental processes come first. For him, language comes first. In our material-object language we postulate and constitute a public physical world, and in our language about sensations, mental processes and the like we postulate and constitute an inner world of mind: but in the last resort there is nothing but the facts about our linguistic practices, and the ways in which they are interwoven with the forms of life they have been developed to serve.

One of these forms of life is the religious life. The overview method, by which we look at religious language and try to see clearly how it works in the religious life, shows us that a religious faith functions as a guidance-system. It provides us with a body of images, standards for self-assessment and goals that we can use as an itinerary to find our way through life. The overview does not provide any glimpse of a heavenly realm or any religious metaphysics: it returns us simply to the practice of religion. When Wittgenstein says that the religion of the future will have to be extremely ascetical, he means that it must learn to be content with practice alone, because in the end that is all we have in any sphere.

Evaluation

Near the end of his life, while packing his notebooks and manuscripts in a hotel in Dublin, Wittgenstein said to a friend:

> Bach wrote on the title page of his *Orgenbuchlein*, 'To the glory of the most high God, and that my neighbour may be benefited thereby.' That is what I would have liked to say about my own work.

This remark reflects the influence on him of Spengler's *The Decline of the West* (1918–22). In a vigorous culture with a strong public realm there are analogies and interconnections between all the great domains of human concern – religion, art, social organisation, mathematics and so on. A person who contributed to one of them contributed to all of them, adding a stone with his own name on it to the public building. So long as the unity of the culture is maintained, the work of individuals gets taken up into the public realm, and they can dedicate it 'to the glory of God and the benefit of my neighbour'. But Western culture has for generations been in decay through the dissolution of the analogies and connections between its different forms of life, and it is now no longer possible to dedicate one's work to the glory of God in the old way. We live, Wittgenstein believed, in an age without culture, in which men work for purely private ends.

The complaint is familiar to us by now, and Wittgenstein follows his predecessors in blaming the disaster on the rise of scientific-industrial civilisation with its tawdry belief in technical progress and its superficial conception of knowledge. Much of his philosophy can be seen as an attempt to provide a remedy: but it is a strangely ambiguous remedy.

Wittgenstein's thinking *can* be portrayed as deeply conservative. The terminology may be novel, but the argument is very like Edmund Burke's. Wittgenstein always sought to limit the pretensions and the destructive effects of science and to show that our whole lives, with all our own thoughts and beliefs, are inextricably bound up with historically-developed communal language-games and forms of life. The philosopher's job is to cure us of the illusion that we can escape from them. Deviants who think they can break out of the existing institutions have to be shown that there is nowhere for them to escape to. They thought they could see a way out; but in every case they can be shown that they had merely confused two different language-games. The only transcendence permitted is the one that allows you to see the deep wisdom of the status quo. Similarly, in religion, Wittgenstein *can* be seen as just one more nostalgic and impotent *emigré*, of the sort that may be seen attending the Orthodox liturgy in the West. Such a man disdains liberal and modernising theology and prefers to cling to what he regards as the genuine article, even though he is himself half-sceptical about it and his allegiance has become a private matter that he can no longer effectively integrate into the mainstream of his real life. Nietzsche would say harshly that such a man is haunted by God's ghost and feels a compulsion to go along each week and lay flowers on God's grave.

It is clearly possible, then, to portray Wittgenstein's teaching as being highly reactionary. It is directed towards understanding our world, and seems to leave no scope for changing it. Unlike Nietzsche, he has little to say about whether or how a creative individual can bring about fundamental change in art, or religion, or politics. Yet there is another side to him. He is also a Modernist and a radical humanist. He acknowledges the need to restore our sense of the unity of culture, but because he knows that the age of metaphysics is past and that henceforth the philosopher's task will be to reconcile us to a new situation, his proposed reunification of culture centres not around the idea of 'the glory of God', but around man and language. Although he could never be a Party man nor accept Marxist historicism and scientism, there were some things in Marxism that he admired, such as its moral passion, its exaltation of manual work, and its abhorrence of class distinctions. And he was sufficiently attracted to Russia to learn the language, to think of settling there, and to visit it in 1935.

Perhaps these conflicting interpretations of Wittgenstein merely reflect the fact that conservative and Marxist social thinking are Jacob and Esau, rivals and brothers. I have suggested that Wittgenstein's sense that a deep religious imperative requires us to renounce the illusions of metaphysics and accept the primacy of the practical and of our common life was derived from the Judaeo-Christian tradition; but as we have also seen, a similar move was made by Feuerbach in his use of the doctrine of the Incarnation to transform Christianity into radical humanism. Here and at a number of other points Wittgenstein reflects long-standing polarities in Western thought, between the individual and society, between conservatism and radicalism, between God-centred and man-centred outlooks, and between established order and radical creative freedom. Sometimes we think he has achieved, or at least points to, a wholly original synthesis; but at other times we feel his pessimism and sense of strain. His eremitical religious temperament is not quite at ease with the voluntaristic, social kind of humanism to which his thought has led him. He has re-established the primacy of the public realm, but has not quite been able to show how our contribution to it can still be offered 'to the glory of God'.

My own belief is that his ideas about religion were too conservative and nostalgic. He was left with a kind of mystical inertia, inherited from Schopenhauer, which expressed the utmost admiration for the highest levels of religious achievement, but declared them to be indescribable and beyond the reach of ordinary mortals here below. They were to be venerated from afar – which means, left marooned and ineffectual. In his return to the human and the practical, Wittgenstein left them behind so that they should not be profaned. His motive for doing this was certainly religious, but it was not Christian. God dies on the cross, outside the camp: that is, in Christianity the sacred precisely does not remain fenced-off and inviolable in the sanctuary, but unhesitatingly and unreservedly profanes itself. Had Wittgenstein been able deliberately to profane the sacred more thoroughly, his final outlook might have been more satis-factory to him, for he could have put religious ideas to a more creative, energetic and public use. As it was, his radical humanism remained tinged by a faint but unmistakable note of religious frustration and melancholy. He did not quite succeed in bringing about the full synthesis of faith and modernity.

Chapter 8
THE TURN OF THE TIDE

The liberation of faith

We have cleared the ground and collected some useful materials. It is time to start building the house. Where are the plans?

At the end of chapter 2 we ran into a paradox: René Descartes had an objective metaphysical God whose existence he had proved by pure reason, and yet he was not a conspicuously religious man at all. Blaise Pascal, by contrast, was intensely religious, the sort of person who will pay whatever price is asked for the saving kind of faith that his soul demands – and the price turned out to be that he must forfeit any rationally grounded assurance of objectivity. Here, we suggested, was an early example of a theme that is often met in modern religious thought: the claims of theological realism and the claims of religious seriousness pull in opposite directions. That is why a line of German theologians influenced by Kierkegaard have declared war on what they called objectifying theology, as if it were bad for religion that God should become too real.

How can this be? If we look back at Kierkegaard, the answer seems to be that if you have a God who provides for you an objective metaphysical resolution of the spiritual tensions of your life, then he makes you less religious. You have offloaded the polarities on to God, and you let him do the work of reconciling them; whereas Kierkegaard regards this as paganism and says that in Christianity the movement is in the opposite direction. For him, Christianity demands that we become subjective. The polarities and tensions of life ought not to be pushed away and resolved metaphysically, but should be internalised and experienced subjectively to the highest degree, so that we are forced to undergo the inner spiritual transformation which is Christianity's demand and promise. Following Luther, Kierkegaard insists that everything must be internalised. The problems of religion must not be solved abstractly in thought, but concretely in human existence. Theology must be translated into spirituality. Hence the attack on metaphysics and objectivity, and in the long run the development of a non-realist interpretation of religious belief.

If this is so, then Christianity's own inner logic points in the direction of an anthropocentric and voluntarist view of life, a radical Christian humanism. But, as Wittgenstein says, it is here walking on a tightrope and must be very careful about each step, for the progress of Hegel, Feuerbach and Marx out of Christianity towards radical *secular* humanism runs so closely parallel and uses so many of the same arguments. It is all too easy to slip from one to the other. Complaints about liberation theology and about Christian atheism arise when people suspect, rightly or wrongly, that the tightrope worker has taken a false step. Yet the risks must be taken. 'An honest religious thinker is like a tightrope walker': to be honest, you must walk the tightrope; to be religious, you must not fall off it.

The movement of thought involved here is towards non-realism, and we undertook to bear the question of realist versus non-realist interpretations of religious belief constantly in mind. We have done so, and can now begin to see quite new perspectives opening up.

Consider to begin with three twentieth-century figures whom we have met, Jung, Schweitzer and Wittgenstein. They were approximate contemporaries, German in linguistic and cultural background, and all of them influenced by Kant. Kant had been a metaphysical agnostic who had argued that our knowledge cannot be extended beyond the limits of possible experience, so that the existence of God as transcendent Creator cannot be proved by theoretical reason. God should rather be interpreted as a guiding ideal, not given in experience but instead functioning as the ultimate focus and goal of our intellectual and moral life.

Jung interprets Kant's teaching in accordance with his own psychological interests. He accepts the metaphysical agnosticism, and concerns himself solely with the human idea of God. Because the psyche is an organism it is self-balancing and also goal-seeking. It has its own inner tendency to correct its course and keep moving towards its proper fulfilment. God is the Self, the goal of a fully integrated and unified personality towards which our psychic life tends. But the Self is not merely an inert ideal limit, for because Jung's thinking is teleological he sees the Self as being already present and active in our psyches as an archetype. In his official *Collected Works* (1953–71) Jung always means by God simply the immanent God-image in the psyche, though in his popular works, and especially in the beautiful *Memories, Dreams and*

Reflections (1963), he accommodates his language to popular usage and seems to speak of God in more nearly realistic terms. The concession is, however, only apparent, and does not imply any change in Jung's position. He justifies it on the ground that his own internalised and psychological interpretation of God is after all the true one, and fully expresses the substance of what the ordinary person means by God. From the religious point of view it does not matter very much that the ordinary person does not make a clear distinction between mythical and ontological realities, and Jung is willing to use the popular language – provided that he can use it to convey the true inward meaning of God.

However, people grasped enough of what was going on here to become curious about Jung's real position. Their question was regularly posed in the form, 'Does Jung really believe in God?' Yet putting the question in this way was an example of approaching a religious issue with fixed and ready-made religious meanings in one's mind. So to frame it was to assume that we all of us already know what is meant by God, to assume that the realist view of the meaning of God is in possession of the field, to assume that anyone who is not as willing as we are to take it for granted is being ambiguous and evasive and needs to be pinned down, and to assume that the only real problem is to compel Jung to come clean and say on which side of the line he really stands. In short: 'Is he one of Us, or one of Them; is he with us or against us?' Realism is political, in the sense that people frame religious questions in realist terms because they feel a need to draw lines, to classify, and to divide the sheep from the goats. The hidden motive behind the question, 'Does Jung really believe in God or not?' was to find out whether he was friend or foe, and as such the question was philistine, for at a deeper level it showed a wilful reluctance to allow Jung to explain himself on his own terms. As we have said before, people are much more deeply conservative and harder to shift in their perception of religious meanings than they are over matters of religious truth. Many a person is converted into Christianity, or out of it, without ever properly examining his own view of religious *meanings* at all. A theologian who tries to change people's perception of the meaning of some doctrine will be much more sharply attacked than one who simply denies its truth. Nevertheless, the question that should be asked of Jung is not, 'Does he believe in God?' but, 'What does Jung mean by God, and what part does the idea of God play in Jung's thinking and in his conception of the religious life?' The question about meaning is much more interesting than the question of truth, and is prior to it. Indeed, when it is fully answered there is nothing left to ask.

If we turn next to Albert Schweitzer, we find a very different character. As a student he wrote a dissertation on Kant's philosophy of religion, and was also much influenced by Goethe, by Schopenhauer's view of nature, and by Nietzsche's diagnosis of the state of European culture. At the same time Schweitzer was always a Protestant minister. However far-out he became he still liked to preach, and he led prayers readily. Most remarkably of all, he was a Protestant rationalist in the heroic mould and of a type now extinct, for it was second nature to him to assume that so long as he was uncompromisingly loyal to truth he could not be being disloyal to Christ. Finally, Schweitzer was a man of the will, whose life was given to an ethical deed.

In Schweitzer's version of Kantianism, therefore, God is primarily the personified ground of the ethical will in us. Yet because he is a theologian Schweitzer also feels the need for at least a minimal cosmological idea of God. His answer is in effect to identify God with Schopenhauer's 'will', everywhere present in nature and in ourselves as an amoral striving will-to-live or Life Force, a power that is riven with conflict and internally at odds with itself. The believer's task in life is thus fundamentally ethical. He must throw himself into an unavailing ethical struggle to unify God and to make his goodness actual, by attempting to bring nature's blind and amoral will to live into subjection to the ethical will to love. This heroic but inevitably unsuccessful ethical battle to bring the world into line with the requirements of morality is for Schweitzer the very essence of faith in God. It echoes Jesus' tragic heroism in being willing to go voluntarily to his death in the vain but morally necessary hope that by doing so he might force the arrival of the Kingdom of God, and it also echoes the Kantian hope that in the long run nature and morality may be brought into harmony. Yet Schweitzer continues to insist on the tragic character of his conception of faith by his dual emphasis on Jesus' failure to bring in the Kingdom and on his own inability to see any good providence or moral order in the course of world events. The ethic of Reverence for Life remains a cry of protest, and an obligatory impossibility.

If this interpretation of Schweitzer's view of God is correct, as I think it is, then it is one of the most remarkable pieces of 'radical theology' in the history of Christian thought, and perhaps the most purely voluntaristic. But again it is philistine to ask, 'Well then, does Schweitzer really believe in God: does he think that God exists?', for the question is ill-framed. He is another non-realist, although quite different from Jung; and to do him justice we must study him with an open mind and find out how the idea of God actually works in his thinking.

The cases of Jung and Schweitzer help us to see why in the later

Annie Besant, shortly
after her marriage

Vivekananda,
photographed in
Chicago in 1893

Nietzsche in the last
year of his life, 1900

The house at Sils
Maria, where Nietzsche
lodged in the summers
of the 1880s

Ludwig Wittgenstein

Gustav Klimt's portrait
of Wittgenstein's sister
Margarethe, painted in
1905

The house designed and
built by Wittgenstein
for his sister in Vienna,
1926–8

From the same period,
Wittgenstein's only
known work of
sculpture, a bronze
made in the studio of
his friend Michael
Dobril

In the 1930s
Wittgenstein conducted
his seminars in his own
rooms in Trinity
College, Cambridge,
here refurnished for
filming. His way of life
was austere

Left In a medieval
cathedral worshippers
are arranged as if in a
procession led by the
clergy and the choir.
The church is *in via*, on
the way; and this life is
seen as a pilgrimage
towards the heavenly
world above, Jerusalem
the Golden.

Above In a modern
cathedral (as here at
Liverpool) the focus of
worship is not located
beyond the congre-
gation in a transcendent
world above, but at the
centre of the community's
life in this world. In the
Middle Ages – as in
Dante – only the worship
of Heaven had this
circular layout. It seems
that with the disappear-
ance of the old linear
progression (vestibule,
nave, chancel, sanctuary)

the old two-worlds
cosmology has been
abandoned. Heaven
has come to earth

An unfinished agenda:
Christian art produced
thousands of images of
a mother rejoicing in
her infant son. Similar
representations of a
mother with a daughter
are rare, as this example
(St Anne with her
daughter, the Virgin
Mary, by Murillo)
reminds us. Through
the figure of Christ, the
male nude was invested
with religious value
from the Middle Ages;
whereas the female
nude remained secular
or pagan.

One of the very rare
examples of a female
nude treated with
compassion and
religious feeling: an
early drawing by
Van Gogh, expressing
his concern about the
condition of women in
his time

Wittgenstein concern for meaning entirely replaces the traditional concerns for objective existence and knowledge of what exists. Always we must ask what kind of job the idea of God does in the language and what role it plays in the way people shape their lives. Religion in the twentieth century has become entirely human: Jung's God is part of what Jung is, and Schweitzer's God is part of what Schweitzer is, and there is no third party. Each has to be studied on his own terms, and we may find ourselves responding to the one or the other as we seek to work out our own view; but however that might be, Jung's God is logically embedded in Jung's thought, and Schweitzer's in his; and in each case we need to get a clear overview of the working of the life-and-thought totality in question.

That is not always easy. In Jung's case I for one feel a need to press on and to ask if all his talk about the psyche, the collective unconscious, the archetypes and the rest has a coherent logic and makes a sense that I can make my own. In fact, I have some doubts; but supposing that I were able to satisfy myself on these points and to gain a full and clear understanding of the role of God in Jung's thinking, then I would have gone as far as it is possible to go. There is no further *question* to ask, because God's existence as a topic does not arise: all that remains is the *decision* as to how far I wish to make this way of speaking and living my own. On Wittgenstein's view, shared by many modern philosophers, philosophy is not a superscience that finds out superfacts beyond the reach of other sciences: it is essentially a quest for understanding of things that are already before us, plain to view. It assembles reminders, reshuffles the elements of the problem – and that is all. Meaning is everything.

On Wittgenstein's personal position, a former student wrote in 1955:

> . . . I do not know whether he can be said to have been 'religious' in any but a trivial sense of the word. Certainly he did not have a Christian faith. But neither was his view of life pagan, un-Christian, as was Goethe's. To say that Wittgenstein was not a pantheist is to say something important. 'God does not reveal himself *in* the world', he wrote in the *Tractatus*. The thought of God, he said, was above all for him the thought of the fearful judge.

More recently published evidence now obliges us to modify that verdict. In the early Norway notebooks Wittgenstein does in fact at least toy with pantheism. Later, the Kantian and anthropocentric heritage is certainly very strong, and there is no doubt that Wittgenstein never believed Christian dogma in the realist way. Dogma 'puts a brake on thinking', and makes the crude mistake of suggesting that religious beliefs are theoretically or objectively true. Thus one can indeed say that he never held Christian *beliefs*, in the plural. Yet, on the other hand, his practical response to Christianity was usually wholehearted and direct:

> ... Christianity says that sound doctrines are all useless. That you have to change your life. (Or the *direction* of your life.)

Wittgenstein's biography, taken with his concurrent personal notes, shows that he made repeated attempts all through his life to answer that call. Furthermore, his notes show that religious states were familiar to him:

> Christianity is not a doctrine, not, I mean, a theory about what has happened and will happen to the human soul, but a description of something that actually takes place in human life. For 'consciousness of sin' is a real event and so are despair and salvation through faith.

A believer is a person who in 'infinite torment' hears religion's practical demand, 'Do this! Think like that!' It offers him 'rules of life dressed up in pictures'. If, and only if, he is desperate enough will he recognise in these rules and pictures a Gospel of salvation, and will 'penitently open his heart' and seize them for himself.

The account is non-realist and voluntarist, but it is not religiously impoverished. 'What inclines even me to believe in Christ's resurrection?', asks Wittgenstein in a note of 1937; and he replies almost in the voice of Pascal. A dead Christ would be unable to help, and it is help that is needed. This help is found, not through speculation, but by an act of the heart – that is, of the will and the passions. 'It is *love* that believes the Resurrection. . . . What combats doubt is, as it were, *redemption*.' The believer who cleaves to Christ in his heart, not in a theoretical but in a practical way, becomes like someone whose weight is now suspended from heaven rather than being planted on the earth. His position appears to be the same as the next man's, but he can act quite differently.

Wittgenstein is tightrope-walking again, for what he has just said runs perilously close to the French sceptic Renan's statement that it was his disciples' love for him that had the divine power to bring about the resurrection of Jesus. What keeps Wittgenstein on his tightrope is his non-realism. He is not pretending that his thoughts are leading him towards dogmatic fideism. Dogmatic fideism is an attempt to argue from the heart's need to dogmatic truth. It says: 'Reason cannot determine whether the doctrines are true or not, so I am at liberty simply to choose, and nobody else is in any position to blame me for my choice: so I choose to believe in the dogmatic truth of the Resurrection, because of the faith-experience that it has made possible for me'.

Wittgenstein, however, is not saying this. He is a voluntarist, and not a dogmatic fideist. He thinks that dogmatic fideism is irrational, rejects the idea that dogmas can be theoretically true, and treats them instead as being no more than expressive symbols of states of the soul. As such, they are 'inexpressibly wonderful'. Thus Wittgenstein at least sometimes knows the states of soul and practises the faith inwardly; but he is not a fideist, for he does not believe the theology – or rather, he sees the theology as providing a symbolic vocabulary for *expressing* the states of soul, but not as providing a theoretical *justification* for religious experience and practice. He gives religion precedence over theology, the creed being simply the expression of faith.

Most orthodox believers work the other way round, deducing their religion from their theology. As they see it, the theoretical truth of the theology justifies the practice of the religion. The way of life is deduced from the supernatural facts, the 'ought' from the 'is'. Wittgenstein reverses the order: for him the primary reality is the states, acts and experiences of the soul, and the theology is no more than a linguistic expression of it. Religion is to theology as the performed symphony is to the musical score: a musical notation is doubtless a very clever invention and a most useful thing, but the score is after all only a set of instructions for performing the music. It is not itself the music, and it is a logical error to suppose that it adds anything to the music. It exists merely to facilitate repetition of the music in other performances, just as the baptismal Creed was a device for transmitting the Christian life. The musical score provides useful material for discussion, at least among people who can read music and imagine what a real performance would be like, but it does not *justify* the performances that are based on it: it merely provides directions for them. As it is in music, so it is in religion: the performed life is the primary thing, and the doctrine is merely a set of rules. Wittgenstein was after all a musician.

Another analogy: imagine a believer who suffers, as many have done, a total loss of the older dogmatic type of faith and comes instead to think that we are merely the ephemeral products of an indifferent universe that will in due course extinguish us and everything that we hold dear. He experiences a sense of transience, worthlessness, despair and a desperate need for value ('How can I, in the little time that I have, become something of real worth?') – and through these thoughts finds himself, to his own astonishment, beginning to become a Christian all over again, but in a quite new way. His deeply-felt encounter with the inexorable limits of the human condition has actually brought about within him the first movements of the soul towards faith, and he is now ready to grasp it with an entirely fresh zeal because never before did he feel so great a need of it. It is only by passionately committing his life to this way, these rules, these pictures, that he can find the worth and the deliverance from futility that he needs. So he becomes a believer, but in the frank recognition that everything is now a different way round from the way it was before. Yet he does not have any feeling of inferiority about this reversal. Quite the opposite, for he now sees that over the centuries the old dogmatic theology that was so comforting (so very comforting) had in fact grown so big, so highly-coloured and so objectified that it had turned into a great painted screen that people used to shield themselves from the truth of life. Its collapse was long overdue and a blessing in disguise, for it had forced him back to the primal experiences from which authentic faith always had begun. The dogmatic theology, ideally, ought to have remained simply a representation of those experiences which would force people to confront them, enable them to recognise them, and show the path through them. Unfortunately, over time and for reasons to do with institutional power and our human timorousness and love of ease and security, it had allowed itself to become horribly perverted from its proper function. Eventually, people urge all sorts of reasons for keeping that screen, reasons pastoral, aesthetic and conservationist, and they fight hard to keep it. Yet whether they like it or not, the time will come when a religious iconoclast will rise up and say that it is now better to knock the screen down than to go on struggling to prop it up. Hence a Luther arises to attack late-medieval Catholicism, and then later, a Kierkegaard to attack in turn the illusions of bourgeois Lutheranism.

In the English-speaking world the first explicit and consciously non-realist philosophies of religion began to be put forward in the late 1950s. They were neither numerous nor worked out in any great detail, and it was then widely assumed that they were merely reductionist, and could be dismissed as being no more than last-ditch attempts to save something of religious values and attitudes on the part of people who were on the way out, having already lost the main substance of religious belief. Indeed, that is probably the majority opinion to this day, in spite of the fact that Christianity has been developing for so long in a non-realist direction. Consciousness of what is actually happening is resisted until the very last minute, even on the part of those who are themselves leading the advance. It is as if we climb slowly through the mist for generations before at long last the day comes when the air clears enough for us to be able to look back over the ground we have traversed. Only in the last few years has the non-realist point of view finally gained enough altitude and confidence to look around and see more clearly where it is and where it has come from. To its amazement, it sees a whole new landscape. It has after all a pedigree, and even a very ancient one. The Old Testament can now be seen to have profoundly voluntaristic and expressive in its use of religious language, as we remarked in chapter 3. Old theological maxims like *lex orandi, lex credendi* (that is, the nature of true belief is determined by the nature of true piety) and the rejection of gnosticism stand out as landmarks. So does the mystical tradition, with its emphasis on the limits of religious language, the need to go beyond religious objectification, and the ultimate supersession of knowledge by love.

Still more important, the new vantage-point shows up more clearly than before the full diversity and richness of religious thought in the critical period, especially since Kant. As we have seen in the cases of Jung, Schweitzer and Wittgenstein, the way to get the best out of them is not to ask the plain man's political-realist question, 'Does this man think that God exists or not?', a question that narrows and deforms the issues, but instead to set aside *existence* in favour of *meaning* and ask the much more illuminating question, 'What job does God do, what part does he play, to what use is the idea of God put in this man's thought?' From the new non-realist viewpoint a person believes in God if the idea of God does some real work and plays a constitutive part in his thinking and in shaping his way of life; for as Wittgenstein says, a word that does no real work is like an idle cog in a machine. It can be removed without making any difference. And when we looked at the part God plays in the thought of each of those three figures we found that he was important to all of them, but in very different ways. Modern non-realist theologies are in fact extremely diverse, in a way that is completely hidden by the philistine judgment that all three of those men were, in traditional realist terms, mere 'atheists'. The non-realist way of looking at them shows that however heterodox they may be in traditional terms they are in fact genuine twentieth-century believers, and very interestingly different from each other.

All of which shows that we already live and have been living for a long time in the new era, the age of the artist-theologian who offers us a personal vision of the religious life. Realism is long dead and gone: we live in a time when religion has become fully human, when theology is like art, and when we use the available resources as aids to our own spiritual formation, but must in the last resort find each of us his own unique voice.

Critics will complain that I have prejudged the issue by choosing as my examples a group of deviant and marginal figures. In fact, though, the result would have been just the same if I had taken a group of mainline theologians of the modern period. Among the best and most representative names are Karl Barth, Rudolf Bultmann, Paul Tillich, Karl Rahner and Wolfhart Pannenberg. But those five, also, have produced highly diverse and similarly incommensurable theologies, each of which has to be studied as if were an individual and more or less autonomous work of art that expresses a personal vision: is it not the case that in the modern period we have come to speak of 'creative' theologians? In each of the five cases there is a philosophical background that shapes the thought at a deep level, and in which Kant, Hegel and Kierkegaard inevitably bulk large. But the fact is that Barth's way of talking about God is intelligible only internally and on Barth's own terms, and Bultmann's way of talking about God is similarly intelligible only on Bultmann's own terms, and so on. So markedly internal are the criteria of meaning in each case that it no longer makes sense to assess them as realists; that is, as if they were offering recognisable portraits in slightly different styles of an objective Being with known lineaments who is independently established in the language. Barth's God is part of Barth's theology, and Bultmann's of Bultmann's, and that is that. In short, they are artist-theologians. In art, as in theology, there was indeed once a time when there was an established public symbolic language that people understood, and the individual painter who presented his personal celebration of some great public fact or theme was content to operate within fairly tight limits. He did not see his own work as a personal expression, but was content to act in the service of a great publicly-established reality that existed independently of him. Today, though, that is no longer the case. The art-work is not measured against a great public mythic reality that it exists to celebrate and to glorify, but is assessed as a personal creative expression. So it now is with theology also.

Yet, if in the modern period people's varied personal visions of God are no longer connected together by any agreed public metaphysical referent, if there is no longer any hub that the spokes run to and which holds them all together, is not our talk of God becoming hopelessly vague and equivocal? I imagine this objection being raised, because I guess that the old realist Adam in you will not lie down. (He would still keep raising his head, even if I wrote a thousand pages.) But the objection shows how realism confuses people about the true meaning of the word God. The common factor is in fact still there, and is the same as it always was; for a man's god is that which he worships, that which has over-riding authority in his life, that which matters most to him, that which most profoundly determines his sense of himself and the aim of his life, that which expresses the deepest truth of what he is. There are people, says St Paul sourly, 'whose god is their belly', and he is here using the word 'God' in this primal sense. Many writers of the eighteenth century recognised it, and called it the 'relative' use of the word. A man's talk of God reveals what Paul Tillich, whose thought ran close to non-realism, called his 'ultimate concern'. Show me your God, runs an old saying, and you show me what you are. Hence the intimate connection in Kierkegaard between faith in God and our life-task of 'becoming an individual': every human being who is serious about existence, who is not content to drift with the crowd towards death but seeks to set himself high ideals and to make his life something of worth, must formulate his own idea of God as the unifying symbol of the life-aim to which he is devoted.

It is possible for people, and even for a whole society, to lose faith in God. How can this happen? It happens, not primarily because they have decided that something they used to think existed does not after all exist, but because the available language about God has been allowed to become too narrow, stale and spiritually obsolete, and no longer functions as a satisfactory vehicle through which people can articulate their highest life-aims. The work of creative religious personalities is continually to enrich, to enlarge and sometimes to purge the available stock of religious symbols and idioms so that faith in God shall continue to be possible. Certainly if faith in God is to flourish in a society as diverse and rapidly-changing as our own, then the more diverse religious thought becomes the better; whereas if on the other hand it is confined to a ghetto, closely policed and told to restrict itself to reiterating the idioms of the past, then faith in God will die.

Unhappily, in many of the Churches today that is just what is happening. A nostalgic realist theology, whose spiritual life is far too narrow and which has lost the original breadth of the idea of God, is functioning as an ideology of decline. Decline created it, and it in turn perpetuates the decline. By contrast, all vital modern religious thought since Kant has been (unconsciously, more often than consciously) creative, expressive and non-realist.

Nor is there any mystery about why the change in religious thought should have begun just then. In pre-critical philosophy people believed in an objective intelligible order, to which the human mind sought to accommodate itself. For Plato this order was the world of Ideas, the noumenal world; Christians included it all within the Divine Mind. But Kant's great critical examination of knowledge, his enquiry into the process by which the human mind converts raw and formless experience into ordered objective knowledge, had led him to a revolutionary change of viewpoint. He found that the mind does not receive objectivity: it confers it. Certainly there is a world of ideas, a great set of intelligible principles and essences by which the world of sense is compelled to become an ordered cosmos. It includes the principles of logic and mathematics, moral values, categories, theories, laws and so on. Only, it is not in a world above, but in our own heads. In Kantian jargon, it is not *transcendent*, located in a supernatural world, but *transcendental*, demonstrable by analysis as a condition of the possibility of our knowledge of this world. It is not *beyond*, on the far side of experience, but tucked away unnoticed on the *near* side of experience.

In Kant's own analysis, we must be committed to just one particular set of principles and categories by which we order our experience to make our world. Later critical philosophy is more cautious: we cannot prove that we are right to construct our world in just the way we do; we can only show that it is just a fact that our culture and our language order the world thus and not otherwise. Either way, the crucial point is that the power that orders the world and turns chaos into cosmos is no longer ascribed to an objective metaphysical Creator, but simply to the human mind. There is no fixed and eternal intelligible world-order prior to us; there is only our own historically developed construction of the world order.

This 'Copernican revolution', as Kant called it, spelled the end of the old realist metaphysical notion of God. The objective God of realism was inseparably bound up with the Platonic idea of an objective and eternal intelligible order. When that order came to be seen as a human product, when for example it was realised that scientific theories are not discoveries but inventions, then the God of realism came to be seen as a mythic projection of the human mind. Feuerbach, Marx and others could regard the believer's objective God only as his own magnified mirror-image. To them it seemed that religious belief was necessarily pre-critical in outlook, for it insisted on crediting God with cosmos-ordering and legislative powers that Kant had proved to be in fact our own.

As a result, theologians found themselves in a very awkward position. They wished to claim that their own thinking was also critical, and yet they (or many of them) wished to continue to defend some version of the realist view of God. How could this be done? Hegel's philosophy portrayed God as immanent within the creative world-ordering powers of the human mind itself; but because over the millennia human beings have had many different forms of consciousness and have constructed their worlds in many different ways, those who wish to make God immanent within human thinking will have to make God into an historically evolving being – a very considerable transformation of the traditional idea of God, which ends by making God into little more than a personification of the developing collective mind of all humanity. If Hegel is the principal father of the liberal theology which tries to keep a cosmic idea of God, he also reveals the reason why it amounts in the end to little more than a vapidly optimistic metaphor. Hegel's *Geist* is the mere ghost of God: because he is no more than a personification of the way things are actually going, he makes no serious demands upon us.

Hegel is the chief begetter of liberal theology; and Kierkegaard is the classic case of radical theology's revolt against it in the attempt to restore religious seriousness. Kierkegaard is the sworn enemy of all those who see religion as merging the individual into a larger Whole within which the polarities of life are objectively reconciled. He detests everything objective, metaphysical, cosmic and world-historical. He insists that Christianity requires us to fulfil the fundamental human life-task of becoming individuals, and must not be presented in any way that encourages us to offload the responsibility for that task. Any promised objective metaphysical resolution of life's spirtual tensions that makes things easier for us must be fought as a temptation. Kierkegaard is seeking to go beneath realist ideas of God to the primal meaning of God as *my* God, my life-aim, my spiritual task and goal; and '*my* God' is not a metaphysical being but the expression of my spiritual commitment to my life-aim. Most of modern religious thought derives from Hegel and Kierkegaard. Hegel shows a realist idea of God becoming so fuzzy, metaphorical and indefinite that it eventually dissolves away altogether. Kierkegaard shows that the way to restore religious seriousness and depth to life is to give up the cosmic and metaphysical side of theistic belief, and to make faith in God subjective and existential. In so doing he points to modern non-realism; but the task of liberating faith from the Babylonian captivity of realism was very onerous, and he shows a degree of strain and inner disturbance that repels many people. Only much later could it become clear to us that we have moved out into a larger and freer atmosphere.

Critical spirituality

Many religions began as ways of transcendence, attempts to see the human self and its world as if from outside, and as a whole. The Teacher sought to compel his audience to make an imaginative leap and consider how their lives might look when seen from an absolute viewpoint, such as the all-seeing eye of a God about to come in Judgment. If it could be made abruptly enough, the sudden shift from a worldly to an eternal standpoint for self-assessment was intensely consciousness-raising or awakening. People saw that their lives hitherto had been absurd, futile and lacking in integrity of aim. It was urgently necessary to repent and to begin living a new, examined life.

If an act of self-criticism was in this way an essential step to religious awakening, one might have expected religion to welcome as an ally the huge development of critical ways of thinking in modern times. If critical thinking sets out to question assumptions, expose pretensions, demystify institutions and rigorously to test everything that passes for knowledge, then surely it is only doing in a modern way the kind of demolition-job that was done by the prophets and teachers of old? It ought to be welcomed as our modern 'natural theology' that prepares the way for the Gospel of the New Life.

Furthermore, religion itself insists that this process of self-examination and purification must continue unceasingly. The believer must learn to recognise the imperfection and inadequacy of all human religious ideas, and to follow an inner path of renunciation and progressive purging of illusions. Unless the life of faith is a continual effort of self-criticism and self-transcendence, religion quickly decays into rigidity and becomes superstitious and unspiritual.

Yet in spite of all this a strange reversal seems to have taken place, as if religion having gained its initial victory thereafter resists criticism to protect its own position. People fear the corrosive power of critical thinking and see it as hostile to faith. Whereas critical thinking can never simply accept the prevailing assumptions but must always ask for explanations and reasons, religion comes to be used precisely to protect a community's set of basic assumptions against questioning. Religion is seen as being sacred, revealed, authoritative, communal and traditional. It sets up and protects the reality that people live by, and treats doubt as impious and sinful. It instinctively regards the critical thinker as a subversive, and is willing to mobilise formidable sanctions against him.

Many years ago I debated religious questions publicly with a Muslim. He gave firm and clear answers to every question that was raised, by citing the Qu'ran. I pointed out to him that if I were also a Muslim I would indeed share his dogmatic belief in the authority of the Qu'ran over all religious questions, and we might then join in an internal Islamic debate about his exegesis of the Qu'ran; but since I was not a Muslim it was surely unreasonable for him to expect me to be persuaded by a simple appeal to the Qu'ran's dogmatic authority. At the very least he owed it to me as a non-Muslim to give me some reasons for taking the Qu'ran to be authoritative. His reply was simply to cite the Qu'ran in support of its own authority, just as some fundamentalist Christians cite biblical texts to prove the authority of the Bible. It is hard to see what else he could have done, because Islam seems to rule out in principle any suggestion that there might be a higher court of appeal by which the Qu'ran could be judged and vindicated. The Qu'ran is itself the ultimate court of appeal and criterion of truth.

When different religions and cultures meet it is very easy for each of them to perceive the dogmatism of the other. I would have taken a further step and have become a critical thinker if after my encounter with the Muslim I had said to myself, 'I wonder if perhaps my own thinking is similarly constrained by deep assumptions of which I am unaware?', and had set out to look for them.

This may be done at various levels. I can by introspection seek out my basic presuppositions, question them, and so work backwards in search of simple and lucid criteria of genuine knowledge. I may reflect on the nature of perception and understanding, and so try to discover from within the nature and limits of the knowledge possible to me. Or I may conduct my enquiry at a more communal level by beginning with language, on the ground that all my thought and communication is so mediated by language that the limits of the language available to me must determine what is knowable by me. But however I proceed, I am sure to move towards the conclusion that the theory of the nature and limits of the knowable must precede and determine the theory of what there is; and this in turn will lead me towards an anthropocentric outlook. Both of these two points are very important for religion.

The theory of knowledge comes first, I say, because critical thinking demands that all knowledge-claims without exception be tested by criteria that can be established and applied within the domain of common human thought and experience. Critical thinking works within the human realm, and the longer we examine our cognitive powers and our language, the more clearly we see that human knowledge is just human knowledge, provisional, fallible and man-made; so that there is no sense in supposing that we might somehow transcend the limits of human thought and experience. I can take off my spectacles and see how the world looks without them, but I cannot take off my mind and see the world from an absolute point of view, nor can I step outside the limits of language and describe the relation of language to reality in non-linguistic terms; and if I reflect about this situation a little longer I see that there can be no cause for lament here, for I cannot imagine how things could be otherwise. Human knowledge is human knowledge, and the world exists for us only within the sphere of the humanly knowable. Pre-critical thinking often began by laying down what there is out there in reality, and then introduced human beings and asked how they could come to a

THE SEA OF FAITH

true knowledge of it, by accommodating themselves to the real. But
critical thinking abandons realism and reverses the order. It begins with
our cognitive powers, our language and our social relations and then
shows that our world must have the general features that they prescribe.

Critical historians and anthropologists nowadays regularly work in
this way when they are interpreting some remote or exotic period or
tribe. They show how the language, the thought-forms, the culture, the
beliefs and the view of the world held in that milieu make up what is, on
its own terms, an intelligible and coherent human totality. Beliefs are
datable human products, with provenances as obvious to a specialist as
they are in the case of any other human product. And not only that, but
historians, being self-critical people, are well aware that their own books
are also period pieces; so that an experienced medievalist, for example,
after having read a work of medieval history, will have no difficulty in
saying when it was written and what was the ideological standpoint of its
author.

Our hypothetical historian is well aware of the extent to which his
colleagues and predecessors viewed their data in the light of theories, and
this brings me to another characteristic of critical thinking: it has become
highly conscious of theory. It recognises that we see the world in terms of
theories, that most theories are pretty short-lived, and that they are
themselves among the most typical products of the ages in which they
reign. This realisation has been very consciousness-raising. Critical
thinking is thinking that it is conscious of itself and its limitations,
conscious of its own theories, and conscious that all theory is man-made
and provisional. A critical thinker seeks to emancipate his own thinking
from the tyranny of theory. He learns regularly to perform little thought-
experiments in which he sets aside the theory in terms of which he usually
looks at the phenomena, and tries looking at them in the light of another
theory. Theories become for him not shackles but tools, to be picked up,
tried out, used where they are helpful, and discarded as soon as they
become unhelpful. Thus his view of theory is pragmatic rather than
dogmatic.

As we see most clearly in the case of the scientific method, critical
thinking uses methodical doubt as a way to truth. Knowledge grows by
the negative method of eliminating errors. There are those who see
religious belief as drawing its strength from steadfast adherence to a
single framework of belief. If they are right, they have to reckon with the
fact that science draws its peculiar strength from precisely the opposite
temper of mind. Open, sceptical and puritanical, it is (or should be)
systematically dedicated to self-criticism. It demythologises, it detects

and discards illusions with almost obsessive zeal. In terms of traditional dogmatic thinking such a temper of mind is subversive, destructive and nihilistic. It seems to recognise nothing as 'sacred', in the sense of being exempt from criticism; and yet it has proved to be the most powerful way to knowledge yet devised.

What happens when this spirit is applied to human affairs, to ethics, politics and religion? The idea that human beings may and do progressively advance in consciousness and freedom by critically diagnosing and discarding their own illusions was developed by Bruno Bauer, a follower of Hegel. Subsequently, Karl Marx produced a critical theory of society which aimed to show how the social relations in which we are embedded constrain our thinking in ways in which we ourselves unwittingly collude, with the result that we are systematically deceived as to our true interests. Sigmund Freud rather similarly set out to show how we may become disabled by self-imposed psychological constraints of whose true nature we are unaware. Both thinkers proposed practical paths to deliverance, by following which we can come to a clearer view of our situation and our real interests, and so act more rationally and effectively.

Like Martin Luther, Marx and Freud see the natural man as being in a state of captivity, in which his understanding is darkened and his will in bondage to powers beyond his conscious control. But they were both vehement opponents of dogmatic religion. For them, it was critical thinking that opened the way from bondage to freedom. But lest we be thought to treat them with too much respect, let us add one last feature of critical thinking. It is especially suspicious of theories that are too comprehensive, that explain everything, that fill out the world and resist refutation because they have taken care to anticipate all the objections that can be brought against them. Such theories are sometimes described as incorporating 'blocks to falsifiability', in the form of explanations of why anyone should disagree with them and arguments prepared in advance to dispose of any counter-evidence that may be adduced. In so far as either Marxism or psychoanalysis is converted into an all-encompassing and irrefutable body of dogma of this kind, it of course ceases to be truly critical.

We have looked at some of the main features of critical thinking. It is free enquiry, which does not accept any premises dogmatically. For it 'nothing is sacred', in the significant use of that phrase to mean 'exempt from scrutiny' or sacrosanct. It typically operates independently of established social authority, seeking to free itself from any kind of coercion by power-interests. It follows the negative method of doubt as a way of truth, and because critical thinking must above all be self-critical, a critical thinker is often introspective. He seeks out unexamined prejudices and social or psychological constraints which may be distorting his own thinking. As Schopenhauer has finely said,

> What is most opposed to the discovery of truth is not the false appearance that proceeds from things and leads to error, nor even directly a weakness of the intellect. On the contrary, it is preconceived opinion, the prejudice, which as a spurious *a priori*, is opposed to truth. It is then like a contrary wind that drives the ship back from the direction in which the wind lies, so that rudder and sail now work to no purpose.

Critical thinking begins with the theory of knowledge and is typically anthropocentric in outlook. It accepts without complaint the fact that human knowledge is after all just human knowledge, man-made, provisional, fallible. What else could it be? And the correct attitude to theory is neither sceptical nor dogmatic, but pragmatic. We must have theories, but each and every theory is no more than a tool with a limited range of usefulness. Critical thinking seeks emancipation from the tyranny of theories that have become dogmas. Its spirit is light, supple, clearheaded and mobile, like Wisdom in ancient Judaism, and the Tao in China.

Early Buddhism provides one of the most striking anticipations of critical spirituality in ancient thought. The Buddha's path requires a very high degree of inner detachment and freedom, a state that has been summarised as 'clinging to the void and practising compassion'. He was willing to teach a few metaphysical doctrines, such as the 'no-self' doctrine, that he regarded as being directly helpful in producing the kind of spirituality he sought. But he was deliberately silent about many classical issues in dogmatic metaphysics, such as whether there is a First Cause, whether the world is eternal, whether the soul is identical with the body, and whether the saint continues to live after his death. Sometimes he says that such questions are ill-framed and unprofitable, and must be set aside. Sometimes he answers with a 'fourfold negation': it is not correct to say that there is a First Cause, or that there is not, or that there both is and is not, or that there neither is nor is not. The Buddhas teaching is not agnostic, if by 'agnosticism' we mean the view that the questions of God and immortality are indeed very important and intelligible questions, but questions which unhappily we are in no position to determine. Rather, he seems to wish to lead his disciples to a standpoint where such questions *will no longer trouble them*. The pursuit of his spiritual path is therapeutic; it cures us of every kind of discontent, including metaphysical discontent. And there is here an interesting resemblance to the later thought of Wittgenstein, whose philosophy was also therapeutic. Wittgenstein sought to show that the world of human practices and speech can be so described from within that it becomes plainly a mistake to hanker after any external points of support for it. It simply is what it is.

In seeking thus to cure us of any desire to seek external metaphysical backing for our practices, Wittgenstein seems to have been pushing the critical principle to its limit. As we have seen, critical thinking takes a pragmatic view of theory. Scientists and historians alike, looking at the history of their own subjects, come to see that all theories are man-made interpretative tools with each a limited lifespan and range of usefulness. But realism or objectivism always depends upon a theory. So critical thinking can never rest for long in any sort of realism: 'reality' changes as theory changes, and theory does undeniably change. Thus, in the long run, no more can be said than that the worlds that people live in are constituted for them by the currently prevailing forms of life and speech, and of course these things change. So it seems that everything 'out there' is eliminated, and only human practices and human speech remain.

If critical thinking thus leads to radical anthropocentrism, Wittgenstein leaves us a little perplexed as to its religious implications. There is, we argued earlier, a Hebraic religious motif in his teaching which seeks to return us to the common human world. There is even perhaps a Buddhist strain, which argues not merely that it is possible to take up the religious life on a basis of metaphysical agnosticism, but also that the religious life is purest when it reaches a standpoint for which metaphysical questions do not even arise. On the other hand there is another Wittgenstein who grits his teeth, says farewell to metaphysics, makes himself a therapist, and sets out to persuade us that we must accept a purely human world. Here Wittgenstein the pessimist is preparing us spiritually for a post-metaphysical Ice Age, showing us that it can and must be accepted without complaint because because no alternative to it is clearly conceivable. In this mood he so deeply embeds our thought and action in the prevailing language-games and forms of life that it is hard to see any possibility of creative action to change current realities.

Perhaps even at the end of his career Wittgenstein was still torn between Judaic voluntarism and Schopenhauerian resignation as his final spiritual attitudes. At any rate, critical faith must decide whether in the end it seeks merely to interpret the world, or to change it.

The move to anthropocentrism is equally apparent within the field of theology proper. Over a period of two centuries or so biblical criticism developed in such a way that the perceived contribution of supernatural agency to the formation of the Bible grew smaller and smaller, and the contribution of historically and culturally conditioned human religious psychology grew larger and larger. Originally, in the doctrinal definitions of sixteenth-century Protestantism and Catholicism alike, Scripture was seen as dictated by God, and the believer studying God's word felt himself to be directly addressed by the divine voice, clear, golden, authoritative and timeless, speaking immediately to his heart. But critical thinking has remorselessly whittled away that pure and simple objectivity. It points out that most of the biblical books do after all purport to be occasional writings addressed by human authors to their own contemporaries, so that they must be open to assessment and interpretation at that purely historical level. It then draws attention to doctrinal differences and historical disagreements between and within the various biblical books. It notices the very diverse literary character of the texts. It makes us see to what a great extent the biblical authors were dominated by cosmological and other beliefs that are very strange to us. It insists that no historical judgment can ever be more than probably true, and it shows us how very precarious is any argument to the effect that some supposedly historical event could have been brought about only by a benevolent supernatural agent; and then it caps this by showing that the supernatural elements in, for example, the Gospels can be sufficiently explained in terms of the purposes, the cultural resources and the literary techniques of their writers. In such ways as these what was originally a pure and simple divine revelation has been progressively converted into a historically conditioned human religious expression, much more clearly understood now, and undoubtedly moving, extraordinary, and of great religious value, but nonetheless entirely human.

More recently – since the mid-nineteenth century, in fact – the same process has happened in the case of Christian doctrine. It, too, is a human expression, with a human history which can be traced in great detail as critical historical research displays the cultural settings, the human needs and the power-interests that produced and established it.

Younger still is the comparative study of religions by the critical historical method, which examines on a global scale the fabulous diversity of religions, their historical changes, and their relations to their cultural settings. Traditional supernaturalism had almost nothing more interesting to say about all this than that the gods of the heathen were demons, an outlook which had to be discarded before the subject could begin at all. Attempts to discover cross-cultural religious universals, or to impose tidy evolutionary schemes upon the material, have fared little better, but some rather looser and vaguer interpretative ideas may remain useful. Thus the fact that we speak of Greek gods, Norse gods and Hindu gods suggests that a people's religion gives symbolic expression to their corporate identity, the sacredness of their traditions and their allegiance to their values. The Jungians draw attention to widespread cross-cultural patterns of symbolism, and suggest that they reflect certain deep predispositions in the human psyche. Others are impressed by formal resemblances in the ways religious concepts move, and in the shape of the mystical life, in widely dispersed traditions. But most scholars in the field are at present wary of stating their own theoretical positions. We are left with the general impression that the majority of them take some form of anthropocentric view of religion, and could hardly do otherwise. Theology may declare that the gods made men, but all that the critical historian can see is that human societies postulate gods, establish their cults, ascribe to them attributes drawn from the human realm, and imagine them speaking in human languages, issuing laws, ruling their domains and occasionally intervening to help their human subjects. Naturally, critical thinking can perceive in religion only a human expression, and in so far as this way of thinking becomes completely dominant in our culture it seems to leave no room for the old innocent pre-critical practice of religion. Critical self-consciousness seems to make us wallflowers at the dance, lamenting our inhibitions but unable to shake them off.

As I have already hinted, I do not take so pessimistic a view, because I believe that critical thinking is itself an essential part of the religious life, and because I do not think that the practice of religion has to depend upon the acceptance of a body of dogmatic beliefs. Of course it commonly does so depend; but it need not do so, and indeed it ought not to do so.

I can claim some historical support for this view. Because of its association with the myths of the pagan poets, Christian writers were in early times suspicious about the word 'theology'. They felt a closer affinity with the philosophers, but it must be remembered that in those days the word 'philosophy' signified not so much a body of teachings (*dogmata*) as an active striving after wisdom which required a whole-hearted commitment to a pure and ascetical way of life. Similarly, St Augustine regarded Church teachings as wisdom, not knowledge; *sapientia*, rather than *scientia*. And when the Greek Fathers used the term 'theology', they also meant by it something like spirituality, a commitment of one's life to the quest for divine wisdom. Thus the original felt affinity between Christianity and philosophy was *an affinity between two spiritualities* rather than a matter of commonly-held metaphysical dogmas. At the level of metaphysical dogma, biblical faith and Platonism have indeed rather little in common: what first drew Christians and philosophers together was mutual respect for each other's spirituality and a common dislike of popular superstition. Only much later, in Paris in about the year 1200, did Christian teaching

257

become a university subject, an objectified body of dogmas for which the status of a science was claimed.

The establishment of theology in the universities as a branch of knowledge naturally encouraged the development of a realist and dogmatic view of the nature of religious belief, especially where Christian teaching was married to Aristotelian metaphysics, or where the influence of the Design Argument led people to view God as a kind of scientific hypothesis. Nor has objectification been confined to Christianity; partly under Western influence, it has tended to spread in other traditions as well.

Dogmatic realism helped to give the Church crisp formulas around which it could rally to defend its identity in times of rapid change, but it also committed the Church to a long and ultimately unsuccessful rearguard action against critical thinking. The older tradition suggests a way out of this impasse. If in the early centuries the affinity between Christianity and Platonism was not a dogmatic affinity, but rather an affinity between two spiritualities, then it may be that if we today can come to see religion primarily as spirituality we may be able to perceive an affinity between Christianity and critical thinking. All of Western thought has now become critical, and religious thought must therefore also become critical. But, as we have seen, critical thinking puts epistemology before ontology (or, in its most modern form, language before reality), holding that the limits of what there can be for us are shown by the cognitive and linguistic resources available to us. Similarly, critical religious thinking must put the nature of faith before the object of faith. It must regard a correct determination of the nature of religious faith as showing all that can be shown of the nature of the object of faith. Get the spirituality right, and it will have been shown what talk of God means; for the meaning of talk of God is given by the part it plays in shaping the spiritual life. What faith is shows what God is.

On this view, which was first clearly stated by Kierkegaard, Christian faith is not an ideology but a form of life, a passionate commitment to the quest for deliverance from the world, for salvation and spiritual perfection. Religious teachings prescribe the itinerary; they show the course of the Path. They are to be used instrumentally, as tools and guides. Understood dogmatically, they mystify us and may become enslaving and religiously damaging illusions; but understood spiritually they become means to inner liberation. God becomes our Saviour in so far as religious doctrines no longer constrain us externally but inspire and guide us inwardly.

Someone who takes a realist metaphysical view of God as a cosmos-transcending being 'out there' will always find it difficult to explain what can be meant by talk of union with God and having God dwell in one's heart. How does the God out there become *my God*, who shows me the path to true selfhood? But if spirituality is put first, we can see the point of such idioms. For mystical thinking moves in the opposite direction from mythical, dogmatic thinking. Mythical thought projects religious realities outwards, objectifies them and pictures them in the form of an invisible world of supernatural beings and forces and causes of events. The believer then becomes the servant of the very things that he has himself postulated. But mystical thinking draws them back within the self. It internalises and spiritualises. It interprets religious ideas not descriptively but regulatively, regarding them not as giving supernatural information but as prescribing the form of the religious life. Mystical thinking carries out a kind of inner critique through which the self is purged, purified, emancipated from bondage to dogmatic illusions, illuminated and transformed into freedom and godlikeness. The mystic attempts to overcome dogma, insisting that God, Christ and heaven are not 'up there' but are to be found in the heart by desire, by love, by the will; that is, by a path of inner purification. Thus we are instructed to 'let nothing live in thy working mind but a naked intent stretching into God'; and this naked intent must be nothing else but 'a naked thought and a blind feeling of thine own being', for God 'is thy being and in him thou art that thou art'. Such language was not perceived as heretical until after the triumph of dogmatism in the Church, which inevitably led to the persecution of a long line of mystics. In earlier times, just as the spiritual meaning of Scripture was higher than the literal, so the mystical, internalised, non-realist interpretation of doctrine was recognised as a higher truth than its popular realist interpretation.

The stronghold of dogmatic realism is no doubt the doctrine of Creation, and the postulation of an objective metaphysical God as world-ground. However, such a theology faces the perennial difficulty that if it cannot solve the problem of evil it falls to the ground; and if it can solve it then it cuts the nerve of the doctrine of redemption, for the world is perceived as being already the expression of the will of an all-good and all-powerful God, and therefore in no need of betterment. But in fact God was not at first so perceived in either Testament. The God of the Old Testament was perceived as the basis of the nation's identity, the prescriber of its rituals, the embodiment of its values and hopes: the creation-theme became explicit only later and secondarily, in connection with the hope of redemption from the Babylonian captivity – and as it became more explicit, the problem of evil came to the forefront. In the New Testament the infant Church was a society of people committed to the hope of a new humanity in a new world to be brought in by Jesus. In neither Testament was religious belief primarily a matter of holding a theory about the metaphysical ground of the present world-order. Although New Testament faith in God was undoubtedly realist – it would be absurd to suggest otherwise – we must not suppose it to have been more metaphysical and objectified than it was. For the New Testament writers evil never became a primarily theoretical problem, to be solved by producing arguments of the kinds that became popular in later times. On the contrary, the early Christian faith was emphatically a religion of redemption. It has nothing to do with the kind of cosmological theism that attempts to justify the present world-order. It began with a hostile diagnosis of this present world, seeing in the present prevalence of evil not a secondarily arising and theoretical threat to cosmological faith, but that which makes faith necessary in the first place. Many of our objectified modern theologies feel they must attempt to explain away evil, but Christianity began as a hope that it would soon be conquered and that a new humanity would be inaugurated. The kind of human being it aims at is symbolised by Christ, the society it hopes to see is called the Kingdom of God, and the transcendent ideal goal of its spirituality is God. The whole is essentially not a dogmatic system or ideology, but an ethical project aimed at human emancipation.

Understood in this way as an ethical project and a spirituality, religious belief is no longer at odds with critical thinking but on the contrary can readily enter into alliance with it. Both seek freedom from the tyranny of the world, the fetishism of objectivity; both gain that freedom by learning always to use theory instrumentally rather than dogmatically; both stress self-examination and seek to clarify consciousness and enhance freedom by recognising and discarding inner blocks; both are in the long run profoundly anthropocentric; and for both our life is a continual quest after an ideal which we may never claim to have finally attained. What truth is for critical thinking, God is for Christian spirituality – simply, life's goal.

The joyful wisdom

A key factor in compelling people to seek a new understanding of religious belief has been the gradual fading of the expectation of an afterlife. For about two millennia, roughly from 500 BC to AD 1500, much religious thought and action was dominated by the contrast between this fleeting and wretched world below in which we must spend our brief lives and the eternal heavenly world above which is the soul's true home. This life was merely a state of probation during which the soul prepared itself for the life to come. All the norms of thought and action were located in the supernatural world, religious attention was concentrated upon it, and religious action was understood as being traffic with it. The world of the dead and of heavenly beings was immensely more 'real' than this world, and it was important to assist souls in purgatory with masses, indulgences and prayers, and to invoke the intercession of the saints. Belief in life after death was strong because the whole orientation of religion was towards the supernatural world above, and the belief was realist because it expected post-mortem verification.

Then with the Reformation there came a revolt. Protestantism rejected the old hierarchies that claimed to mediate to mankind a hope of ultimate salvation in the world above, and instead offered the believer a solid foretaste and assurance of salvation that he could attain by a personal act of faith here and now, in this present life. The chief interest of religious action switched away from ascetical preparation for death, Judgment and life in the world above, and towards the realisation of religious values in social life in this world. As their service books show, the Reformers drastically pruned back all rituals concerned with the dead. Nothing was left except the funeral service, which itself now took the form of an exhortation to those still alive that they should fear Judgment, repent and put their trust in God's final triumph over evil at the General Resurrection. As for the soul of the deceased, no more was said of it than that the mourners hoped that the dead person 'rested in God'. No religious act was performed on the dead person's behalf, nor was there any hint that he continued living and active in such a way that there might perhaps be communication or interaction between the dead and the living.

Protestant funerary rites thus had the effect of discouraging any vivid and practical belief in life after death. Religious attention was redirected so strongly towards this world and the actualisation of religious values here in this life that the thought of a supernatural world of the dead was bound to fade away, for it was not allowed to play any effective part in the daily practice of religion. The believer was warned that what he was at the moment of death, he would remain eternally. Everything decisive happened before death, and could not be changed after it.

It is in this context that we should set Kierkegaard's turning away from life after death. One of his *Thoughts which Wound from Behind* (1848) is about the resurrection of the dead. He rejects all speculative concern for personal immortality:

> Immortality is the Judgment. There is not a word more to be said about immortality. . . . Immortality is not a life indefinitely prolonged, nor even a life somehow prolonged into eternity, but immortality is the eternal separation between the just and the unjust. Immortality is not a continuation which follows as a matter of course, but it is a separation which follows as a consequence of the past.

In effect, all talk about what is to come 'after' death must be understood solely in terms of the way it bears upon the will here and now:

> Eternity is the distinction between right and wrong, hence immortality is the separation between the just and the unjust. . . . It is an idle, indolent, effeminate thought to wish for a life after death in the sense of a long life. Eternity's thought is that in this earthly life men differ, in eternity occurs the separation.

Kierkegaard's Protestant emphasis on the here and now is equally apparent in his explanation of what is to live according to the Sermon on the Mount. He contrasts three different spiritualities, typified by the birds of the air who live a purely natural life, 'the Gentiles' who represent ordinary rational human beings, and the Christian. The birds know nothing of the morrow, nothing of either time or eternity, but simply live and are what they are in the present moment. The Gentiles, being rational and reflective, are aware of time and even terrorised by it, for they live burdened by the past, with a feeling that their time is slipping away, and consumed with anxiety about the future. The Christian is a person who has passed through the Gentile stage and has returned to something closer to the condition of the birds, for he lives eternally in the present moment. But his faith is not simple immediacy; it is immediacy after reflection. Because a human being properly understood is a compound of time and eternity he should neither expect nor seek the simple immediacy of the birds, but through faith he should so relate himself continually to eternity that he lives in a regained immediacy, after reflection. In this state he no longer has occasion to think about death, for his whole life is lived on the basis of having already overcome it. It is in the moment, in the here and now, that the believer has passed through Judgment and entered upon Eternal Life.

Thus from Kierkegaard's point of view the medieval believer who spent his life in anxious preparation for death and Judgment was one of the Gentiles, and no true Christian. Kierkegaard shows very clearly that Protestantism, with its revolt against all post-dated religious cheques and its urgent demand that everything must be cashed in practice *now*, tends by its own inner logic towards existentialism. It was in this spirit that Wittgenstein, when dying of cancer, remarked to a friend:

Isn't it curious that, although I know that I have not long to live, I never find myself thinking about a 'future life'. All my interest is still on this life and the writing I am still able to do.

All religious doctrines and themes thus become present imperatives which, if they are functioning properly and with their full force, simply cure the believer of anxiety. He no longer gives death and the future life a thought: he feels no need to think of them. A person who has become fully a Christian no longer experiences any kind of metaphysical yearning after any Absolute that lies 'beyond', for he possesses all things now. It is misleading to speak of him as 'anti-metaphysical', or of his faith as 'non-cognitive', as if he were some kind of rejector who holds a reduced faith and denies the metaphysical dogmas that are so precious to others. The truth is rather the other way round: one who has truly become a Christian no longer feels himself to be alienated from religious realities, and therefore no longer needs any credal convictions to connect himself to them. He does not need any beliefs when his whole mode of existence has become pure and absolute affirmation, a Yes now.

To one who has become a Christian the thought of life after death thus appears as a symptom of lack of faith, for faith says to him, 'If you cannot do it now you will never do it; so forget about life after death and live your eternal life now. The whole mentality of preparing for death, of sitting around brooding over the unfortunate shortage of evidence for life after death, poisons life. Through faith, choose life now. Christian life is life after life after death. Eschatological thoughts have no other function than to remind us that our lives are finite, and so to precipitate us into *Now*. When they have done their job, and the Christian lives eternally in the present, beliefs disappear, for there is no remaining lack for them to express.'

Thus when a fully Christian position has been reached, the difference between the Christian and the non-Christian is no longer a disagreement about beliefs but has become simply a difference in spirituality. In recent centuries the factual or descriptive elements of belief have been steadily whittled away, until nothing serious is left of them. When the purge is complete, we see that spirituality is everything. Doctrines that used to be regarded as describing supernatural facts are now seen as prescribing a supernatural mode of existence. Disagreements between different religions and philosophies of life are not disagreements about what is the case, but disagreements about ways of constituting human existence, disagreements about forms of consciousness and moral policies. As such, they remain sharp and real disagreements; but at least we can now say that we have learned to locate their true character correctly.

The greatest and most remarkable gain is that we are at last beginning to grasp the correct solution to the long-fought-over question of God. Even to this day most people are still dominated by a conception of God as a really-existing infinite person, objective, distinct from us and over against us, who has made and controls the world. This idea of God as a really-existing being was linked with and depended upon ideas of him as being causally active. Roughly speaking, the physical world of common-sense and of natural science is seen as a domain of objects that interact with each other. Stars, people and stones all 'exist' because they interact, or may do so. But God was thought of as causing the world to exist, as being himself the ultimate cause of all events, and as occasionally inter-vening in a special way to cause particular events. Thus God also 'existed', albeit in a special sense.

The Greeks, who in general regarded their gods as part of Nature, bequeathed to the Christians various arguments for God of a causal kind, arguments that moved from facts about the world to a factual God. Naturally enough, in times when everything in this world was legitimated from the supernatural world, when monarchical imagery was potent, and when Christian doctrine functioned to legitimate the Christian State, God came to be seen in a very 'realist' way as the King of Kings, a cosmic Emperor. It was easy for Christians to forget that they had once regarded the ruler of this world not as God but as the Devil, a malign and enslaving figure.

The old realist notion of God was breaking down most conspicuously around the time of the French Revolution. Various factors were involved, including the demolition by philosophers of the old causal arguments that had given him his 'existence', and also certain social and political changes. But most important of all was a sense of his religious inadequacy. How does that cosmic realist God ever get to be *my* God – which is after all the heart of the matter? If we pause and go slowly and carefully for a while, asking ourselves precisely what can be *meant* by the various things that are said of God, the answer becomes clear. What can that X be which is such that the thought of X is ever before our minds, X dwells in our hearts, X inspires and guides us, X leads us towards true selfhood and the attainment of X is the chief task and goal of our lives? Clearly, X here represents a personal religious ideal, an image of our life-aim. And if I further speak of X in personal terms as the Lord of my life and the one to whom I pour out my heart, to whose service I devote myself, before whom I express my sense of shortcoming and to whom I pay my gratitude and thanksgiving, then it is evident that I am representing my personal religious ideal in personal terms. Thus religious language does not after all postulate an objective cosmological God, but a personified religious ideal, internal to the spiritual life, who has supreme authority in our lives and shows us the way to true selfhood. And indeed of the traditional theistic proofs the only distinctively Christian one, that put forward by Anselm of Canterbury on the basis of hints in St Augustine, pictures a God who is the ideal of unsurpassable perfection. This ideal is *a priori* and not factual; it is a kind of unknown transcendence that does not foreclose around any object but precisely remains 'that than which greater cannot be thought, and which is greater than can be thought'. Anselm's famous 'definition' of God is not a label, but an arrow: it does not describe an object, but directs the soul's aspiration. And simply to understand this ideal of perfection is to recognise its authority, its spiritual potency and reality as an ideal for me, for my life.

In the case of life after death we saw, briefly, how an other-worldly and realist dogmatic belief has become converted into principles of spirituality that shape the believer's present existence. Something similar has happened with God, and in both cases what has come about is not a loss or reduction of faith but a clearer working out and understanding of faith's own inner meaning. People once thought of God as an objective being in a higher world, but now we realise that the only true God is *our* God, the religious ideal. He is internal to spirituality, and therefore from our anthropocentric point of view a function of human religiousness, but to say as much does not imply any degradation or restriction of scope whatever, for the ideal is still boundless, transcendent, and of over-riding authority. The relinquishment of old illusions about God at last allows the religious ideal to function properly. Religion is an *activity*: it postulates a goal and seeks to attain it. Realist theologies claim that the religious ideal is already actual, being fully attained in the metaphysical realm quite independently of any effort by us; they assure us that our discontent with the world as it is is misplaced, and they cut the nerve of religious striving. They ask of us no more than receptivity. Their day is over.

The movement from an understanding of religion centred on dogmatic belief to one centred in spirituality and ethical activity may seem irresistible. Why do people then resist it so strongly? Because it is coupled with the admission, at last, that religion is entirely human, made by men for men. This admission is now inescapable, and the next stage in the development of religious thought will have to be based upon it: but it need no more imply any reduction in our sense of the ultimate importance of religion in our lives than does the corresponding admission in the case of art. If human beings were capable in the past of collectively generating vast and beautiful systems of religious meaning and many forms of religious life, all in an unconscious way, then how much greater are the possibilities of conscious religious creativity!

The emergence within religion of a clear and active consciousness of what religion is and how it works has been a strangely patchy and erratic business, and even yet remains very incomplete. Faith finds it very difficult to struggle out of the Babylonian captivity, the sheer darkness, of metaphysics, and the history of the dawn of consciousness in and of religion cannot yet be written. (Feuerbach had the equipment, if his thought had only taken a slightly different turn.) There is a kind of prehistory, as the case of Mani, the third-century Iranian prophet who founded Manicheeism, shows. Mani was the first to be aware of the plurality of religions, and to set out consciously to found a new universal faith. He was the first consciously to set himself to write the scriptures of a faith, consciously to work up a system of doctrine and to lay down a pattern of church organisation. He made a faith that touched millions and flourished for over a thousand years, and if it is dead today the reason is perhaps that he was too conscious in some ways and not conscious enough in others. He has about him a little of the air of the intellectual of late antiquity who plans a faith for other people and designs an enthrallingly exotic and eclectic system of doctrine – and he therefore seems to us to be dated. He has not passed through the fires of criticism, scepticism and radical anthropocentrism that have cured us of the impulse to build systems of doctrine like castles in the clouds. Because we can know only the human person, the world he constructs around himself and the spiritual project he sets before himself, our religious task in the modern period is more searchingly existential, creative and ethical. Our search for new ways of achieving true selfhood, of gaining immediacy after reflection, of at last 'becoming a Christian', cannot be just a thought-experiment cast in the form of doctrinal speculation; it has to be performed in reality and in deed. We have been forced back to the human, the practical and the concrete. Demythologised, religion becomes hard work again.

For us, then, the religious task has become the task of attaining true selfhood. The formation of a creative artist provides the best image of this task, and also an indication of its difficulty, for it often takes such a person some fifteen or twenty years of unremitting labour to find his mature style, his distinctive voice – and we have to do it not in art, but in life. We shall need help, the help of our vision of God and of Christ as God's self-expression in human form, the help of rituals and of companions on the journey and so on. Such help is available.

There are those who protest about the allegedly excessive individualism of an age in which each person sees it as his own primary task in life to become a self. They point back to ages when a person could confidently and piously see himself as predestined by God and Nature to be just this cell in the social body, just this stone in the social edifice, and was content simply to enact his appointed role. Where people are thus happy to accept a socially-assigned identity, then it is possible to build a cohesive and enduring society out of them. But, Nietzsche remarks, those days are past:

> What will not be built any more henceforth, and *cannot* be built any more, is – a society in the old sense of the that word; to build that, everything is lacking, above all the material. *All of us are no longer material for a society*; this is a truth for which the time has come. . . .

Do we regret this? Do we think that Paul Gauguin and Paul Cézanne were wrong to labour so long and ruthlessly at the task of making themselves into 'Gauguin' and 'Cézanne'? Yet if they were 'egoists', they were also public benefactors who have enriched the lives of millions. Furthermore, the idea that our personal identity is not naturally determinate, but is rather our religious project and task, is itself of Christian origin. In baptism and some other sacramental acts the individual is given a personal name that signifies his unique relation to God and his personal religious destiny. My personal name *is* my relation to God; stands, that is, for the self that is known to God and which with God's help I am to become. The biblical ideal of the New Covenant and the Kingdom of God signified a world in which the claims of society and of personal individuation were no longer opposed but synthesised, at a higher level than had ever been achieved in the past:

> And no longer shall each man teach his neighbour and each his brother, saying, 'Know the Lord', for they shall all know me, from the least of them to the greatest, says the Lord. . . .

It is because the Kingdom of God is so much more modern than the Church that it has come increasingly to the fore in recent Christian thought. Because of the way it is organised, the Church's social ideal still seems relatively medieval. Each of us, it seems, is expected to find his personal fulfilment in performing the duties of his rank, or in making his contribution as a cell in the functioning of the whole body. But in the Kingdom of God these organic and pyramidal metaphors disappear, and each gives most to the whole only in and through becoming most fully and uniquely himself.

In this vision of the world there is nothing predetermined, and nothing wholly non-human. Prior to human activity, nature and human nature are formless chaos, mere possibility. Through human creativity guided by the Christian religious ideal the world is to be wholly human-ised, and all Nature turned into art. Thus at last the world becomes – a divine Creation.

Chapter 9
CONCLUSION

The road has been long and winding, but the conclusions to which it has led are in one way simple. The way we construct our world, and even the way we constitute our own selves, depends on the set of values to which we commit ourselves. Our preferences reveal what we are, and are reflected in the world we establish around ourselves. The outer world reflects the inner, and the constitution of both is ultimately ethical. In many world-views metaphysics comes first, and then ethics finds a place as best it can: but the truth is rather the other way round. Ethics comes first; and religion is our way of representing to ourselves, and renewing our commitment to, the complex of moral and spiritual values through which we shape our world, constitute ourselves, gain our identity and give worth to our lives.

God (and this is a definition) is the sum of our values, representing to us their ideal unity, their claims upon us and their creative power. Mythologically, he has been portrayed as an objective being, because ancient thought tended to personify values in the belief that important words must stand for things. Plato, whose thought was still half-mythological, considered that words like truth, beauty and justice must designate real beings existing in a timeless, heavenly world above. His metaphysics was a semi-abstract mythology, and we now see that he made a philosophical mistake. Values do not have to be independently and objectively existent beings in order to be able to claim our allegiance. We can, after all, recognise that duty calls or that *noblesse oblige* without supposing that duty or *noblesse* are real beings. Indeed, thinking of values as objective beings out there does not help us in any way to progress towards a clearer understanding of the special part they play in our lives. We can do without that mythological idea.

Dominated by the belief that each important word must name a

269

being, Plato went on to fill up his heavenly world with an odd consortium of values, logical ideas, mathematical objects, common nouns, human souls and qualities. Today, with the increasing differentiation of our knowledge, our discriminations have become too refined to tolerate such a quaint mythological jumble. We try instead to sort out the confusion by looking carefully at the various different ways in which language is actually used. The old reifying habit of mind which populated the universe with a host of occult beings is now obsolete. Talk of moral values can be better explained in other ways.

As with values, so with God, because God's status in the language is very close to that of values. God simply *is* the ideal unity of all value, its claim upon us, and its creative power. (God is indeed the creator, for value indeed makes the world.) But the Platonic notion of God as an objective being, out there in a higher world, does nothing to explain the way he functions as *our* God, chosen by us, our religious ideal, our life-aim and the inner meaning of our identity. Just as you should not think of justice and truth as independent beings, so you should not think of God as an objectively existing superperson. That is a mythological and confusing way of thinking. The truth, we now see, is that the idea of God is imperative, not indicative. To speak of God is to speak about the moral and spiritual goals we ought to be aiming at, and about what we ought to become. The meaning of 'God' is religious, not metaphysical, even though unfortunately a deeply engrained habit of self-mystification leads most people, most of the time, radically to misconstrue the true meaning of religious language. The true God is not God as picturesque supernatural fact, but God as our religious ideal.

The view that religious belief consists in holding that a number of picturesque supernatural propositions are descriptively true is encouraged by the continuing grip on people's minds of a decadent and mystifying dogmatic theology. In effect I am arguing that for the sake of clarity it should be discarded entirely, and replaced by the practice of religion – ethics and spirituality – and the philosophy of religion. Then religion can become itself again, with a clear intellectual conscience at last.

Does this amount to saying that God is simply a humanly constructed ideal, such that when there are no human beings any longer there will be no God any longer? This question is improper, because it is framed from the obsolete realist point of view. The suggestion that the idea of God is man-made would only seem startling if we could point by contrast to something that has *not* been made by men. But since our thought shapes all its objects, we cannot. In an innocuous sense, all our normative ideas have been posited by ourselves, including the truths of logic and mathematics as well as all our ideals and values. How else could we have acquired them? Thus God is man-made only in the non-startling sense that everything is. That is modern anthropocentrism. But even on my account God is as real for us as anything else can be, and more primally authoritative than anything else is.

With historical change, people change, and so the idea of God is in continual change. This is a good and necessary thing, because there is no task in life more important than that of working out our own personal vision of God, a task which each person must undertake for himself. But there is another incentive to the task, for someone who believes in God aspires after an ultimate unity and harmony of moral and spiritual values; and this we cannot have, because life is tragic. We will never succeed in working out and living contentedly by a fully coherent set of values and ideals. There will always be internal conflicts within our idea of God, such as the very ancient one between justice and mercy which so tormented some of the Israelite prophets. Thus faith in God, commanding us to seek a value-unity which cannot be had, is tragic – and being tragic is creative, for one is compelled to struggle to overcome the contradiction. That struggle is true religion, the religion of Israel, 'the one who strives with God'.

If metaphysical theism were true, the tragic vision would be overcome and the comic vision would prevail. There would be no real scope for religious struggle and creativity (apart from the struggle to persuade oneself to accept the comic vision, that all is well). But in axiological theism the tragic vision comes to the fore and acts as a spur to creativity and to the distinctively religious kind of achievement.

For the Christian, this task of working out a vision of God takes the more human and concrete form of framing a personal vision of Christ, who is our own ideal *alter ego*, our true Self that we are to become, our religious ideal actualised in human form. But he also, as Western Christians have always known, is tragic. The image that most reminds us of him is the Cross.

When we have fully accepted these ideas and have freed ourselves from nostalgia for a cosmic Father Christmas, then our faith can at last become fully human, existential, voluntary, pure, and free from superstition. To reach this goal is Christianity's destiny, now approaching.

What could be simpler? Why did I not say all this at the outset? Because after all it is *not* simple: the revolution in our form of religious consciousness needed in order to reach the new point of view is traumatic. So far as I know, only a few people are yet prepared for it. The majority of people reject it as being incomprehensibly thin and barren after the richer fare that they have been accustomed to. They hear us say that faith is no longer a guided pilgrimage to a guaranteed destination, but has become instead a way of creatively framing one's own life as a spiritual project. They hear that the only true God is the thought of God, shaping our whole lives, and that the objective God many people believe in is an oppressive pagan notion – in fact, the Devil. They are told that all the doctrines of faith are not indicatives but symbol-clad imperatives; so that the doctrine of resurrection, for example, does not promise another life hereafter but tells us to live now a new life that has left the fear of death behind. Rightly understood, the doctrine is not a set of supernatural facts that generate the ethic and the spirituality: the doctrine just *is* the ethic and the spirituality, with no gap between. And on hearing all this, they recoil in revulsion. Even if they darkly suspect that a fully traditional dogmatic kind of faith would nowadays be impossibly cranky, they find the proferred alternative to it, an undogmatic and wholly existential faith, to be shockingly naked and neither rationally justifiable nor practically sustainable. If our basic stance in life can have no objective foundation, then why choose one such stance rather than any other?

There is an answer to this question. To find it, consider some community – a prosperous suburb in modern West Germany, perhaps – where the basic material and social needs of life are met as adequately and efficiently as they have ever been. Here, people seem to have everything – and we become all the more aware that the real questions of life have not been touched. People's poverty is absolute, for they are spiritually lost, feeling that their lives are aimless and worthless. To promise metaphysical consolations to such people is worse than useless, when their problem is that they are already doped to the eyebrows with the various sorts of spiritual Valium that flood the market. What is needed is an awakening of the will, the courage and the ambition to discipline oneself for high achievement and to make of one's own life a personal spiritual project. Only the modern autonomous kind of faith, based on a ruthless rejection of illusions, can help. The other sort of faith merely confirms the state of impotence and illusion, and cannot give the necessary stimulus to break out of it.

And why choose one form of religious life rather than another? Kierkegaard has given the answer, and shown the form a modern apologetic must take. His method is to expound each particular form of life from within, like a novelist. He does not need to test it against any supposed metaphysical realities external to it. It is sufficient to explore its values, its inner logic, and the life-possibilities that it opens up. By this method we may be able to show purely from within that a particular way of life eventually runs into difficulties that can be solved only by making a transition to another one (this is all that is meant by Kierkegaard's allegedly irrational 'leap of faith'). I for one believe that if in this way we were to explore Nietzschean humanism and Buddhism we might be able to show that each has its limits and both are fulfilled in a Christian spirituality that can unite the radical humanism of the one with the high spiritual attainment of the other.

However that may be, the general point is that the new conception of faith is by no means irrational: quite the opposite. And if the impression of loss persists, it will be only temporary. After a while, continuity reappears and everything returns. What was given up comes back, though transformed and seen now from a new viewpoint. We see that religion is wholly of this world, wholly human, wholly our own responsibility, and that it has become ethically active and militant. It is religion that has raised us out of the dark, chaotic unconsciousness of Nature and has made us human; for religion just is our values, expressed in our social institutions and our practices. Its earlier forms tended to be more collectivist; its newer forms are more concerned with self-realisation. As it has progressed, so the old dogmatic consolations, with their outworn associated structures of oppressive social and psychological power, are inevitably passing away. But the historic task of religion, of embodying our values, witnessing to them, conserving them, setting them forth in symbols and securing their realisation in human life, remains unchanged. It will be performed all the better after the painted veil of illusion, that has hitherto hidden its workings, has finally dropped away.

NOTES AND SOURCES

These notes are kept to a minimum, and are intended to supply just enough material to enable the reader to find some of my main sources, or to follow up particular points for himself. The publishers of books referred to are British unless otherwise stated.

Page 7   **Introduction**   Lloyd Geering, *Faith's New Age* (Collins 1980) covers some of the same ground as this book. See also John H. S. Kent, *The End of the Line?* (SCM 1982).

Page 13   **Wojtyla**   See Karol Wojtyla, *The Acting Person* (Dordrecht, Holland: D. Reidel 1979).

Page 14   **Bruno**   See, for example, Alexander Koyré, *From the Closed World to the Infinite Universe* (Baltimore: Johns Hopkins University Press 1969).

Page 15   **Belief in God**   There is a general survey of some of the transformations which the idea of God has been undergoing in the modern period in James Collins, *God in Modern Philosophy* (Greenwood Press 1978).

Page 22   **Dover Beach**   There are many editions of Arnold's poems, such as the Penguin one, first published in 1954. Arnold's books of radical theology are *St Paul and Protestantism* (1870), *Literature and Dogma* (1873), *God and the Bible* (1875) and *Last Essays on Church and Religion* (1877).

Page 22   **Secularism**   This subject is very controversial. See, for various points of view, D. A. Martin, *The Religious and the Secular: Studies in Secularization* (Routledge 1969); Susan Budd, *Sociologists and Religion* (Collier Macmillan 1973); Owen Chadwick, *The Secularization of the European Mind in the Nineteenth Century* (Cambridge University Press 1976); S. S. Acquaviva, *The Decline of the Sacred in Industrial Society* (2nd edition Milan 1966, translated and further updated, Blackwell 1979).

Page 24 *Hook* For Victorian religious statistics, and the full text of Hook's letter, see *English Historical Documents 1833–1874*, edd. G. M. Young and W. D. Hancock (Eyre and Spottiswoode 1956), Part IV.

Page 28 *The later Roman Empire* Alistair Kee, *Constantine versus Christ* (SCM 1982)

Page 28 *Twelfth century* For example, Colin Morris, *The Discovery of the Individual 1050–1200* (SPCK 1980).

Page 29 *The king is a layman* R. W. Southern, *Western Society and the Church in the Middle Ages* (Pelican 1970).

Page 36 *The Mechanical Universe* Hugh Kearney, *Science and Change 1500–1700* (Weidenfeld and Nicolson 1971) has a large bibliography. See also R. S. Westfall, *The Construction of Modern Science* (Cambridge University Press 1978).

Page 37 *The Medieval World* C. S. Lewis, *The Discarded Image* (Cambridge University Press 1964).

Page 40 *Dionysius* See Denys Rutledge, *Cosmic Theology* (Routledge and Kegan Paul 1964).

Page 41 *Galileo* Jerome J. Langford, *Galileo, Science and the Church* (Ann Arbor: University of Michigan Press 1971); Galileo Galilei, *Dialogue Concerning the Two Chief World Systems* (Berkeley: University of California Press 1967).

Page 48 *Pascal* Penguin books publish translations of his *Pensées* and *Provincial Letters*. Background in Robert Mandrou, *From Humanism to Science 1480–1700* (Penguin 1978), c.4.

Page 56 *The biblical world-view* Carmen Blacker and Michael Loewe, *Ancient Cosmologies* (Allen and Unwin 1975), c.3.

Page 57 *imperative* James Muilenberg, *The Way of Israel* (Routledge and Kegan Paul 1962).

Page 60 *William Smith* Smith is mentioned in the standard histories of the rise of geology, such as G. C. Gillespie, *Genesis and Geology* (Cambridge, Mass.: Harvard University Press 1951). Otherwise, the best book is very rare: *William Smith: His Maps and Memoirs*, by Thomas Sheppard (Hull: A. Brown 1920). The leading modern historian of geology, M. J. S. Rudwick, points out in *The Meaning of Fossils* (Elsevier 1973) that though Smith has precedence in point of discovery, it was Cuvier in 1808 and 1811 who first actually published the crucial ideas after studying the geology of the Paris region with his colleague Brogniart. So there occurred one of those enjoyable quarrels between the British and the Continentals about who was first.

Page 64 Darwin *Autobiography and Selected Letters* (New York: Dover 1959); and further reading listed in Jonathan Howard, *Darwin* (Oxford University Press 1982).

Page 67 Schopenhauer Quotations from *The World as Will and Representation* (trans. E. J. Payne, New York: Dover 1967). See also Patrick Gardiner, *Schopenhauer* (Penguin 1963).

Page 68 Freud Begin with Ernest Jones, *The Life of Sigmund Freud* (abridged edition, Penguin 1964); Philip Rieff, *Freud: The Mind of the Moralist* (University of Chicago Press 1979). Among Freud's main discussions of religion are the 1907 paper, '*Obsessive Acts and Religious Practices*', plus *Totem and Taboo* (1913); *The Future of an Illusion* (1928); *Civilization and Its Discontents* (1930); and *New Introductory Lectures* (1932), XXXV.

Page 72 Jung Begin with Anthony Storr, *Jung* (Fontana 1973). Then Jung's *Memories, Dreams and Reflections* (Collins 1967) – a work of beautiful mythology, it must be confessed – and his *Collected Works* (Routledge and Kegan Paul), especially Volume 11.

Page 78 Going By the Book Try consulting W. G. Kümmel, *The New Testament: The History of the Investigation of its Problems* (SCM 1973), very German-academic. The classic is Albert Schweitzer, *The Quest of the Historical Jesus* (Black 1910: reprinted SCM 1981).

Page 80 Pusey H. P. Liddon, *The Life of Edward Bouverie Pusey*, vol. I (Longmans 1893).

Page 92 Strauss Horton Harris, *David Friedrich Strauss and His Theology* (Cambridge University Press 1973).

Page 96 The System of Terrorism Geoffrey Faber, *Jowett* (Faber 1957), cc.XI-XII.

Page 98 The trial of Robertson Smith J. S. Black and G. W. Chrystal, *William Robertson Smith* (Black 1912).

Page 102 Schweitzer Werner Picht, *Albert Schweitzer* (Allen and Unwin 1964); Albert Schweitzer, *My Life And Thought* (Allen and Unwin 1954).

Page 113 Many actions addressed to God E. E. Evans-Pritchard, *Nuer Religion* (Oxford University Press 1956): 'Sacrifice is made to separate God and man, not to unite them', p. 275.

Page 114 The Morning Star John Gray, *Near Eastern Mythology* (Hamlyn 1970).

Page 131 Descartes There are many translations of Descartes. Best short study for beginners: Anthony Kenny, *Descartes* (New York: Random House 1968).

Page 133 Winstanley Gerrard Winstanley, *The Law of Freedom and other Writings* (Cambridge University Press 1983).

Page 134 Paine *The Essential Thomas Paine* (New York: Mentor Books 1969).

Page 136 Kant Kant is difficult, and no really simple and clear introduction to him appears to be available. Try W. H. Walsh, *Kant's Criticism of Metaphysics* (Edinburgh University Press 1975).

Page 139 Marx David McLellan, *Karl Marx* (Macmillan 1973: Paladin 1977); *Karl Marx: Early Texts* (Blackwell 1971).

Page 139 Hegel Charles Taylor, *Hegel* (Cambridge University Press 1975). Sidney Hook, *From Hegel to Marx* (1936; reprinted Ann Arbor: University of Michigan Press 1962) is still useful. Marx W. Wartofsky, *Feuerbach* (Cambridge University Press 1977).

Page 146 Kierkegaard Still much misunderstood. Reading him, begin with the *Journals*, of which there are various anthologies. Try Gregor Malantschuk, *Kierkegaard's Thought* (Princeton, N.J.: Princeton Univeristy Press 1974); Mark C. Taylor, *Journeys to Selfhood: Hegel and Kierkegaard* (Berkeley: California University Press 1980); John Elrod, *Kierkegaard and Christendom* (Princeton, N.J.: Princeton University Press 1981).

Page 157 Birmingham John Hick, *God has Many Names* (Macmillan 1980).

Page 161 *Toleration*   See Mandell Creighton, *Persecution and Tolerance* (1895), by a great Victorian liberal churchman and historian.

Page 165 *China*   Brief account in Hans Küng, *Does God Exist?* (Collins 1980), pp. 588 ff.

Page 166 *Translations*   Eric J. Sharpe, *Comparative Religion: A History* (Duckworth 1975).

Page 166 *Schopenhauer*   See the note to page 67, above.

Page 171 *Annie Besant*   See her *Autobiography*, and note the verdict of Professor R. C. Zaehner, *Hinduism* (Oxford University Press 1962): 'no single person did so much to revive the Hindu's pride in his religious heritage as did she', page 212.

Page 174 *Gandhi*   His *Autobiography* has been reissued by Penguin (1982).

Page 174 *Vivekananda*   Swami Nikhilananda, *Vivekananda: A Biography* (Calcutta: Advaita Ashrama 1971).

Page 186 *Jung*   Reprinted in *Modern Man in Search of a Soul* (Routledge and Kegan Paul 1970).

Page 189 *Mackie*   For example, *The Miracle of Theism* (Oxford University Press 1982).

Page 190 *Modernity and belief in God*   One of the very few writers who put forward a view close to ours is Rubem A. Alves of Brazil. See his 'What does it Mean to say the Truth?', in A. R. Peacocke (ed.), *The Sciences and Theology in the Twentieth Century* (Oriel Press 1982).

Page 190 *Nietzsche*   New and better translations of his works have been produced in recent years by Walter Kaufmann in the USA, and by R. J. Hollingdale in Britain. Bibliography in Ronald Hayman, *Nietzsche* (Weidenfeld and Nicolson 1980: Quartet Books 1981). The best studies are by Karl Jaspers (Berlin 1936: University of Arizona Press 1965), George A. Morgan (Cambridge, Mass.: Harvard University Press 1941), F. A. Lea (Methuen 1957) and Walter Kaufmann (Princeton, N.J.: Princeton University Press 4th edn. 1974).

Page 213 *Wittgenstein*   His works are published by Basil Blackwell of Oxford. Begin with *Philosophical Investigations* 1973), pp. 1–51.

Then *On Certainty* (1975), and *Culture and Value* (1980). Biographical material in Allan Janik and Stephen Toulmin, *Wittgenstein's Vienna* (New York: Simon and Schuster 1973) and Rush Rhees (ed.), *Ludwig Wittgenstein: Personal Recollections* (Blackwell 1981). There are innumerable studies: try works by K. T. Fann, David Pears, Anthony Kenny and P. M. S. Hacker. On the house built for Gretl, Bernhard Leitner, *The Architecture of Ludwig Wittgenstein* (Studio International 1973). No really up-to-date appraisal of Wittgenstein on religion yet exists.

Page 241 *Wittgenstein's personal position*   Quoted from G. H. von Wright, in Norman Malcolm, *Ludwig Wittgenstein: A Memoir* (New York: Oxford University Press; Galaxy Books 1958). The quotations that follow are from *Culture and Value*.

Page 244 *Non-realist philosophies of religion*   Further comments on them in my *The World to Come* (SCM 1982), c.2.

Page 254 *The Buddha*   See Edward Conze, *Buddhist Scriptures* (Penguin 1969); E. J. Thomas, *Buddhist Scriptures* (London 1913).

Page 256 *Christian doctrine*   Beginning with D. F. Strauss, *Die Christliche Glaubenslehre* (Tübingen 1840–1).

Page 256 *Comparative study*   Surveyed in Eric J. Sharpe, *Comparative Religion : A History* (Duckworth 1975).

Page 257 *Theology*   Wolfhart Pannenberg, *Theology and the Philosophy of Science* (Darton, Longman and Todd 1977), pp.7–12.

Page 258 *Objectification*   W. Cantwell Smith, *The Meaning and End of Religion* (New York 1962; London SPCK 1978).

Page 259 *'Let nothing live . . .'*   These phrases are from *The Cloud of Unknowing* (14th cent., English).

Page 261 *Thoughts which Wound*   From the *Christian Discourses*.

Page 263 *Life after death*   See D. Z. Phillips, *Death and Immortality* (Macmillan 1970).

Page 264 *The Question of God*   See my *Taking Leave of God* (SCM 1980).

Page 266 *Mani* See W. Cantwell Smith, cited above (p.258).

Page 267 *Nietzsche* I here use ideas from *The Gay Science*.

Page 267 *'And no longer . . .'* Jeremiah 31 : 34.

ACKNOWLEDGEMENTS

Gerard Evans did me a service by showing me the faults of an early draft of this book, and Dennis Nineham and Hugh Dawes made valuable comments on the typescript of the present version – though neither my views nor my errors should be imputed to them. Susan Kennedy of BBC Publications successfully urged a number of desirable modifications to the text, and Elizabeth Cartmale found the illustrations as well as doing much of the picture research for the documentary films. To them all, many thanks.

A newcomer soon learns that the making of a television series is a large-scale collaborative enterprise. Peter Armstrong, who is named in the dedication, was the chief instigator of the whole project, but it could not have been completed without the extensive and varied skills of Peter Dale, Anthea Cridlan, Kate Payne, Carole Porter, John McGlashan and Niall Kennedy, Rex Maidment, David Feig, George Cassedy, Cecilia Brereton, Chris Lysaght, Philippa Daniel, Henrietta Gilpin, Rosemary Turner, the composer Nigel Osborne and many others too numerous to mention individually. To them all I owe a debt of gratitude.

PICTURE CREDITS

INDEX